'CONNE*X*ION'

Foreword

Many and varied are the experiences that shape our lives.

Our parents, siblings, education, friendships, role models, first love… for most of us, these are universal influences, and it's hardly surprising how our lives unfold.

Then there are the influences of religion and travel. Even here, life remains relatively predictable when we stay close to familiar traditions, follow the patterns of our upbringing, or venture only into like-minded cultures.

But what happens when, by design or circumstance, we are thrown into the deep end of human turmoil - forced to live and breathe experiences we might wish we hadn't? What inner compass do we rely on then? And is the outcome ever assured?

In *ConneXion*, the author shares a journey far from the ordinary. He has survived hateful prejudice and witnessed, first-hand, the brutal realities of war. Yet, through a rich tapestry of global travel and the quiet wisdom offered by nature, he rises—stronger, wiser, and profoundly connected.

I commend this book to those old enough to reflect on adventures and misadventures the youth of today may find almost unbelievable. And equally, I offer it to the young and curious, ready to discover a story that is anything but ordinary.

— A friend

"Neutrality in the face of such evil is complicity"

In Memory of:

Shiba Prince – who will always be my girl – 26.04.2011 – 22.09.2025

Evelyn Dolly Somai (nee Prince) 30.06.1933 – 30.09 2025 – My mother!

As a tribute to:
All those who walk through this world with a quiet courage, protecting and uplifting the lives of others.
To the humanitarian workers who stand where hope is fragile, offering steadiness in the midst of chaos.
To the guardians whose souls seem called to service, moving through life

2

with a purpose that feels older than themselves.

To the mentors, healers, and guides who help others rise, gently shaping the best versions of who we might become.

And to the seekers — those who pause to question their path, leaning into the mystery of why they are here and what their journey means.

May their compassion, resilience, and inner light continue to weave threads of humanity through the darkest and brightest places on Earth.

Preface

I have called this book *Connexion* . The title embodies the threads of my narrative - the way I see, hear, smell, and touch the world shaped by my experiences. Each of us carries our own unique narrative, woven from the fabric of life's challenges, triumphs, and insights. It speaks to the universality of storytelling, inviting readers to reflect on how their senses and experiences shape their personal journeys.

My hope is that the contents of this book inspire others to claim their story and share it. Writing your own story can also be part of your own healing journey. For future generations, your narrative becomes a beacon - a way for you to understand who you were, rather than letting your story be told or assumed by others. The book highlights the importance of legacy and authenticity, resonating with the interconnected nature of identity which I have explored in the book.

For me, understanding my past has been vital. It has illuminated who I am today and how the events of my life - and the lives of my ancestors—have forged my existence.

I believe that our physical bodies are merely vessels, shapes and forms that carry our souls through a journey planned long before we were born. When our physical form succumbs to mortality, the soul endures. It continues to live, to experience, and to grow, completing its predetermined journey across lifetimes."

I believe that every problem has a solution - though it may not always be obvious, it exists as part of the fabric of our journey.

I believe that we are never truly alone. Angels surround us in many forms—sometimes as strangers, friends, or fleeting moments of guidance. There are no coincidences; every encounter is planned, a link in the chain of life's connections.

There are three important gifts I hope to share with you through this book. Firstly, is to be a giver as well as a receiver, for balance in life comes from the interplay of generosity and gratitude.

Secondly is to know that words are powerful. They can build bridges or tear them down, uplift or destroy. In the wrong hands, they are weapons; in the right hands, they are healing tools.

Lastly and most importantly, do not surrender your thoughts to another. Be your own judge, discovering truth through learning and experience.

Introduction

Life is a tapestry of connections, threads woven through time, space, and experience. Each thread tells a story - of identity, belonging, struggle, and triumph. This book, *Connexion*, is my story. It is a reflection of the moments, places, and people that have shaped me, a journey across cultures, continents, and the ever-shifting landscapes of the heart and soul.

Born in Brixton, London, to parents of French and Guyanese heritage, my life began in a melting pot of diversity. My early years were shaped by the rhythms of the neighbourhood, the whispers of the Windrush generation, and the complexities of growing up at the crossroads of cultures. Brixton was more than a place; it was a vibrant, sometimes challenging, microcosm of humanity that taught me the importance of resilience, identity, and community.

Connexion is not merely a recounting of events; it is an exploration of the forces that bind us. From the struggles of my family to the lessons learned in war zones, I have witnessed humanity in its rawest forms. As a nurse and humanitarian, my work took me to conflict zones across the globe, where I saw the very best and worst of what it means to be human. These experiences have been both a privilege and a burden, shaping my understanding of life, loss, and the profound interconnectedness of all things.

This book also reflects my deep connection to nature. From the Australian bush to the African savannah, the landscapes I have traversed are more than backdrops; they are characters in this story. The roar of lions in the wild, the rustle of eucalyptus leaves in the wind, and the quiet majesty of unspoiled wilderness have provided solace and perspective, reminding me of the intricate web of life to which we all belong.

Connexion is a celebration of stories - mine, yours, and those yet to be told. It is a call to own your narrative, to honour the threads that weave your life together. Writing this book has been an act of discovery, a way to make sense of my past and its influence on my present. It is my hope that in reading it, you too will be inspired to reflect on your journey, to see how your experiences, challenges, and insights have shaped the person you are today.

Above all, this book is a reminder that we are never alone. The connections we make - to people, places, and even to ourselves - are what give life its meaning. Whether through moments of serendipity, the wisdom of ancestors, or the unspoken understanding between strangers, these connections are evidence of a larger, more profound truth: that we are all intertwined, part of something greater than ourselves.

As you turn these pages, I invite you to look beyond the surface, to explore the deeper truths that lie beneath. In sharing my story, I hope to encourage you to share yours, for it is through our shared humanity that we find purpose, understanding, and hope.

Welcome to *ConneXion*.

Essences

I was born in Brixton, Lambeth, in August 1961 to a British-Guianese father and a French mother. I was the fifth child of six, with siblings from different marriages. Though home births were common at the time, only I was born at home; my younger sister and older brother were born in hospital. My brother, just a year older than me, had health issues at birth - likely encephalitis - and stayed in the hospital until he recovered. My parents married before I was born, although both he and I were conceived out of wedlock.

Living with us were two half-siblings from my father's previous marriage to a Guyanese woman. My eldest sister, born in East Berbice, Guyana, was eleven years older than me. We shared the same birthday, and it was often joked that I was her gift! My eldest brother, six years older, also came from that earlier marriage. Another half-sister, closer to my age, was the daughter of a relationship my mother had during her first year as a student nurse.

Our home, a three-story Victorian terrace on Beechdale Road, was owned by my father. In those days, Brixton was a lower-income neighbourhood, a far cry from the "upmarket" area it's considered today. My memories of that house are vivid and somewhat unpleasant than pleasant. We lived on the upper two floors, which held a small kitchen- dinning room, a front living room, three bedrooms, a separate bathroom and toilet. My maternal grandfather lived downstairs with his new French partner and their four children at the time, who were technically our aunts and uncles, though close to us in age.

The kitchen, though cramped, was the heart of our home where we would gather as a family. My mother would place me in a blue hammock strung across the room while she cooked, keeping me close as she moved around.

My father arrived in the UK in the early 1950s with his first wife from Georgetown, British Guiana. His cousin, Cheddi Jagan, a leader in the People's Progressive Party (PPP) and a pivotal figure in British Guiana's political history, helped him establish roots. Unlike Cheddi, who studied to become a dentist in Washington, D.C., and retained his Hindu faith, my father converted to Christianity, opening a door into British society. Yet I always sensed he still carried his Hindu roots, one as a shield, the other as a compass.

The British Nationality Act of 1948 had opened doors for Commonwealth citizens, providing work opportunities and pathways to citizenship. Though familiar with British customs, many migrants struggled to adapt. The government even organised classes on everything from queuing at bus stops to hailing buses. To fit in, many adopted British accents and personas. Commonwealth citizens, being British subjects, were generally more accepted than "aliens" from Europe, though tensions rose as West Indian, Guyanese, and Indian communities grew.

Born in Corentyne, East Berbice, British Guiana, my father was the grandson of indentured labourers from Uttar Pradesh, India, brought to replace slave labour after the trade's abolition in the 19th century. His family, of the Kurmi caste, was known for their agricultural skill and work ethic, traits my father carried into his life in the UK. Rather than working in sugar cane plantations as many indentured families did, he worked as dental assistant for his cousin Cheddi and had aspirations to become a dentist or a helicopter pilot. He often spoke of becoming a yogi and how the soul was separate to the physical body. He believed that the soul in each person's had a plan and that it would choose different people and life experience to complete its journey.

In the UK, he worked tirelessly for London Transport, where he remained until retirement, taking pride in his role as a union representative.

My maternal grandfather, whom we called "Papa," was French-Canadian with British roots in northeast England. He came from a family of stevedores, working the docks between Le Havre, France and New York. He settled in Le Havre, where he met my grandmother and where my mother was born. For the duration of the war he was interned in Paris. My grandmother died in an Allied bombing during WWII, while attending a German dance in occupied France—a means of survival for some women during those years. After the war, Papa was displaced and eventually settled in the UK, where my father helped him secure work laying and preparing railway tracks.

Papa and my father shared a tense relationship. Of Aryan descent, Papa openly expressed racist views and resented relying on my father, a Black man, for support. Despite this, Papa and I shared a bond. His love for cacti, clocks, stamps, and odd mechanical items fascinated me. Proud and rugged, he reminded me of John Wayne—a figure admired but rarely understood. He kept his softer side hidden, fearing it might reveal a weakness.

During childhood, Brixton felt like a world all its own, filled with people from the West Indies, British Guiana, India, and beyond - the "Windrush Generation"—who took on essential roles in hospitals, public transport, engineering, and hospitality. The area became a colourful blend of Caribbean, Indian, and various other influences. I remember the smell of curries and spices from our Guyanese relatives blending with my mother's French dishes as she learned to cook "Guyanese style." Brixton wasn't just a neighbourhood; it was a tapestry of stories from across the empire, each scent and flavour a part of who I was becoming.

The Brixton market, bustling and vibrant, looked as though it had sprung straight from the Caribbean. People walked among the stalls in bright clothing, some sporting dreadlocks and Rastafarian hats, others wearing traditional attire like shalwar kameez, saris, and beaded jewellery. Bob Marley tunes blasted from speakers, adding a reggae rhythm to the scene. The market overflowed with foods you couldn't find anywhere else in the UK but straight from the British colonies: mangoes, yams, plantains, guinips, chilies, peppers, and other exotic produce. There were great drums of ground spices in earthy tones reminiscent of North African markets and people making fresh roti, filling the air with a rich fusion of Caribbean, Guyanese, and Indian aromas.

Occasionally, you'd spot a lone bobby making his rounds, looking quite out of place in this spirited, lively scene. Brixton was a sublime melting pot of cultures, people, food, textures, languages, and smells - a place that offered a sense of home to so many migrants who had journeyed far in search of work, bringing pieces of their homelands with them.

From our house, you could walk to the centre of town - a bit of a trek for a young child, which usually meant either riding in a pushchair or walking close beside Mum or my eldest sister, securely harnessed so they could tug me back if I wandered too near the road. Our house on Beechdale Road was just one block from the main street. A left turn took you toward the prison, while a right led you to the busy shopping district and market. One shop that stands out in my memory is Bon Marché, a department store that seemed to have everything under its roof.

All the houses in our neighbourhood were built from dark grey bricks and topped with grey slate roofs, smoke drifting from chimneys that punctuated every home. The terraced houses on Beechdale Road looked nearly identical, each with a small entrance porch adorned with reddish brown tiles and a small courtyard bordered by a mosaic patterned tile with a modest hedge protected by black cast iron railings. Entry into the courtyard and patio was through a cast iron gate painted black.

The front door was typical yet substantial - a solid, heavy structure with a filled lower section, flanked by glass panels on either side. Between them, an ornate black door knocker and a decorative, rose-shaped knob and brass letter box centred themselves in the space between the lower and middle sections of the door, adding a touch of elegance. The upper part of the door featured a wide pane of frosted glass, gently filtering light into the corridor. Painted directly onto this glass was the house number – *Number 20* - a simple yet defining mark of identity. Opening this door greeted you with a distinctive scent, one that etched itself deeply into memory. Over time, this scent became a trigger, capable of transporting you back to that place, to that era. While fragrances from cooking, air fresheners, incense, perfume, or fresh flowers might mask it for a while, the underlying scent always reclaimed its presence, a subtle yet persistent reminder of the house's essence. Each house held its own unique scent, as distinct as the people who lived within its walls. The house became a part of its inhabitants, just as they became part of it. This is why, years later, even the faintest scent can evoke a feeling - a moment of comfort, nostalgia, or perhaps discomfort - bringing you back to a time and place forever etched into your being.

Entering the house, you'd immediately see a staircase on the right, leading up to a large heavy white door with black sprung hinges. This was the door that divided upstairs and downstairs. Downstairs to the left of the stairs was a double door to the left opening on to a large double room, which could be divided into a sitting room and a bedroom. This room had a big, central fireplace, and the back section opened to a small courtyard and garden. Further down the corridor lay the kitchen and bathroom, though the toilet was outside, as was typical of the time. I was too young to remember exactly where everyone slept, but Papa, his new wife—close to my mum's age - and their four children managed to occupy the lower floor whilst the eight of us lived upstairs.

At the end of the downstairs corridor, a door led to the cellar - a dark and mysterious place that seemed frightening to any child. Years later, as a teenager, we watched *10 Rillington Place* together in the family sitting room, a film about a serial killer who buried his victims in his garden and behind the walls. My father offhandedly mentioned that he used to frequent the same café as the killer, John Christie. I couldn't help but imagine bodies hidden in the cellar of our old house on Beechdale.

Inside the house, a faintly musty scent mixed with the aroma of furniture polish. The stairs were carpeted grey with a reddish pattern with runners, and the high walls were covered with embossed wallpaper, painted over layer by layer rather than being stripped. Nothing in the house was new. The sash windows rattled in the wind, the boiler in the bathroom was gas-powered, and so was the hot water in the kitchen. From the kitchen window, my mother would hang out the washing to dry on a pulley line over the backyard. All the washing was done by hand, and we had an old mangle to wring out the clothes. I think I learnt the hard way of not putting your fingers too close and that it was not a toy! By today's standards, it seems like a hard life; the hardships of that time, though, have a certain dignity compared to today's comforts.

As you reached the upstairs landing, the first two rooms on the left were the bathroom and a separate toilet, leading down to the kitchen. Indoor toilets were considered a luxury at the time, so I suppose we were quite "modern"! The fixtures in these rooms were almost works of art, adorned with intricate patterns. Unlike today's lightweight, mass-produced fittings, each cistern made from cast iron that was so hefty it took two people to lift. The cisterns hung high above the toilet, with a chain to the left. I remember hearing that chain pulled repeatedly in frustration, as the flush was minimal. The cistern took its time refilling, and it was a wait before you'd get a proper flush.

To the left of the landing was the first bedroom on the right - this was where I slept with my brothers. Next to us, at the front of the house, was the largest room, which doubled as my parents' bedroom and our sitting room. Of the few fond memories I have of Beechdale is of that space; it was where we celebrated Christmas, watched my father's cinefilms, and listened to recordings he'd made of us talking or singing. One such recording was my brother in his pyjamas with a microphone in hand singing '*she lups you yeah yeah yeah*', AKA – 'She Loves You' by the Beetles whilst the rest of us were sitting on the dark red settee speckled with black dots that made it look like a giant ladybird!

On the landing was another smaller set of stairs led up to a modest room on the left, then a few more steps to the topmost room, similar to an attic. These rooms were where my half-sisters slept, although as we got older, my parents eventually separated their bedroom from the sitting area.

There was a distinct painting I still recall, one that often appears in my dreams. It depicted an Indigenous chief against a backdrop of white clouds, blue skies, and pine trees, resembling the Canadian Rockies. I think Papa may have brought it from his time in Canada.

I also remember a board game my eldest brother had, though he doesn't recall it now. Each card in the game had a unique face representing a different person—a sheriff, a convict with dark eyes and a stubble, a soldier similar dress to the American Civil war, a Canadian Mounty, a banker, a Native American with a rifle and a cowboy. I was too young to understand the objective of the game, just an observer, yet the images left a lasting impression on my mind.

A particularly unsettling memory from early childhood was watching the remains of a large, straw-stuffed teddy bear burning in the fireplace downstairs, where Papa and his new partner (who was technically my step grandma or nana) lived. I wasn't certain if they were married - Papa hadn't married my mother's mother, nor my mum's younger sister's mother. His new partner was a few years younger than my mum, and I imagined it must have been challenging for her, living in a house technically owned by her stepdaughter who was also Papa's eldest daughter, my mother.

Yet it was this woman's cultural connection and shared language that seemed to appeal most to my mother. It offered her a chance to speak in her native tongue and to share conversations away from my father's ears. The French had this way about them - they'd speak English when you were around, only to shift into French for discussions meant to remain private. At times, it felt like a kind of elitism or exclusion.

Nowadays, it might be seen as a wonderful gift to be raised bilingual, yet my mother didn't encourage it for us children. I wasn't sure if this was due to my father's perhaps typical British disdain for the French, or if it was my mother's own way of placing a barrier between us and our French heritage. She could move between both worlds, but we were to belong to only one.

The teddy bear, large and cream-colored, wasn't actually mine but belonged to my eldest half brother; I remember bits of straw spilling from its loose stitches and its dark eyes with one of them hanging by a thread, but watching it burn left me inconsolable. I remember crying, asking why it had to be thrown in the fire. My mother told me it was falling apart and had given it to my step-grandmother to burn. My own teddy, a golden-orange one I called Sooty, went everywhere with me, though I'm not sure where he eventually disappeared. Other treasures from those days included a pull-along train and a soft knitted blue and grey toy elephant—simple comforts from a time when loyalties and belonging felt far less complicated.

A recurring memory - or perhaps a dream - lingers of tumbling down the stairs, pursued by a noisy cylinder-shaped vacuum cleaner resembling a giant dachshund. I remember its head and rear in black and a warm orange-brown in the middle. Somehow, in this memory, the vacuum, my fall, and a broom are strangely linked. May it was the broom stick that I struck before tumbling.

The "hammock" also left a strong impression on me; it may have just been a blue sheet knotted across the room, but it felt magical. I think it was in that hammock where I first tasted whisky, given to me by Papa to quiet my endless cries. I was told as I was a screamer. However this may have been attributed to constant earaches I had as a child and below average hearing. This was later resolved with the removal of my tonsils and adenoids. It was only a sip, yet I screamed even louder afterward. As they say, if you loathe something at first, it might end up becoming a future passion. For me, this was certainly true for whisky - I'm quite partial to a single malt now. Marmite, however, was a different story; force fed one spoonful was enough to turn me into a lifelong Vegemite devotee, spread thin over butter on toast.

Few other memories are as vivid. The small back garden comes to mind, where, like most children, I enjoyed hours of play. We even had a sandpit, and I'd play there with my aunt, who was only a few weeks younger than me! My hair then was a light brown, soft curls tied in a ponytail - a detail I know well thanks to family photos. I'm told my parents were hoping for a girl after my brother, and though I might not have chosen the style, I certainly didn't have a say in it! Later, my curls were cut and preserved as keepsakes, which I likely wouldn't have voted for either.

The garden also reminds me of my uncle, just a year older than me. He was a rambunctious kid who had a strange fascination with torturing insects and pulling the shells off tortoises, yet he was a good-hearted troublemaker. I remember when he broke his leg and came home with it in a plaster cast. Later in life, he joined the French Foreign Legion, which felt entirely fitting.

Then there was "Remember, Remember the Fifth of November" - my first Guy Fawkes bonfire night. I ended up with some minor burns from the sparks at the local bonfire in the nearby park. My mother had to lay me down on her bed that night. One firework, the Catherine wheel, still sticks in my mind with a hint of unease; it spun and whistled as it sprayed sparks. Those might have been the very sparks that left little burns on my hands, as they did on my eldest sister's head.

This house was my 'home for four and a half years from birth, or nearly five if you count the months in my mother's womb. The essence of this house would later test loyalties, relationships, cause division and opportunities for to those who called it a home.

"Perhaps I'll Arrive"

Sunlight streamed through skylights set high above the tin roofs, blending with the warm glow of large bell-shaped lamps hanging from the rafters. The beams of light, filtered by suspended dust motes that muffled sounds, created an ambiance reminiscent of an East End market. The terminal was stirring to life with the early dawn as buyers and sellers - or so it seemed - began to gather.

Scattered around were wooden desks, rustic and worn, adorned with tags, labels, and blank rectangular cards. Crates, parcels wrapped in striped plastic, and trolleys piled with goods formed a chaotic yet purposeful arrangement. Behind each desk stood a large weighing scale, its clock-like face marked in pounds, ounces, kilos, and grams, with a bold red arrow needle fixed toward what would be a 12 o'clock position. These scales, once a familiar sight in Woolworths stores where the public paid a penny to weigh themselves, were now pressed into a far more utilitarian role.

But this wasn't a market. It was the arrival and departure terminal of Lahore Airport, Pakistan. The modest building, its utilitarian charm beginning to show its age, was soon to be replaced by a new terminal under construction. For now, however, this served as the gateway for my departure to Peshawar, nestled in the North-West Frontier of Pakistan, where I would spend a night before embarking on a road trip to Kabul, Afghanistan

The terminal buzzed with activity. Travelers jostled for space, ready to have their bags checked, weighed, and tagged by hand. Boarding passes, handwritten on blank cards, were issued at makeshift counters. Luggage was weighed on the repurposed 'Woolworth' scales and then loaded into crates, pushed manually across the concrete floor. Automation was a distant luxury; here, every movement pulsed with the rhythm of human effort.

Men in traditional shalwar kameez, some with brown woollen shawls draped over their shoulders or adorned with distinctive caps, mingled with uniformed officials. Small stalls offered steaming cups of tea, fizzy drinks, sweets, crisps, fruit cake, and local delicacies resembling miniature bhajis. In the centre of the hangar-like terminal, rows of wooden seats, resembling long church pews with individual divisions, provided resting places. A vibrant mix of people occupied these seats: a mother adjusting her plain coloured scarf as her children ran around her, men in blue uniforms sporting a blue beret deep in conversation, elderly gentlemen sporting henna-dyed beards, and young men dressed smartly in open-necked white shirts and trousers.

A steady hum of voices filled the air, underscored by the occasional scrape of brooms against the floor. The cleaning was perfunctory at best—each sweep sent the dust into brief, swirling dances before it resettled. Even this seemingly mundane task served a dual purpose: a subtle way to observe the crowd while maintaining an appearance of order amid the chaos.

The hangar-like building served as both a check-in area and a departure lounge—though calling it a "lounge" was generous. It felt more like a Victorian built train station without the trains or perhaps a large barn devoid of hay or produce. Check-in was straightforward. I placed my bags on a wooden desk, handed over my passport, and presented a letter from my employer explaining the purpose of my trip. A series of yes-or-no questions followed, delivered in a monotone by the customs officer, who also doubled as the check-in staff and baggage handler. He barely glanced at me as he chatted with his colleague, seeming almost oblivious to my presence.

As he filled out a small card that would serve as my boarding pass, my bags were hauled onto a wooden cart. With the formalities complete, I found a seat on one of the wooden benches that passed as "lounge chairs." The design, with dividers separating each seat, ensured no one could stretch out. Not that this stopped a few people from napping on the floor, too stubborn - or too heavy - to be moved aside by the cleaner's broom.

Looking around, I noticed the occasional "European" - a collective term I used for anyone who didn't look local. Most were men, typically in their thirties or older, well-groomed and in reasonable shape. Their attire was predictable: trekking cargo pants in muted tones, plain or checked shirts, and wrap-around belt pouches likely stuffed with passports, wallets, and other essentials. A few carried small backpacks, briefcases, or even simple plastic duty-free bags - more likely filled with cigarettes than alcohol, given our flight's destination.

Opposite me sat a man in his mid-to-late thirties, clean-shaven with short, medium-brown hair. He looked perfectly at case in this setting, as though he had made this journey many times before. A brief nod served as our greeting. He asked, in a northern English accent, where I was headed.

"Peshawar," I replied.

"Ah, with the UN?" he asked.

"No, with the International Red Cross," I said.

When I asked about his work, he mentioned he was working with the British Council.

Our conversation was interrupted by an announcement: a flight number followed by the call to board at Gate 1. The flight prefix was "PIA," which prompted the man to quip, "Perhaps I'll Arrive." His comment wasn't entirely out of place. Pakistan International Airlines had recently faced a string of crashes, near-misses, and delays. Perhaps he also meant their infamous flight cancellations.

Despite the jest, my own experiences with PIA were positive. Over the next year, I would regularly fly on their small, propeller-driven planes, cruising low over the majestic Hindu Kush mountains. Navigating the region's challenging flying conditions - mountain thermals and sudden swirls - was a feat in itself. Their pilots took pride in their skill, often pointing out the scenery and tilting the aircraft so passengers could take in the breathtaking views.

After passing into the boarding area, I encountered the usual carry-on baggage check. My bag went through an X-ray machine, and another officer in blue but sporting a belt with a pistol and decorative service awards above his breast pocket performed a quick pat-down before waving me through. This was pre-9/11, so security was remarkably lax by today's standards.

A female PIA staff member, dressed smartly in the airline's green and white uniform with a neatly tied neck scarf, ushered us through a glass door. Outside, we followed a marked path, looping around red-and-white plastic safety poles and ropes, to our aircraft - a Fokker F27 Turbo Prop. It had been years since I'd flown on a propeller-driven plane, and I had forgotten how deafeningly loud they could be. My last flight on a prop plane was as a tourist flying over the Nazca Line in Peru where I was given a front seat next to the pilot!

Inside, the cramped cabin bore the marks of countless journeys. Seats were narrow, the overhead bins modest, and the windows offered glimpses of the fading sunlight as the plane prepared for take-off. While taxiing to the runway, I noticed a few Hercules C130 Aircraft, a few white coloured propellor driven plans with the word UN marked in blue and two white airplanes with the familiar emblem of the '*Comité International de la Croix-Rouge*'. By now, the fatigue of travel weighed heavily on me—hours spent in the terminal, preceded by a long-haul flight from Zurich, had taken their toll.

As the plane ascended, the landscape unfolded below - a patchwork of fields, villages, and winding rivers that gradually gave way to rugged snow-capped mountains. The sound of the engines was deafening, but it was a sound that would become a familiar companion and relief in the months to come.

The stewardess whom I sure was the same person who I saw at the gate, stills impeccably dressed in green and white with her neatly tied neck scarf, approached with a trolley. She handed me a box of refreshments: a piece of fruitcake, bhajilike snacks, and a small carton of orange juice. The simplicity of the meal was unexpectedly comforting, a reminder of the terminal's offerings. For a fleeting moment, I thought, *Swiss Air—you're forgiven.*

A tradition I kept on my travels was to ask if they had a pack of playing cards. My mother, an avid collector of mementoes from around the world, cherished these small tokens from my journeys. Over time, as I visited nearly 80 countries, her collection grew significantly—though thankfully, she wasn't using them for endless games of 52-card pick-up! Not all airlines carried branded playing cards, but PIA did, and I was pleased to purchase a pack to take back to the UK.

We finally arrived in Peshawar just before dusk. Relief washed over me—I was glad to have reached my destination and looked forward to a nights' rest before embarking on my next journey: a rugged trip by Land Cruiser to Kabul, traversing the historic Khyber Pass.

Passing through customs and retrieving my luggage was uneventful. I scanned the crowd for any familiar faces but saw none. Traveling alone, this marked the first of many 'missions' or 'deployments' with the International Red Cross. Neither term felt entirely appropriate - 'mission' carried religious connotations, while 'deployment' evoked military undertones. As a humanitarian organisation, our work focused on assisting people affected by armed conflict, often in active war zones.

Then, a welcome sight emerged. A man in a grey shalwar kameez, a navy vest, and a traditional grey woollen cap stood holding a small banner with my name alongside the Red Cross emblem. A large badge with the organisation's logo

24

adorned his chest. His smile was broad, radiating relief that mirrored my own. He extended his hand warmly and said, *"Salam alaykum."* I returned the gesture, replying, *"Alaykum salaam".*

After collecting my luggage, the Red Cross national employee—my driver—escorted me through the crowded terminal to a reserved parking spot for Red Cross vehicles. It was evident that the International Red Cross was both well-known and highly respected in this region.

I climbed into the passenger seat, fastening my seatbelt, and noticed a large brown envelope with my name on the dashboard. The driver handed it to me, explaining that I could read its contents once I reached my accommodation.

As we drove, we exchanged pleasantries in broken English. Although I was in an Islamic country, my Arabic - learned during nearly seven years in Saudi Arabia commencing during the first Gulf War in 1991 - was of little use beyond religious phrases. Most Pakistanis didn't speak Arabic unless they had worked in Arabic-speaking countries. His mother tongue was Urdu, which I didn't speak, so English became our default means of communication.

Arriving at dusk, with night falling, was always disorienting. The faint glow of yellow streetlights and neon signs from countless shops blurred my surroundings. Electricity poles and tangles of wires framed the view, interspersed with three- and four-story houses and apartments. As we turned off the bustling main road onto quieter neighbourhood streets, the atmosphere changed. The air felt less polluted, the noise of car horns and diesel engines faded, and towering, vibrantly decorated trucks - each uniquely adorned with dazzling lights and intricate designs - became a fleeting memory.

The driver stopped in front of my pre-booked guest house. A porter emerged, took my suitcase, and offered to carry my bag as well. I declined, keeping it with me, and followed him inside. The driver exchanged a few words with the porter, assured me he'd see me in the morning, and drove away.

The guest house was modest but welcoming, its entrance painted in a warm cinnamon hue with simple yet homely decorations. My room, however, was less inviting. Located on the first floor - adhering to Red Cross security guidelines of avoiding ground and high floors - it was dimly lit and sparsely furnished, with only a bed, a dresser, and an adjoining bathroom.

The bed featured a polished wooden headboard, plain sheets, and a simple bedspread. A vase of plastic flowers sat on a small coffee table next to a glass ashtray, and on the ceiling, an arrow pointed toward Mecca. Security measures were evident: all accommodations used by the Red Cross underwent strict assessments, requiring guards and adherence to minimum safety standards.

Before settling in, I opened the brown envelope marked "Confidential" beneath my name. Inside was a 'welcome' briefing pack containing security information, a list of contact numbers, instructions for the following morning, and a note confirming an 8 a.m. pickup for briefings at the Red Cross sub-delegation in Peshawar. From there, we would travel in a convoy of Land Cruisers toward Kabul.

Disoriented and uneasy, I checked my luggage and documents, took a quick shower, and climbed into bed. Sleep came, but it was shallow - my heightened alertness and unfamiliar surroundings keeping me on edge.

Around 1 a.m., a muffled explosion shook me awake, followed by the staccato bursts of gunfire. My heart raced as I strained my ears to listen intently, clutching the bedclothes. The gunfire was sporadic, punctuated by distant shouting and chanting. It didn't seem to be moving closer. The explosions then sounded more like fireworks, though my heightened state made me fear street fighting was breaking out nearby.

Gradually, the noise subsided, replaced by the hum of distant traffic. Exhaustion won out, and I drifted back to sleep.

At 7 a.m., I was up promptly, showered, and dressed in attire befitting a Red Cross delegate. Breakfast awaited downstairs: Afghan-style bread, honey, cream cheese, boiled eggs, and slices of melon, papaya, and banana. I savoured the black tea, with milk and sugar. I asked the host what the noise was last night. He said there had been a celebration and it was common to shoot in the air and set off firework crackers. It was a bit of an anti-climax to what I was expecting him to say!

The driver arrived on schedule, and for the first time, I could see my surroundings in daylight with pink, white and dark red bougainvillea flowing over fences and entrances and balconies with potted pink geraniums . Peshawar revealed itself as a modest frontier town. Some areas had a rugged charm, while others were meticulously maintained, with regimental squares that reflected a proud military history.

The British army's influence was unmistakable, evident in the ranking systems and the proudly displayed coats of arms of each regiment.

I soon arrived at the sub-delegation office where I was to meet the head of the sub-delegation and a few of my companions most of whom were seasoned delegates that would journey with me to Kabul. From Kabul I would then travel to Kandahar in the south to begin my role as a surgical ward nurse at a Hospital administered by the International Red Cross.

Half-Bloods

Our family numbered eight: Mum, Dad, and six children spanning a 15-year age gap between the eldest and youngest. I had an older brother, Adam, just 13 months my senior, and a younger sister nearly four years younger. We three were the biological children of my parents, Abraham and Dolly. Abraham also had two children from a previous marriage, Kumari and Mark, while my mother had a daughter, Charlotte, with a traveller. Charlotte would later become one of the most important people in my life.

Each of my half-siblings carried stories of their own - tales of hurt, abuse, abandonment, perseverance, tragedy, adversity, and triumph.

Kumari, who I will call by her stage name Kumi, was born in Berbice, then British Guiana, on the mainland of South America. Though geographically part of Latin America, the culture, language, food, religion, and lifestyle of British Guiana were heavily shaped by English colonialism, agricultural traditions, and the Indian subcontinent. It was culturally closer to the West and East Indies than to the Spanish- and Portuguese-speaking countries of Central and South America. Sandwiched between Brazil and Venezuela, and sharing a coastline with French and Dutch Guianas, British Guiana served as an outpost for 18th- and 19th-century naval and trading powers—primarily Britain, France, and the Netherlands—while countering the influence of Spain and Portugal.

Kumi and I shared a birthday, exactly 11 years apart. It was often remarked that I was her "gift." I'm unsure of the exact year she arrived in the UK, but it may have been with my father or her mother in the early 1950s, before their divorce. At 11 years of age, Kumi likely mimicked parenthood by caring for a doll, as many girls did in that era. When I was born, I replaced the plastic doll with real cries, soiled nappies, laughter, and emotions.

This dual parenthood - biological from my mother and pseudo-parenthood from Kumi - initially seemed harmless. However, it sparked jealousy between them and created a veneer of harmony for the outside world. The competition may have begun early. Around the age of two or three, I recall calling out for either "mum" after finishing my business in the toilet. By all accounts, I was a cute child; my mother even wanted to enter me into a 'Pears Soap' competition. My mixed heritage - a blend of Indian and French Aryan blood - gave me an uncommon appearance when cultural mixing was rare at the time. People were often categorised as Black, Brown, White, or Yellow (a term then used for East Asians). Later, I'd be labelled "half-caste" by those intent on categorising others.

My sister once told me that my mother threw a jealous tantrum when I wanted to go with her instead of with her. Such moments reflect the emotional toll on children when adults fail to grasp how their actions shape young, impressionable minds.

I adored both my sister and my mother, sometimes unsure of who my "real" mother was. Kumi, though petite, was athletic and strikingly attractive. Her figure drew wolf whistles from workmen and passing cars. She emphasised her well-endowed chest with tight T-shirts and hot pants when walking down the street. If I walked beside her, many assumed I was her child. Between the ages of six and ten, I even felt proud of having such a young, vibrant "mum." She even once attended our school athletics day at junior school with both her and my dad blitzing the field in their respective mothers and fathers race. It seemed strange that no one questioned whether she was my mother or not! In contrast to being considered 'old' enough to pass as an adult, Kumi also imitated being a young teenage to gain access to my younger sister's gymnastics club. Kumi was probably chronologically older than the female gym instructor who probably thought how well endowed my sister was for her age. I think my sister had to dumb down her intellect and conversation appropriate for someone who was around 14 years rather than being around 25 years old. She was a great actor and carried it off – Oscar style!

In Brixton, Kumi dressed modestly and wore her hair short, resembling a dowdy older sister. That changed when we moved to South Croydon. There, she embraced the swinging sixties with long hair, colourful mini-skirts, a fondness for older men, and a free-spirited personality. We shared much in common: both Leos, musical, outgoing, playful, and sporty.

Kumi took up judo and trained as a masseuse while studying physiotherapy. She quickly became the apple of my father's eye. Her judo skills gave her an unusual authority in the household. Only she could calm my father's frequent tempers. When my parents fought, my siblings and I would tremble, praying for her return. She'd confront my father and somehow defuse his anger, confident in her ability to physically handle him if needed.

31

Kumi's bedroom, overlooking the garden, was her sanctuary. She personalised it with paintings of world flags and had her own sink. Her artistic touch remained even after my brothers inherited the room. Visiting Kumi's room was a treat, especially on Sunday mornings when she cleaned and invited us in. She had a record player and a growing collection of classical 33 rpm vinyl records and 45 rpm pop and chant singles by the Beatles, the Casuals and classical pop. My love for classical music began there. She enthralled me with vivid descriptions of scenes behind the music, like Edward Grieg's programmatic music to Ibsen's play *Peer Gynt*. To this day, I frequently request the original Edward Grieg's *Peer Gynt* on ABC Classic FM, particularly the Wedding March which led to Peer Gynt's trials and tribulations. I've yet to hear it played except for his 'suites' which were not in sequence to the Ibsen's play. I did, however, find the same vinyl recording she owned with the Royal Philharmonic Orchestra and chorus conducted by Sir Thomas Beecham.

Kumi didn't always live with her parents before joining us. During or after their divorce, she lived in a Salvation Army-run home. She often lamented that period, yet spoke fondly of her time there, sometimes preferring it to home life.

Kumi left our South Croydon home around age 24 or 25 years much to our sadness but would often return. I remember our trip to Euston or maybe it was Liverpool Steet train station to say a tearful goodbye as she began her overseas journey. She had been the glue of our family, uniting us. There seemed nothing she couldn't do - painting, storytelling, sports, cooking with minimal ingredients, or even climbing trees. She played football with the Crystal Palace ladies, swam brilliantly (fond memories for Streatham public baths with her, my dad and Charlotte), sang, danced, and created life wherever she went. She was an actress which may have been self-nurtured as a child imagining herself as something different to who she was, her ancestry and upbringing.

Her secretarial job near Victoria Station led to a position at a U.S. military base in Karlsruhe, West Germany. There, she met an American soldier named John, who seemed much older than her. All accounts were that he was married and had a wife and kids in Texas, USA. My mother disliked him and spread rumours about him being abusive, which I doubt were true. I imagined him as my sister's husband. Loud, confident, and handsome, he joined us for Christmas one year, giving Kumi a horsewhip as a gift - fuel for my mother's claims.

Kumi spent three years in West Germany before returning to us, briefly restoring our family's unity. Now speaking some German, I think this sparked a further interest in languages and she soon began learning and speaking French at a higher level. Those years were a testament to her resilience and ability to adapt, yet they also marked the beginning of a shift in our family's dynamics. Whilst Kumi's passion for literature, music and seemingly endless vocabulary including teaching us rarely used words such as 'thrasonical', 'contumacious,' 'cantankerous', 'belligerent', 'reiterative', 'imbecile' and 'quidnunc'– it all seemed as though it was to escape our modest and working class background and that she was ' above' us both academically, culturally and linguistically. I even combined all the words together when calling someone a name not really knowing what I was saying. It could have been French to anyone hearing it , or gobbledegook, and I remember replying to a question in the language lab at school by reciting all these words as a phrase.

When asked to explain by my French teacher who had a Mauritian background, I replied naively that my sister had taught me some French words and what I said was a French phrase. I don't think she really understood what it was I said! No kid could use these words yet alone understand them and maybe she thought I had been duped!

Kumi somewhat appeared ashamed of her heritage disguising her Indian roots or claiming to be of a high caste or Brahmin as well as having some Jewish and Spanish descent. I never questioned this at the time but became increasingly under her influence adopting much of her tastes, pretentiousness and free spirit which would lead to some of my family calling me a snob or excluding me from more grounded and commoner activities such as football. I was a hockey player, a tennis player, a rugby player – all sports that tended to be played by the more privileged with soccer played by the working class! Yet I love football and follow the team of my childhood to this day – Liverpool!

Yet, I had a strong bond with Kumi and would make trips on my own to her house the other side of the River Thames on the bus Route 68 that travelled all the way from South Croydon bus garage to Chalk Farm Station or from East Croydon to Victoria on British Rail, change to the Underground train run by London Transport, take the Victoria Line (Light Blue) to Warren Street station and the Northern Line (Black) to Camden Town. It was then a short walk passing through Camden Markets to her house in Kentish Town! Strangely enough her house number was '68'. My favourite underground trains were the ones that went deep underground like the Central Line (the Red line on the map) which were called the 'Tube'!

With my father working for London transport I learnt very early the ways of travelling through London using trains and buses. I was street smart and as a young boy I could confidently travel on my own through the network of underground trains, learning all the different lines, connections and bus routes and garages and spend a day on the top deck of a Routemaster bus going all over London. A feat rarely allowed today by parents but would later serve me well in my search for hidden bars, clubs and haunts and my humanitarian work and travels.

Mark was the name given to my eldest brother, who shared the same parents as Kumi. In character, however, he couldn't have been more different from our sister - polar opposites in many ways. Six years my senior, Mark was by definition my "big brother," but often, I felt like his older brother and mentor. My expectations of what a big brother should be, shaped by my relationship with my biological brother, Adam, just a year older than me, clashed with the reality of Mark's unique personality.

Mark was an undeniably handsome young man, perhaps the most striking among us. His Indian heritage gifted him deep brown eyes and a well-proportioned physique. Like most of us, he was on the shorter side, but his perfect proportions made height irrelevant. His looks bore an uncanny resemblance to a young Maradona - the iconic Argentinian soccer player famous for his "Hand of God" goal that broke English hearts during the 1986 World Cup quarterfinals.

But Mark's similarities to Maradona went beyond physical appearance. On the soccer pitch, he displayed the same dramatic tendencies and was once told that when throwing the Javelin at school it went backwards! When not playing truant, being expelled from school and reports of trying to set fire to the toilets at school, off the field, he had what could only be described as a natural gift for persuasion - a showman and a born salesman starting with selling second hand cars, owning his own car sales pitch who could, as the saying goes, "sell a coffin to his grandmother." Mark exuded charisma, often adopting a mafia-esque demeanour, playing pranks, and wearing his emotions unabashedly on his sleeve. His heart often ruled his head, sometimes leading him into conflicts with authority and bringing moments of shame to our family.

In many ways, Mark was a Ricky Gervais of his time— outspoken, crude, and unapologetically forthright. The opposite of being 'woke' he didn't filter or mince words, called a spade a spade, and tolerated no nonsense. Yet he balanced this brashness with a flair for sophistication. He had a taste for the finer things in life: designer clothes, luxury cars, elegant jewellery, original paintings, and a home adorned with opulent (and sometimes faux) ornaments and "bling." Gold, in particular, was his weakness. Luxury defined him, whether it was lavish holidays, fine dining, or entertaining guests. Mark demanded perfection and wasn't afraid to confront anyone who fell short, even waitstaff. He refused to feel embarrassed—appearances mattered deeply to him, as though he sought to project the abundance he may have lacked as a child.

Mark's desire to be loved and acknowledged manifested in his relentless drive to succeed. He worked hard to build his business empire, showering others with generosity, especially us as children and our parents. Today, he is arguably the most successful member of our family, both in material wealth and stability. He married his childhood sweetheart, who remains his anchor, raised two boys, and is now a proud grandfather. His choice of career—owning and managing nursing homes—reflects his deep empathy, using his charm and natural salesmanship to care for others in a meaningful way.

Not completing high school, leaving at fifteen years without any school certificates and rejecting fully the academic gifts that came naturally to him, Mark was the epitome of success without qualifications. My parents feared his reputation would disadvantage both my brother Adam and myself which led to them enrolling us in schools a fair distance away!

Unlike Kumi, Mark was effortlessly gifted as a young child. My parents envisioned him as an officer in the Navy or excelling in a profession befitting his higher-than-average IQ. He breezed through his Eleven-Plus exams, earning a coveted place at the London Nautical School. What exactly happened for Mark to reject what would have been an easy path to success, I don't know. Maybe it was part of his souls plan!

Despite his potential, our relationship as children was strained. Mark seemed to view me as weak, a mummy's boy and effeminate and would sometimes ridicule me and exclude me from the typical "boy" activities like football at the local park or joining Sunday league games. Instead, he gravitated toward Adam, who became his playmate and mentee. Together, they played Subbuteo (always Spurs versus the Eagles), watched *Match of the Day*, and bonded over football (and farts!). Mark even introduced Adam to the pub scene and enlisted him to help as a milkman.

However, as time passed, Mark became immensely proud of my achievements. I believe, deep down, he recognised the struggles I faced in my teens - the unspoken battles with my sexual identity, the loss of loved ones, exclusion from family events where you could be equal and bring your 'loved ones', the fear of the AIDS crisis, and the constraints that kept me from becoming my true self. Though he couldn't express it then, his pride grew as I broke free from those shackles to forge my own identity. Somehow, through a mix of grace, determination, an illness and a touch of luck, I found my way, and Mark has always respected and encouraged me on that journey.

Mark's struggles adapting to life as a child with his father and stepmother shaped much of who he would become in later years. Whether it was the lingering ghost of racism rooted in my mother's Aryan lineage or the influence of my grandfather, "Papa," it was clear that Mark was seen as needing to be "whipped" into shape—both figuratively and, sadly, quite literally. His dramatic and rebellious nature became a constant thorn in both my parents' lives. To them, Mark embodied the archetype of a "young hooligan," the very example of what Adam and I were never to emulate.

Similar to Kumi, Mark didn't seem to embrace his Indian heritage. In all but appearance he was British or more specifically 'English'. He developed an exaggerated South London accent infused with phrases of East London cockney. Explicitly he was Indo-Guyanese but implicitly was Anglo-Saxon – or a coconut – Dark brown on the outside and 'White' on the inside. Like many first generation migrants (especially from British Commonwealth states), they would become more 'British than the British' and openly demonstrated a nationalistic persona. They had little attachment or interest to their parents heritage almost to the point of rejection of their culture and values. This would later challenge the second generation who wanted to reclaim their lost heritage, find out and seek knowledge of their ancestral roots adopting some of this cultural practice into their everyday lives. Many found it frustratingly hard to integrate into the UK that externally was multicultural but inwardly still colonial and had visions that Britain still ruled the waves!

For my father, Mark and many migrants and first generation it was about 'fitting in' to be accepted into British society and 'assimilating' rather than embracing multiculturism. 'High Tea' was a regular Sunday afternoon event for us. I read a report following the Brexit report that the Windrush and post second world migrants and their children were overrepresented in the Yes (to coming out of the European market) camp and many voting toward centre right political parties.

My mother, openly voiced her disdain for Mark and Kumi to "her" children. She failed to grasp how her harsh words and actions planted seeds of bias in young, impressionable minds—biases that would later echo in our own behaviours and beliefs. Her inability to see the ripple effects of her actions only deepened the divide between us as siblings.

Mark's early childhood was profoundly shaped by his time in foster care following the divorce of his biological parents. Yet, unlike the stereotypical narratives of trauma or shame that often surround such experiences, Mark remembered his time in foster care with the Gray family as a source of genuine love and belonging. For him, the Gray's represented stability, warmth, and a sense of family that his biological home could not provide.

This fondness for the Gray's lingered well into adulthood, driving Mark to search for them across decades. His journey to reconnect involved pouring over immigration records, ship passenger lists, and even newspaper archives. Eventually, he succeeded in tracing the family to Canada. Tragically, by the time he located them, his beloved foster mother had already passed away. However, he was able to speak with the Gray's daughter, a connection that, while bittersweet, brought him a sense of closure.

I believe this search for his lost "family" was more than just a quest for nostalgia. It was Mark's way of reconciling the wounds of his past, a testament to his enduring need for love, connexion, and the acknowledgment of those formative years when he felt truly valued. The Gray's, even in their absence, were a reminder of what family could and should be—a contrast to the fractured dynamics of his biological home and a reflection of the deep resilience that has always defined him.

Yet, Mark's intentions were always rooted in love and a deep desire to prove himself - a relentless determination to overcome the setbacks of his childhood and build a successful life. One memory that stands out vividly is the night a large house up the road went up in flames. The glow of the fire illuminated the night sky, visible from the Windsor pub where Mark was at the time. Fearing it might be our house, he ran home as fast as he could, ready to rescue us children while both Mum and Dad were working their respective night shifts.

Then there was another, almost comical moment that highlighted his complexities. After a family evening out visiting one of Dad's friends, a drunken stranger made unwelcome advances toward Mum as we arrived home late at night. This escalated into a heated street brawl, waking up the neighbours with Dad defending her honour. Mark - who had the strength to knock both men to the ground if he'd been inclined - remained blissfully asleep in his room through all the yelling and chaos. His capacity for heroic action and his ability to completely disengage were quintessentially Mark, always surprising and never predictable.

The only thing that was predictable was Mark having a reserved seat at every Crystal Palace FC soccer match! Go the Eagles!

The last of my half siblings is Charlotte born in 1958 to my mother and whom I will call a traveller. Charlotte will I hope one day write about her own story as my story will be my memory and will not do justice to her own personal journey. She deserves a chapter on her own which is a bit further along as you move through this book.

The Road to Kabul

Following a series of country-level briefings at the Peshawar Sub-Delegation Office that expanded on the global and regional overviews I had attended at the British Red Cross headquarters in Grosvenor Square, Hyde Park Corner, and later at the International Committee of the Red Cross headquarters in Geneva, we prepared to depart. We boarded our respective Land Cruisers, ready to face the unpredictable terrain ahead.

The white 4WD, manual gear Toyota Series 75 Land Cruisers were the backbone of the ICRC and many other international humanitarian organisations operating in conflict zones. These versatile vehicles came in various configurations tailored to their intended purposes. Most were long-wheelbase models with seating for three in the front - two passengers and a driver. Behind the front seats, some vehicles featured front-facing seats with storage space at the rear, while others, like those I often used, were equipped with side fold-up "trooper" seats. This design provided greater cargo capacity, allowing stretchers to be carried in the back. However, enduring a four-to-eight-hour journey over rough terrain on those bench seats often left you with a numb backside and an unsteady gait. As a first-time delegate and one of the younger members of the team, I had little chance of claiming a front seat. These prized spots were typically reserved for the head and deputy head of delegation, department leads, and, in keeping with an era of chivalry, female or senior colleagues.

This was my first deployment as a surgical ward nurse - the beginning of a transformative chapter in my life. Among a convoy of seasoned professionals, I was the sole medical team member, both an observer and an active participant in a high-stakes environment. As our vehicles set off, each manned by Afghan drivers and field officers - often from tribal backgrounds aligned with the regions we were entering - a steady stream of radio exchanges began. The lead vehicle relayed updates to a designated base, using only call signs for vehicles and locations; personal names and specific places were never mentioned. These communications detailed our movements - current position, destination, estimated departure and arrival times, passenger count, and status updates such as "all is well" or, at times, more foreboding alternatives.

Depending on the level of risk, we adjusted our visibility: flags were either prominently displayed or removed entirely. I recall one particular occasion when we travelled in a convoy of four Land Cruisers, each bearing a Red Cross flag—its stark white background the reverse of the Swiss flag - fluttering at the rear. We were en route to a prison that resembled a medieval fortress, perched atop a hill with a winding road leading to a drawbridge and an arched entrance. From the narrow slit windows of the prison, the sight of our convoy - four vehicles with banners unfurling in the wind - must have evoked the image of crusaders returning to a castle, our armoured steeds replaced by Land Cruisers. The exception was the reversal of the white and red!

Each diesel-powered vehicle was equipped for resilience and survival. They featured snorkels for fording rivers, UHF and VHF radios with aerials, fire extinguishers, first-aid kits, and a critical supply of water. Personal snacks were a staple, and it was tradition for new arrivals to share "tastes of home." I had brought Swiss chocolates and snacks, a small but welcome gesture that bridged cultural divides in the field. The vehicles bore the unmistakable emblem of the International Red Cross, a marker of neutrality and protection under the Geneva Conventions. These emblems indicated medical support or personnel, and under international law, they were to be respected, their work unhindered. Vehicles were further marked with identification numbers visible from above and Geneva-issued license plates.

On each vehicle on the back door and side window was a sticker – showing a cross against a rifle. This was to indicate that no weapons or armed escorts were permitted within or accompanying the Red Cross. Our protection was our emblem and mandate.

It was 1998, and tobacco smoking was still an ingrained habit among colleagues. Meetings, briefings, and even the confines of vehicles often swirled with cigarette smoke - a stark contrast to today, where non-smokers would be the norm. A pack of cigarettes, I quickly learned, was a useful currency at checkpoints.

Our first major stop was the Torkham Border Crossing, near the historic Khyber Pass. This crossing, a critical entry point for humanitarian organisations into Afghanistan, carried an air of heightened tension. On the Pakistani side, a long steel and wooden bridge stretched over a "no man's land" section dividing the two countries. The scene was chaotic - peeling light-blue buildings housed barred windows, uniformed officials moved among a throng of civilians carrying goods, suitcases, and children. Most crossings were made on foot or bicycle, with buses, Utes (pick-up trucks), and mini-vans depositing passengers on one side, only for them to board similar vehicles on the other.

Here, I saw my first "light blue" burqa - a full-body and head covering worn by Afghan women that to outsiders symbolised the suppression of women. The garment's small slits or mesh panels for the eyes seemed confining, yet I couldn't help but note the anonymity it provided amidst the crowded border chaos.

The border was a hub of commerce and survival. Local communities carried goods bought in Pakistan for trade or personal use in Afghanistan. Processes moved at a glacial pace, often interrupted by prayer calls, meal breaks, or the unpredictable whims of officials. However, working with the Red Cross and leveraging their well-established contacts, our crossing was relatively smooth. Passports were collected *en masse*, shuffled through a series of officers, and returned with a stamp marking our departure from Pakistan.

The Afghan side of the border presented a stark contrast— an eerily quiet, desolate landscape, buildings with broken glass that had come under mortar attack. We were now in Taliban run country! The bustling activity of Torkham gave way to an oppressive stillness, a harbinger of the challenges that lay ahead in this war-ravaged nation.

Entering Afghanistan was surprisingly straightforward. The senior delegates and field officers efficiently handled the process, exchanging documents and coordinating approvals before our passports were stamped. At the time, I carried a United Kingdom-issued passport alongside a "mission" passport provided by the International Red Cross. While the latter lacked the diplomatic immunity of a UN pass, it symbolised our humanitarian status, grounded in the Red Cross's principles and its unique form of diplomacy.

The eastern region of Afghanistan greeted us with a climate reminiscent of the Mediterranean in early winter - still mild dotted with fruit trees. Although the fruit had long been picked, the orchards were varieties familiar to me, such as stone fruits, persimmons, and even subtropical bananas. Our convoy was bound for Jalalabad, a bustling market town with a businesslike energy that contrasted sharply with the quieter, more subdued settlements I would visit later.

As we travelled, we frequently passed crowded Utes packed with soldiers, their weapons and ammunition loosely slung over their shoulders, and the occasional troop carrier rumbling toward the front lines. The road itself bore the scars of conflict and neglect, cratered by mortar strikes and years of limited or no maintenance. What should have been a short journey stretched into hours, the vehicles bouncing and lurching over the uneven terrain and craters by dropped bombs giving a feeling that you were riding on a boat over choppy seas rather than in a car. The asphalt had long since worn away, leaving a sandy, gravelly surface that sent dust billowing into the air with every passing truck.

While the idea of opening the windows to let in the fresh countryside air—and vent the cigarette smoke - was tempting, the fine dust that poured into the cabin made it impossible. There was no standard for "right" or "left" on these roads; drivers swerved and weaved around craters, dodging each other in a chaotic dance.

Occasionally, we encountered young men and boys working on the road. Armed with spades, they enthusiastically filled potholes with piles of stones just before our vehicles arrived. As we passed, they would step aside, standing at attention with shovels in hand, waiting for a tip in local currency. Their enterprise was striking—not just a means to earn a living but a clever system. I couldn't help but wonder if, during the lulls between vehicles, they removed the stones and repeated the process for the next passing convoy. It was, after all, a business and their way of scraping together a livelihood in this fractured landscape.

After what felt like an eternity, we finally arrived at the sub-delegation office in Jalalabad - a place I would later return to as my duty station. Our arrival was met with warm greetings and, soon after, a traditional Afghan lunch. Grilled, skewered meats cooked over coals were served alongside freshly baked Afghan bread and tangy pickled vegetables. The unspoken rule was to avoid anything that wasn't peeled or thoroughly cooked - a precaution I quickly came to appreciate.

Red Cross sub-delegations and premises operated with a level of precision that ensured both safety and functionality. Local staff, including cooks, housekeepers, and various support personnel, worked seamlessly alongside international delegates. Behind the scenes, teams of logisticians and administrative staff negotiated and maintained minimum standards for accommodations, offices, and other facilities. These efforts provided a secure and supportive environment for technical staff like myself to focus on our work.

As was customary in Geneva, meals played a significant role in fostering community. The main meal of the day, referred to as "dinner," was served in the early afternoon and held in a designated delegate residence. This wasn't a simple lunch but a substantial, thoughtfully prepared meal designed to sustain us through the demands of the day. A lighter supper, often self-prepared with housemates, followed in the evening. Breakfast and "dinner" were the cornerstone meals, with dinner serving as both nourishment and a ritual of connection.

The midday dinner was a formal affair, emphasising dress, etiquette, and light conversation. It was deliberately not a setting for briefings or debriefings but rather a moment to step back from the intensity of our work and engage with colleagues as equals. Evening meals called supper, by contrast, were more casual and intimate. Housemates and occasional guests would gather, sharing the responsibility of preparing a simple meal, allowing for easy, unguarded conversation—a quiet reprieve in a demanding and unpredictable environment.

Due to both the local and organisational curfews, which required us to reach our destination before nightfall, we bid farewell to our hosts and boarded our vehicles for the final leg to Kabul. Driving through Jalalabad town, we navigated its bustling streets lined with shops that resembled makeshift shacks. Signs advertised goods and services, while their wares were prominently displayed for passing traffic. Butchers hung meat on hooks, swarming with flies, alongside carpet and tea vendors, clothing shops, bakeries selling freshly baked flatbread, and restaurants offering kebabs and other traditional Afghan dishes.

The carpet shops were particularly memorable. Sellers would lay carpets on the road for vehicles to drive over, giving them a weathered, antique appearance that increased their perceived value. When tanks passed through, it was like rolling out a VIP red carpet - the immense weight of the machinery adding an air of authenticity to the "aging" process. Many of these carpets, intricate in design and reminiscent of Persian rugs, incorporated motifs like helicopters, rifles or tanks woven into the tapestry, blending tradition with the sobering realities of war.

Before we resumed our journey, I managed to switch to a more comfortable seat, this time behind the front passenger, and even had the luxury of a seatbelt. As we pressed on toward Kabul, the terrain became increasingly rugged, and the temperature dropped sharply, hinting at the winter chill awaiting us in the capital. The side of the roads were littered with remnants of passed conflicts particularly during the Soviet invasion. There were tanks and jeep type vehicle remains with some kids waiving to us whilst sitting one behind the other the gun turret of rusting Soviet built tank!

Not long into the drive, the convoy came to an unexpected halt. Checkpoints were a common occurrence, and most waved us through after a brief exchange. This one, however, was different. Our lead vehicle was in conversation with what appeared to be a senior commander or high-ranking soldier. Identifying combatants was becoming increasingly difficult—few wore anything resembling a military uniform. If not for their ubiquitous AK-47s and ammunition belt, they could easily have been mistaken for civilians or even figures from the era of Genghis Khan. The blurred lines between soldiers and civilians underscored the chaotic nature of the conflict.

A message crackled over the radio from the lead vehicle, summoning my assistance. Two soldiers, lightly injured by shrapnel, needed medical attention, and I was the only trained medic in the convoy. Accompanied by our head of media and communications, I stepped out with my medical kit.

The soldiers sat by the roadside, their injuries superficial but in need of care. With an interpreter and another delegate by my side, I approached them cautiously but professionally. Using the supplies in my kit - saline wash, iodine, Steri-Strips, and bandages - I cleaned and dressed their wounds. The procedure was straightforward, requiring no hospitalisation or major intervention, much to my relief. Yet this simple act carried profound significance, immediately recognised by our communications team. It was a symbolic gesture that would serve us well and protect us in the coming future.

Without asking who they were or questioning their affiliations, I had provided medical care to two Taliban soldiers. In that moment, they were not "the enemy"; they were simply casualties of war. Guided by the Red Cross's principles of neutrality and impartiality, I treated them as I would any other wounded individual.

Such actions, though seemingly small, were pivotal to the organisation's mission and protection. They reinforced the Red Cross's reputation as an impartial humanitarian actor, demonstrating that we took no sides in the conflict. Whatever personal opinions or biases we carried, they were set aside in the face of our professional responsibilities.

It reminded me of the profound ethical commitments shared by professions like law and medicine. Just as a lawyer must defend a perpetrator with the same vigour as a victim, a nurse must provide care regardless of the patient's background—even if it's an abuser injured in a domestic fight. Wearing the uniform of your profession demanded adherence to its oaths and principles, no matter how challenging the circumstances. In that moment, I came face-to-face with the profound weight of this responsibility, realising that even the smallest acts of compassion could carry far-reaching implications.

As Kabul came into view, the landscape gave way to rapid rivers running alongside the road, grey embankments, remnants of recent snowfall, ice and a noticeable drop in temperature. Kabul's temperature can fall below minus five degrees centigrade during the winter months – the time of our arrival.

As we entered the suburbs scars of past and ongoing conflicts became unmistakable. This once vibrant and cosmopolitan city, a hub of Western influence in fashion, education, and culture, had transformed into a city of survival. Unlike the conservative regions governed by tribal chiefs and steeped in local customs, Kabul had been celebrated for its university, which attracted both locals and international travellers. It was a key stop on the famous Hippie Trail, drawing adventurers heading toward the Hindu Kush mountains. The city boasted international hotel chains, swimming pools, diverse cuisines, and a unique blend of 1960s and 1970s fashion—mixing Western, Eastern European, and traditional Afghan styles like the shalwar kameez. Kabul stood in sharp contrast to much of the country, especially the southern provinces, where strict religious codes heavily influenced by tribal traditions prevailed.

However, Kabul's identity was being reshaped by war and the imposition of harsh Islamic and Sharia law. Not long before my arrival, the city under Tajik control had fallen to the Taliban. It was said that whoever controlled Kabul controlled the country. Over the years, Kabul had endured domination by various tribes and foreign invaders, but none wielded the strength or numbers of the Taliban. Predominantly Pashtun—the largest ethnic group in Afghanistan, with roots extending into northern Pakistan—the Taliban now held the city in their grip.

What struck me most was how the population adapted to yet another regime change—this one arguably more stark and contrasting than anything they had faced before. The only reassurance the new regime brought was a sense of security, but this came at the heavy cost of freedom and self-expression.

Amid the chaos, the people's ability to maintain dignity could mislead visitors into underestimating their enduring suffering. Unlike the stark and visible effects of drought and malnutrition seen in Eastern and Central Africa - where gaunt faces, mothers nursing babies on dehydrated breasts, and children with kwashiorkor were unmistakable - the suffering in Kabul was largely hidden. The loose-fitting shalwar kameez and burka were masters of disguise, concealing the toll of hardship. Yet to the observant eye, there were subtler signs. Bare feet trudging through snow and ice. Young adults with faces prematurely aged, their unkempt beards and deeply sunken eyes hinting at lives of relentless struggle.

Afghan faces were unlike any I had seen before - rugged, well-defined, with striking green or hazel eyes and hair ranging from reddish-brown to deep chestnut. Their complexions reflected a unique blend of Celtic, Persian, and Indian ancestry, while their lean, sinewy bodies bore echoes of their Illyrian lineage. Each face seemed to carry the weight of history, a silent testament to survival in the face of unimaginable adversity.

Dolly

Dolly was born in 1933 in Le Harvre, France and lived in Honfleur, a charming fishing port nestled along the Seine estuary. Known for its deep roots in Impressionism, Honfleur inspired artists like Claude Monet and his mentor Eugène Boudin, who was born in the town. It's said that Monet and his contemporaries often gathered at the Ferme Saint-Siméon, perched on a hill overlooking Honfleur, to capture the ethereal light of the estuary.

Dolly's paternal ancestral aunts known as 'maiden sisters' arrived from Brooklyn via the transatlantic trading routes between Le Havre and Brooklyn, New York. Honfleur's ties to North America run deep; it was from this port that Samuel de Champlain, one of France's most celebrated explorers, set sail to establish the city of Quebec. Yet, less celebrated is Honfleur's darker history as a hub for the transatlantic slave trade, which enriched many shipping magnates of the time. Today, the port no longer serves commercial trade but thrives as a tourist destination, its historic waterfront lined with cafés and bars, where modern-day artists still seek to recreate the Impressionists' magic.

The year of Dolly's birth, 1933, was a pivotal moment in history. Franklin D. Roosevelt was inaugurated as the 32nd President of the United States, leading the country through the Great Depression. The Lone Ranger debuted on the radio, and construction began on the Golden Gate Bridge in San Francisco. Across the Atlantic, the Rome-Berlin Axis solidified an alliance between Italy and Germany, signalling ominous times ahead. It was also the year Adolf Hitler rose to power as Germany's dictator, marking the beginning of the Nazi Party's ruthless persecution of minority groups, including Jews, communists, people of colour, and those labelled as "deviants." The first concentration camps opened, and the Holocaust began its grim ascent, a tragedy that would ultimately claim six million Jewish lives over the next eleven years.

Meanwhile, on the other side of the world, Australia witnessed its own milestones. A referendum in Western Australia favoured secession from the Commonwealth, the Australian Antarctic Territory was established, windscreen wipers became mandatory on cars, and Sydney installed its very first traffic lights.

Dolly's mother, Denise Juliette Gosselin, was tragically killed during an Allied bombing raid before the Normandy D-Day Landings in 1944. She had been attending a German officer's dance at the time. Dolly's father, Charles Henri, never married Denise and was later interned in Paris by the Germans during the war. When I asked about photos of her mother and family, Dolly recounted in a letter to me that their home had been destroyed by an incendiary bomb dropped by the 'British' which also destroyed any photographs and possessions she had as a child. Dolly had an older brother, James, from the same parents, and a younger half-sister, Nancy, whose mother was described as a "gypsy"—a term now widely recognised as derogatory when referring to the Roma or traveller communities. In Nancy's case, the term was perhaps a nod to her mother's unconventional lifestyle or perceived mystical abilities.

Charles, whom we called Papa, was the son of Alfred, continuing the family tradition of naming the eldest son Alfred. This meant I also had a great-uncle, Alfred. Papa's younger sister, my great-aunt Mavis, had moved from Winnipeg to Toronto, Canada, many years before and lived to an impressive 100 years. I had the privilege of meeting her on several occasions. Aunt Mavis became a key connection to my maternal family's history, writing to me regularly during my travels and sharing stories that brought our ancestry to life. She often remarked, with a knowing smile, "There are a lot of skeletons in the cupboard." Over the years, I have come to appreciate how true that was.

I am told I most resemble my Uncle James, who I met several times when he travelled from Le Havre to visit our family in Croydon, Surrey. We also visited him during a stop in Le Havre on our way back from a camping trip in Brittany. Uncle James quickly became my favourite uncle. A fellow left-hander like me, he played the violin, mostly by ear, encouraged me to play the piano and had a flair for chess, where his animated and eccentric nature added to the joy of the game. He had six children with his wife who spoke only a few words of English. There was an unusual pattern of alternate blond and ginger hair amongst his children! When his children visited us, his oldest daughters similar in age to myself and my brother were the image of French chic and sang to us Blondie songs in French! Sadly depression has been a regular visitor in our family with his eldest son committing suicide.

At a time when being left-handed was stigmatised, James defied convention. Teachers often tried to "correct" left-handedness by rapping knuckles and forcing children to write with their right hands. But James embraced his natural inclinations, even developing a unique way of writing. His letters were written in reverse, from right to left, with the words mirrored. They could be read more easily when reflected in a mirror. I share this quirk, often reversing certain letters, like N and W, without thinking. As a left-hander, I've faced similar but not nearly the same harsh challenges as my uncle. Writing often smudges as the hand moves across fresh ink, and left-handers tend to adopt a distinctive posture to compensate. James, however, turned what others might have seen as a flaw into a fascinating trait that made him all the more remarkable.

Today, left-handers are often celebrated for their creativity and unique traits, forming a subtle yet tangible bond with others who share this characteristic. Interestingly, what was once viewed with suspicion or even disdain has now become something of a trend, with some parents actively encouraging their children to develop left-handedness, a curious reversal of old stigmas.

In certain professional circles I've been part of, the proportion of left-handers has strikingly exceeded the usual balance of left to right-handers, an observation that has always intrigued me.

On a more personal note, I remember my favourite uncle with fondness, who sadly passed away a few years ago. His later years were marked by struggles - depression and homelessness following a divorce. It pains me that I did not get to see him during those years before he passed, leaving a void in my life that mortality has made permanent.

My mother, Dolly, was just seven years old when war tore through Europe. Her older brother, James, was nine or ten, and her younger sister, Nancy, only four. They lived with my grandmother in northern France when tragedy struck: their mother was killed, leaving the children's world suddenly hollow.

As the German advance from the north pushed southward towards Le Havre - a strategic port vital to the occupation - the fragile order of their lives collapsed. Dolly and Nancy joined a stream of frightened villagers fleeing south, clutching what little they could carry. Along the way, they found brief kindness in farmhouses before eventually being placed in hostels run by Catholic nuns. Their brother James had fled with their father - my grandfather - but where they went was never clear. Perhaps, as a young boy, he was seen as too great a risk to fall into German hands.

The circumstances of their mother's death remained a shadow over Dolly's life. She was killed when Allied bombs struck a German dance hall - an establishment frequented by officers who invited local French women to attend. For many women, these invitations were not about choice but survival: providing comfort to German soldiers away from their homes, their wives or girlfriend or just needing comfort in return for a warm meal, safety, or simply the illusion of normality in a world stripped bare of both comfort and dignity. Whether my grandmother went out of loneliness or necessity, no one could say. What is certain is that the raid obliterated the building - and with it, the fragile existence she had been clinging to. For Dolly, the irony was unbearable: her mother, killed not by the enemy, but by those who claimed to bring liberation.

In the Catholic-run hostels where she and Nancy sought refuge, cruelty replaced comfort. My mother would speak of the nuns' punishments - beatings, shaved heads, solitary confinement - all for the smallest of infractions. Nancy, being younger, endured even harsher treatment. Yet amid this brutality, my mother remembered stepping outside to watch German Luftwaffe planes overhead, entranced by the terrifying beauty of the sky aflame, while the nuns cowered inside, praying through their tears.

She also remembered, with chilling clarity, the sound of Beethoven's *Ode to Joy* echoing through assemblies - its triumphant rhythm turned to mockery by the despair that filled the room. Whether it was in the hostels or her earlier school in Honfleur, that music haunted her forever.

When the tide of war finally turned, Normandy became a battlefield. The D-Day landings marked the beginning of liberation, but they brought devastation in their wake. Le Havre, near Honfleur, was reduced to rubble by Allied bombing. From the chaos, Allied soldiers who had once fled Europe regrouped in Britain as "Free Forces." Among them, the Free Belgian Forces led by Jean-Baptiste Piron - attached to the 1st Canadian Army - became the first to liberate Honfleur.

With their father now in Canada and their mother gone, the three siblings were eventually reunited and evacuated across the North Sea to Great Britain. They were sent to an orphanage in Bridge of Weir, on the outskirts of Glasgow—a home founded in 1876 by philanthropist William Quarrier for destitute and displaced children.

It is little wonder that many French people, including my mother, felt conflicted about the so-called "liberation." The Germans had occupied France but left much of its infrastructure intact. The Allies, by contrast, had brought freedom through destruction. For Dolly, liberation meant loss - her mother's death forever entangled with the victory others celebrated.

Her time in the hostels left scars that never fully healed. Separated from their father, grieving their mother, the children grew up in institutions where punishment replaced care. In the 1930s to 1950s, no laws restricted corporal punishment in such places, and "discipline" was often sanctified as moral duty. The result was predictable: authority untempered by compassion became cruelty disguised as righteousness.

Yet the Scottish orphanage, where Dolly reunited with James, offered a fragile reprieve. For the first time, she felt safe, and food was plentiful compared to the starvation she had known. Later, in England, she would lament the coldness of the institutions and the disdain she felt from the English compared to the Scots. Scotland remained dear to her heart. Even as a child, she spoke with a lilting Scottish accent that softened her Anglo-French tones and often sprinkled her words with Scots slang.

Although her experience in Bridge of Weir was gentler than most, many orphanages of that era became notorious for cruelty. Power, cloaked in piety, often bred oppression.

And so one wonders: how does a person who has known only fear and loss learn tenderness? How do you nurture love when it was never modelled for you? How do you silence the ghosts of the past when they whisper that pain is the only language you know?

Kandahar

After spending a few days at the country delegation in Kabul,
attending numerous meetings and briefings, gaining insight
into the broader Red Cross program, and being introduced
to local counterparts while visiting various hospitals, I
boarded an International Red Cross turb-prop plane bound
for Kandahar. The distinctive Red Cross emblem proudly
displayed on its tail wing and side. Kabul International
Airport, scarred by craters and mortar damage, no longer
facilitated domestic flights. Afghanistan's national airline,
Ariana, had been rendered inoperative, with its fleet
destroyed or grounded. The airspace was restricted to planes
operated by the Red Cross and the UN, as no warplanes
remained active. Instead, the ongoing conflict relied on
mortars, short-range missiles, rocket-propelled grenades,
snipers, and guerrilla warfare.

In Kabul, there was slightly more freedom of movement for
Red Cross staff compared to my destination, as the
organisation had maintained a presence in the city long
before the current crisis. The Red Cross had played a critical
role during the Soviet invasion and the communist regime
that followed, as well as during the subsequent power
struggles among various Mujahideen factions vying for
control of the city. One of my most memorable visits was to
a street known as "Chicken Street." Once a market for live
poultry, it had become the place to purchase traditional
Afghan carpets, including those from surrounding regions. I

developed a particular appreciation for Kazak-style carpets, with their rich, earthy tones and intricate patterns.

Flights operated by the Red Cross or UN were meticulously coordinated between our operations team and local authorities to ensure safety. At the time, the Red Cross program in Afghanistan was its largest worldwide, employing over 900 local staff and 100 international delegates. The operation included a vast fleet of Land Cruisers, tankers, trucks, and warehouses, supported by a robust logistical supply chain. Beyond humanitarian aid, the Red Cross contributed significantly to the local economy, providing employment, paying rent, and hiring chowkidars (watchmen), cooks, cleaners, and logistics staff. Its presence was a vital lifeline for a community grappling with the ongoing consequences of war.

The Red Cross Hospital program in Kandahar was its largest 'hospital and clinical program' currently in operation. The program was part of a five-year initiative aimed at providing care for those impacted by Afghanistan's ongoing internal conflict. It was with this program and my induction to the Red Cross movement as a first-time delegate I would spend the next three months before transferring to Jalalabad for the remainder of my 12-month deployment with a short periods in Panjshir and assessment trips to Bamiyan and other areas affected by armed conflict. The year was 1998!

The overarching goal of the program was to build the knowledge and skills of local Afghans so that, over time, the Red Cross could reduce its involvement, enabling the community to manage the hospital independently. The International Red Cross contributed technical expertise through a diverse team of nurses, doctors, anaesthetists, allied health professionals, and administrators, in addition to supplying critical medical resources.

As a surgical nurse, my role involved teaching and transferring technical skills to Afghan locals who would eventually take over nursing care and support. Many already had practical "field surgical" experience, including skills like suturing, dressing wounds, managing shrapnel injuries, and treating cases involving UXOs (unexploded ordnance) that littered the terrain after decades of warfare. Tragically, most victims of these 'remnants of war' were children drawn to objects that resembled toys and farmers working the land.

Kandahar's weather was noticeably warmer and drier than Kabul, and the landscape was stark—flat and barren, with low-rise housing, government buildings, and rows of modest shops offering basic necessities. Movement around the city was tightly controlled; any excursions required traveling with another delegate and a local field officer. The town, though sparse in material goods, had an unexpected charm: an abundance of roses. The dry climate proved ideal for growing them, and Kandahar's residents lovingly tended to rose bushes that adorned homes, buildings, and even the hospital grounds. These vibrant flowers stood out against the otherwise muted tones of the city, a testament to the resilience and beauty of its people.

Our head nurse, Ingrid, was from Sweden - a seasoned member of the International Red Cross with over two decades of service in some of the world's most challenging environments. Her face bore the quiet strength and depth of experience that came from witnessing both the best and worst of humanity.

My nursing and medical colleagues came from all over the world—Australia, Finland, Norway, Sweden, Switzerland, the Netherlands, Germany, Italy, Japan, and Canada. This diverse team brought a wealth of knowledge, camaraderie, and a shared commitment to the mission, making the harsh realities of Kandahar a little easier to navigate.

Our accommodation was in a walled compound a short distance from the hospital, and transfers to and from the facility were meticulously coordinated for safety. We travelled with our shift colleagues in a shared minibus, even for night shifts, ensuring a reliable and secure commute.

In keeping with local customs, male and female patients were segregated into separate wards. The number of casualties was significantly higher among men, reflected in the greater number of male wards compared to the two female-only wards. Only female members of my team were permitted to work in these wards, supporting local female carers and nurses. However, during night shifts, I was often the only international staff member on duty, tasked with responsibilities such as administering controlled medications. This required a careful approach—before entering the female ward, I would notify the Afghan nurses so they could observe customs like dress codes before I knocked and handed over the necessary medications.

In most cases, I would only ever see their eyes, but over time, I began to recognise each nurse by the unique spark in their gaze or the warmth in their voice when we spoke. I couldn't help but feel a pang of guilt knowing that, without any male presence and within the safety of their female colleagues and patients, the heavy burqas could be removed, allowing them to relax and let their hair down. But even within this relative sanctuary, there were challenges—'vice women,' typically older, more conservative women, kept a vigilant eye on their behaviour. These women had the authority to report any perceived misconduct to local authorities, and the punishments often far exceeded the gravity of the alleged offense.

Kandahar was the first of many missions I undertook while working for the Red Cross and other humanitarian organisations such as UNICEF, UNHCR, Oxfam Australia, and the World Health Organization. It became a crucible for learning, shaping the skills and knowledge that sustained me throughout my career in international humanitarian work.

The contrast between my previous experience at a state-of-the-art military hospital in Riyadh, Saudi Arabia and hospitals in London, UK, and the conditions in Kandahar could not have been starker. In Riyadh, we had access to cutting-edge medical equipment, endless supplies, and a highly skilled international team. Specialist units included a neonatal ward, a "no-touch" burns unit, and even a VIP wing. In war-ravaged Kandahar, however, such luxuries were unimaginable. The hospital was rudimentary, stripped of wealth and resources, barely able to meet the overwhelming needs of a population battered by conflict.

Patients came to us from across the southern provinces, often traveling for days on foot or in makeshift carts. One case remains etched in my memory—a man arrived in a donkey-drawn trailer, his pregnant wife lying inside. She had gone into labour nearly a week earlier, and the baby's legs protruded from her vagina, the birth process stalled. The smell was unbearable, the stench of decay signalling that the infant had been dead for days. Astonishingly, the mother was still alive, though barely—she drifted in and out of consciousness, moaning softly as her breathing laboured.

Out of desperation, her husband had made the arduous journey, clinging to the hope that the Red Cross hospital could save both mother and child. But with such a delayed timeline and the limited services we could offer, their chances were non-existent. Even if the baby had been alive, there was no neonatal or specialist care available. The triage process, so familiar in modern hospitals, was inverted here: those with minor injuries were prioritised over patients needing intensive care or complex trauma management. Gender inequities further complicated matters—men and boys were consistently treated before women and girls, in deference to the dictates of local authorities.

Most international doctors arrived with experience rooted in well-resourced settings, where high-tech equipment and advanced techniques were the norm. Kandahar forced them to confront harsh realities and make agonising ethical decisions. Improvisation became a daily necessity, and any successful procedures were often added to the compendium of war surgery for future reference.

On the day that case arrived, the surgeon on duty had an orthopaedic background—a common specialty given the prevalence of war-related injuries like fractures and amputations. Cases like this, tragically, were not uncommon. The strain of limited resources, cultural constraints, and the relentless tide of human suffering left a profound mark on everyone who served in that desolate place.

Several cases stand out as poignant reminders of the harsh realities faced by those living in conflict zones. One stark truth became evident: we are all victims of our circumstances. In this case, the circumstance was being born into a country where tribal warfare was a part of life, and where culture and religion were dictated by geography and birthright - choices that were not one's own.

As a hospital primarily providing surgical care, with only limited medical support, we treated numerous injured soldiers and civilians caught in the crossfire of war. Above-knee amputations were alarmingly common, and over the years, the Red Cross had developed rehabilitation programs to help survivors adapt to their new realities. These programs aimed to enable Afghans to return to work or train for livelihoods that accommodated their disabilities, such as using prosthetic limbs. The Red Cross also employed many amputees in workshops, where they manufactured prosthetics, bicycles, and other items designed to help restore a degree of dignity and independence to their lives.

War surgery is a field unto itself, demanding creativity, resourcefulness, and resilience. Some of the most skilled war surgeons I encountered were those working within opposing armed groups. Their ability to innovate under extreme constraints often surpassed what could be achieved in more conventional medical settings.

Injuries caused by landmines and unexploded ordnance (UXO) dominated the cases we treated. Over time, the surgical procedures and aftercare for these injuries became almost routine. The approach was aggressive: all amputations were performed above the knee or involved the full limb, even if the initial injury appeared limited to the lower leg. This strategy was not arbitrary; it was a calculated response to the high risk of post-operative infections caused by dirt and debris embedded in wounds. Cleaning and antibiotic therapy were often insufficient, so above-knee amputations reduced infection rates and standardised procedures among staff, improving overall outcomes.

The same principle applied to arm injuries. A severe hand injury that required amputation would typically result in an above-elbow procedure. While this aggressive approach might seem harsh compared to the more conservative techniques used in well-equipped hospitals, it significantly lowered infection risks and provided better long-term results for survivors. These measures reflected the harsh reality of working in a resource-limited environment, where the focus was not just on saving lives but on ensuring patients could have the best possible quality of life afterward.

Working predominantly in the male surgical and burns ward, I observed a striking transformation among young men who had been injured by landmines or weapons. Once removed from the constraints of military uniforms and the rigidity of orders, these young men, now dressed in civilian clothing and sheltered by the relative safety of the hospital, reverted to everyday teenagers. They laughed, joked, and bantered with one another, defying the pain, discomfort, and immobility imposed by their injuries. Despite the dire circumstances, many clung to the hope of miracles, though it was often clear that some wounds, left untreated for too long while awaiting surgical assessment, would not lead to positive outcomes.

The burns unit was particularly harrowing - not just because of the severity of the burns themselves but because of the resource limitations that shaped their treatment. Most burns we treated were first or second-degree; third-degree burns covering more than 27% of the body (by the Rule of Nines) were often fatal in these settings and unlikely make it to the hospital. Treating burns was a multifaceted challenge that encompassed clinical care, pain management, and psychological support. The emotional toll of addressing issues like body image, permanent scarring, and the social stigma burns often carried was immense. For women, in particular, severe burns could mean the loss of any prospects for marriage and the security it might bring, compounding their suffering. The long flowing garments worn by women and given the task of building the fires that would provide evening warmth, hot water and cooking for the family increased their risk of their clothing catching fire and burns. When treating females with burns, their weeping and cries was mixed with a self-sadness that made you wish they could enter mortality and find peace as life fully able and fit was harsh enough on its own without having a deformity.

We accept as truth what is explained by accompanying relatives or the person themselves as you would in the workplace or the hospital emergency department as home, but stories of women purposedly set on fire due to domestic disputes or shame was always in the back of your mind. Whatever the reason, this was a stark reminder of the inequities and how tribal law infiltrates and manifests within religion and contradicts the underlying theme of benevolence, grace, mercy, compassion and forgiveness found in religious doctrine.

Treatment often began with bathing wounds in tepid water to soften dead tissue, followed by the application of creams like silver sulfadiazine and then sterile dressings and bandages. Pain management, however, was strictly monitored due to local authorities' rigid stance on opioid use.

This restriction meant that procedures like debriding dead tissue—a process akin to scrubbing wounds with a cloth resembling a green scouring pad—were excruciatingly painful. Assisting or witnessing such procedures was gut-wrenching, knowing the limited relief we could provide.

Yet, despite the challenges, the resilience of the human body and spirit in such austere conditions was extraordinary. Infection rates, even without routine antibiotics, were surprisingly low—a testament to the body's ability to endure and adapt, even in the harshest environments with minimal access to healthcare.

A particularly distressing event, and one that sadly remains common, involves injuries caused by unexploded ordnance. Such tragedies can occur long after active hostilities have ended, as people return to their daily lives or resume working on farms unknowingly littered with landmines or remnants of war. The victims are often children, innocently playing in fields or drawn to objects that capture their curious minds.

On this day, I was working in our emergency room - a stark, utilitarian space that bore little resemblance to a modern hospital's casualty department. It was a single large room with an examination table, cupboards, and drawers stocked with basic medical supplies: oxygen cylinders, masks, suturing kits, dressing packs, and intubation equipment. These were enough to manage severe bleeding, resuscitate a patient, administer pain relief, and conduct preliminary assessments. An adjoining room provided additional privacy for examinations, although the main room often doubled as a waiting area for relatives, who hovered near their loved ones in various states of anxiety.

A man entered, short in stature and wearing a weathered grey *shalwar kameez*. His long grey beard framed strong features, weathered further by years of hard labour under the unforgiving elements. He likely appeared older than he was; Afghanistan's average life expectancy at the time hovered in the mid-forties to early fifties. He carried his son, a boy of about seven, in his arms. Following close behind was his daughter, a shy five-year-old with wild, untamed hair that brought to mind Tina Turner's character in *Mad Max: Beyond Thunderdome*. She clutched the hem of her father's *kameez*, trailing behind him as he pleaded for help.

The boy was crying, his injuries apparent. Blood trickled down cuts on his arms and legs, evidence of trauma. His sister, in stark contrast, stood silent, her wide eyes darting around the room. The father explained through an interpreter that both children had been playing in a field when they came across a brightly coloured object with wires - an object they had mistaken for a toy. It exploded, sending debris into the boy's limbs—or so we initially thought.

As the boy received attention—his wounds deemed superficial and relatively straightforward to treat - I noticed the girl standing quietly by the wall. Her silence wasn't shyness. Something was wrong. Her neck was visibly swollen, and she appeared to struggle to breathe. I alerted the German anaesthetist, and we quickly shifted focus to her. The boy was sent to the adjoining room with local nurses to have his wounds cleaned and dressed while we turned our full attention to his sister.

The anaesthetist lifted her onto the examination table as her breathing became more laboured. Embedded in her neck were shards of the explosive device, and the swelling was rapidly compromising her airway. She was slipping into unconsciousness. Recognising the urgency, the anaesthetist intubated her to maintain her airway, but it became clear she required ongoing ventilator support—something unavailable in our facility. Manual ventilation was the only option, a temporary solution in the absence of a mechanical ventilator.

The scene was agonising. This little girl could have survived under different circumstances. First, had she not encountered such dangers in a post-conflict environment; second, if her need for care had been prioritised equally, free of the gender biases that overshadowed her father's concern for her brother; and third, if we had access to the necessary medical equipment.

The anaesthetist, a skilled professional from Germany, was particularly shaken. In her home country, this injury would have been entirely treatable - a manageable case with a high likelihood of survival. But here, in Kandahar, the lack of resources and inequities in care claimed yet another life that should not have been lost.

It's hard to imagine, but amidst the distressing scenes in the hospital, there were moments of light-heartedness as well. Maintaining a balance of work, rest, and play was essential to our mental well-being. While opportunities for play were limited, we found solace in gathering for meals, games, and shared activities in the lounge areas of our accommodations. These moments offered a much-needed respite, allowing us to bond and decompress after the challenges of the day.

Our accommodation was a short bus ride from the hospital, located within a large, square compound. The compound comprised four houses used as living quarters and an office building that served as a hub for other Red Cross programs, such as water and sanitation, protection, administration, and logistics. The office building also housed a spacious common room and kitchen, where we came together for breakfast, lunch, and evening relaxation. Each house had a designated colour name - Red, Purple, Green, and Blue—and about six delegates lived in each one. Separating the houses were paths and garden beds with varieties of roses lovingly cared and attended by a gardener who tended to them during the day with a lot of time sitting and drinking local tea. Amongst the chaos that reigned elsewhere with the conflict he espoused peace and resembles a grey wizard with his long white beard, grey flowing robes and a face etched in wisdom. The houses often took turns hosting dinners or events, fostering a sense of community.

One evening, an Australian nurse brought with her a recently released film, *Priscilla, Queen of the Desert*. Given the context of where we were, it was an unexpected yet delightful choice and provided a perfect way to bond and debrief after particularly gruelling days. Australian nurses were among the best colleagues to work with—resilient and resourceful, with their characteristic "she'll be right" attitude that could lift spirits even in the bleakest of circumstances.

The Scandinavians, on the other hand, had a different approach to unwinding. I soon discovered an underground cellar on the compound, which housed a makeshift bar and walls and ceilings covered with graffiti. It was a tradition for every delegate who passed through Kandahar to leave their name there. The typically reserved and stoic Finns, known for their terse, one-word responses during the day, transformed after a few drinks. The change was remarkable—they became animated, loud, and, dare I say, even loquacious!

These moments of camaraderie reminded us of the resilience of the human spirit. In a place so deeply marked by conflict and hardship, our ability to laugh, share stories, and build connections served as a quiet act of defiance against the relentless weight of our surroundings.

Budda and Jam!

"Would you like some bread with that jam?" I asked the young Pashtun member of the Afghan Red Crescent accompanying us. He responded with a toothy grin, his mouth already full of strawberry jam, which he ate straight from the jar as if it were yogurt.

My colleague's alarmed expression deepened when we discovered the same young man casually reaching for his toothbrush. Sharing was assumed, even when it came to personal items, a small but telling glimpse into cultural norms that would mark our journey.

The night before, we had crammed into a former meeting room repurposed as our sleeping quarters in a local administration building. There were fifteen of us in total: myself, a Swiss colleague, our national Afghan Red Cross drivers, field officers, and members of the Afghan Red Crescent Society from Kabul.

The warm, sunny days of Bamiyan surrendered to frosty nights. Thin mattresses and the grey blankets usually reserved for refugees became our only solace, sleeping in close proximity to radiate heat to the surrounds and to each other. Sleep came easily amongst the grunts and snoring before the melodic call to fajr prayer just before dawn woke us. Its sound, rising from the minaret of the nearby mosque, pierced the still air with reverence.

Our Afghan colleagues arose in silence almost simultaneously and those who had covered their heads with the blankets were gently nudged to remind them morning fajr prayers were soon to begin. I got up but not to go to prayer but to witness the still frosty air and the unfolding beauty that comes with dawn. Outside, water had turned to ice and the frozen water bottles hampered those intending to undertake their ablutions and ritual 'wudu' before performing prayers. Some walked to the local mosque others used a quiet covered spot next to the building and used our senior field officer as their Imam, following him in salah and performing a series of *rakah* movements. The frost was an unwelcome reminder of the harshness of our surroundings.

Outside, under the faint crescent moon and a sky still filled with stars, the horizon glowed faintly with the first hints of sunrise. For a moment, peace reigned, and the beauty of the world felt undeniable.

Yet, as always in Afghanistan, serenity was fleeting, overshadowed by the bitter reality of rivalry, war, and control.

In the distance, the shadows of Bamiyan's famous male and female Buddhas, carved into soft sandstone cliffs, loomed over the valley. They stood as silent witnesses to the ebb and flow of history, their presence weaving the past into the present, if only briefly.

After prayers, people walked back in silence. Some returned to sleep, others read the Koran or hadiths or engaged in small talk with each other huddled close together with blankets wrapped around their shoulders. Others started to make tea and prepare for breakfast.

After a communal breakfast of bread, local yoghurt and honey we met for a briefing before packing away our items ready for our day tasks ahead. Our day's purpose was grim but necessary: we were to meet the newly appointed governor and Taliban commanders who had recently seized Bamiyan, displacing the ethnic Hazara population.

In this dynamic, Bamiyan - a Hazara-dominated region - stood at a crossroads. The question of loyalty and survival hung heavy in the air as we approached our meeting, aware that every handshake and promise would be weighed against centuries of history and the immediate needs of those on the ground.

The Taliban had taken over the local Afghan Red Crescent headquarters. The iconic red crescent stitched onto the white flag of the organisation had been removed, leaving only the Taliban's white flag fluttering in its place. The original Hazara staff had fled, and the new Red Crescent team was composed of Pashtuns from Kabul.

We were also there to express condolences and provide financial support to the family of the head of the local Afghan Red Crescent killed during the takeover. This meeting, like many others in conflict zones, was an exercise in navigating the complexities of shifting power. We introduced ourselves, reiterated the principles of the Red Cross Red Crescent Movement, and sought to secure access to prisoners of war and local health facilities.

The district offices were scarred by battle. Bullet holes pocked the walls; overturned furniture and remnants of Rocket Propelled Grenades (RPGs) littered the compound. Even the gates bore traces of the violence—a small stockpile of RPGs sat ominously at the entrance.

Inside the main meeting room, we were greeted with the customary Afghan hospitality, a surreal juxtaposition to the setting. Rugs and cushions were arranged in a semi-circle on the floor, and nails driven into the walls held Kalashnikov or AK47 rifles. A waiter-like figure entered with a tray of freshly brewed Afghan tea, served in small glasses filled with herbs and sugar. In a quiet moment of humour, I thought of the young Pashtun's love for jam and imagined asking, "Would you like tea with your sugar?" Half the glass was undissolved sugar, the trick being to sip it slowly without stirring.

My Swiss colleague and I sat cross-legged in our Levi Docker chinos and checkered shirts, our Red Cross badges affixed neatly, facing Taliban commanders dressed in traditional attire sporting long dark beards and black turbans with long tails . The dialogue, facilitated by interpreters, was courteous and methodical. The interpreters, skilled in neutrality, relayed only the words spoken, avoiding involvement in the content.

The meeting met its objectives. We were granted access to the local prison and the hospital, though both presented their own challenges. The prison likely held Pashtun and Tajik prisoners once captured by Hazara forces, while the hospital previously staffed by health professionals aligned with Iran was largely abandoned after the staff fled, stood as a stark reminder of the precariousness of healthcare in conflict zones.

As we left the compound, I couldn't help but reflect on the contradictions surrounding us. Moments of shared tea and polite conversation with armed men underlined the surrealism of a world where humanity and violence coexisted so uneasily.

The Taliban's rapid territorial gains were palpable, their influence spreading like wildfire across Afghanistan. Regions once dominated by the ethnic strongholds of Tajiks, Uzbeks, and Hazaras were falling under the rule of a predominantly Pashtun movement. Historically, the Pashtuns hailed from the rugged terrains of southern and eastern Afghanistan and parts of northwestern Pakistan, a region collectively known as Pashtunistan.

In these turbulent times, the Taliban's strategy mirrored an age-old practice deeply rooted in Afghan history: the concept of "turncloaking." This was not merely a wartime tactic but a pragmatic survival mechanism. In Alexander the Great's campaigns, as chronicled in Steven Pressfield's *Afghan Campaign*, this method proved pivotal in securing allegiance from local leaders across Central Asia, Persia, and India.

The practice was deceptively simple yet powerful: offer better outcomes—jobs, food security and even stability - and former adversaries would pledge loyalty, often as a matter of survival or 'opportunities'. While ethnicity and tribal identity ran deep, allegiance to a new power was often superficial and transactional. Should a more formidable force arise, allegiances would shift again, like leaves blown by a stronger wind. With the Taliban's expansion it also thinned out their forces so finding allegiance from other ethnic groups was vital.

Having completed our meetings, my Swiss colleague and I took the opportunity to explore the area. We were particularly eager to visit the Buddha statues, monumental sculptures carved into the cliffs of Bamiyan during the late fifth and sixth centuries. These statues stood as a testament to the era when Buddhism flourished in the region, having been a central faith and practice here since the second century. Bamiyan was a vital stop along the Silk Road, the ancient trade route that traversed the Hindu Kush mountains, connecting diverse civilisations. Over centuries, countless pilgrims and travellers paid homage to these sacred statues.

The Bamiyan Valley bore the scars of numerous conquests, its history marked by the arrival of Genghis Khan's forces and later the Mughal emperor Aurangzeb. Whilst one dynasty left the statues untouched the other attempted to erase the statues but failed, their sheer resilience standing as a defiant testament to their creators' skill and devotion. I learned later that over the centuries, invaders often sought to destroy the Buddhas, yet their efforts proved futile. Little did we know during our visit in late 1998 that the statues would soon face their ultimate destruction—not by foreign invaders but by the Taliban.

The reasons behind their destruction are layered and controversial. One explanation suggests it was an act of revenge. The Taliban had reportedly requested that international funds earmarked for the statues' restoration instead be redirected to aid victims of a devastating earthquake in a nearby region, one not under their control. When this request was denied, it allegedly fuelled their decision to demolish the statues stating that how could funding provided to preserving a statue that was in defiance of Islamic scripture be preferred to saving human life? Another explanation, widely documented, ties the destruction to their extremist interpretation of Islamic doctrine. Yet, having spent time observing the Taliban, I found them distinct from other Mujahideen groups, and I remain open to deeper, perhaps less apparent motivations for their actions.

Our field office surprised us by seeking and obtaining permission for us to climb a trail leading to the top of the Buddha statues. The two prominent statues, known as the Western or "male" Buddha and the Eastern or "female" Buddha, stood 55 and 38 meters tall, respectively. Despite centuries of erosion, their grandeur remained awe-inspiring. It struck me as remarkable that even after enduring the elements and repeated assaults by empires like the Mughals, they stood steadfast—silent witnesses to history.

The trail meandered through narrow passages, eventually opening onto breathtaking vantage points overlooking the valley. From this height, I could almost imagine the scene centuries ago: pilgrims arriving from distant lands, their footsteps echoing off the surrounding cliffs. As we ascended, I felt a profound mixture of reverence and sadness, knowing these timeless relics remained vulnerable to the destructive forces of human conflict and ideology.

Upon reaching the summit, we passed through a small passage that emerged beside the statue's head, allowing us to look down its immense length. Faint remnants of blue and ochre paintings clung to the weathered stone, whispering of a grandeur long faded. Our accompanying field officer explained that the statues had once been adorned with precious stones, many stolen or lost over the centuries. As per our protocol, we carried no cameras during official missions, both to minimise security risks and to ensure that what we witnessed remained shared only among us. Our camera was our mind, and the ability to capture images in words would later prove an invaluable skill for future assignments.

Little did I realise that this climb to the heights of the Buddhas would be one of the final opportunities to see them in their full splendour. It is possible we were among the last Westerners to explore their interiors before their violent destruction. In the years that followed, the region descended further into chaos, and the statues fell, casualties of ideological warfare.

Afterward, we wandered through nearby fields, reflecting on our meetings and the hospital visit. Scattered among the fields were remnants of missiles, a grim reminder of the conflict that scarred this place. Our time in Bamiyan was drawing to a close. We prepared to return to Kabul to write our reports and brief the head of delegation.

On leaving Bamiyan, we passed an abandoned stretch of market stalls and shops. Our field officer explained that this had once been the heart of Bamiyan under Tajik control, before the region shifted hands to Hazara mujahideen, and later to the Taliban. The old town had been destroyed and left to decay, replaced by a new central town constructed by the Hazara. Said to be descendants of Genghis Khan's Mongol forces, the Hazara likely trace their heritage to a tapestry of ethnic groups from the region, including Mongols and Turkic peoples of Central Asia.

This fleeting visit, steeped in beauty and tragedy, left an indelible mark, underscoring the fragility of history in the face of relentless change.

Dolly and Charlotte – the early years

After enduring formative years shaped by war and the harsh realities of an orphanage, the people and environment surrounding Dolly became her unintended role models. Was it normal, she often wondered, for such harsh punishments to be meted out for minor infractions? Had the normalisation of such behaviours hardened her resolve, or did it leave her questioning the fairness of a world she was still too young to fully understand?

These questions lingered, often unanswered, until a glimmer of hope appeared in her life. Sometimes, it takes an inner voice - or the serendipitous arrival of someone unexpected -

to challenge ingrained beliefs and steer one toward an alternative path. Could this intervention have been predestined? Perhaps her soul, before its earthly journey, had chosen to endure such trials. But for what purpose? To build resilience, empathy, or something else altogether?

Grace and rescue came to Dolly through the kindness of distant relatives and their friends. This marked the beginning of a period of stability living in Scotland, following years of upheaval defined by separation, loss, war, repatriation, and sorrow. It was a time where she began to find solace, away from the punishing hands of caretakers who had wielded cruelty in the guise of morality. Their methods - harsh punishments meant to "extract Satan" or banish bad spirits - had coincided with her natural transition from child to adolescent.

Puberty, often a time of confusion and discovery, had been marred by a lack of emotional guidance and support. Her body may have matured, but her mind remained tethered to the fears and insecurities of a child, desperately seeking love and safety. Stability was not just a welcome change; it was a lifeline, offering Dolly the chance to heal and begin piecing together an identity forged in survival yet yearning for tenderness and understanding.

Dolly's father, Charles, returned from Canada, where he had fled at the end of the war. He had been released by Allied liberators from a camp in Paris, where the Germans had interned him during the conflict. Upon his return, he visited his children at their relatives' home in Scotland. However, it wasn't long before he returned to Le Havre, France, taking with him his children from a place of relative stability. There,

Charles would soon meet a new partner, start a new family, and begin a different chapter of his life.

Dolly, decided to come back to the UK – this to London to enter nursing school, training to become a State Registered Nurse - the precursor to today's Registered General Nurse. However, it was during this time that the unresolved traumas of her past, coupled with the lack of emotional support in her childhood, began to resurface.

Her sister Nancy remained in France before later returning to Scotland, where she met Walter, a mechanic and a member of the British Territorial Army (reservist) soldier who would become her lifelong partner. Nancy eventually moved to London to complete her enrolled nursing studies and later settled in Hampshire, England.

Dolly was remarkably intelligent, with a love of botany, particularly cacti—a passion she shared with her father. She maintained a journal where she indexed all her plants and cacti complete with their Latin names. She excelled in general knowledge and performed exceptionally well in school, despite English being her second language. In addition to her academic strengths, Dolly had a fondness for collecting stamps and small trinkets, hobbies she pursued with meticulous care. Her stamp collection, which she has maintained to this day, remains impressive. Over the years, I contributed a little to it, especially after moving to Australia, by sending her annual Australian stamp albums.

I always sensed that Dolly felt aggrieved by the circumstances that had constrained her opportunities in life. Like many women of her generation, she seemed to have sacrificed personal ambitions and interests in favour of security through marriage. Her quiet resilience and attention to detail, however, have left a lasting impression on me.

Dolly gained entry into one of London's most prestigious nursing schools, Charing Cross Hospital, which also included placements in Wembley. It was during her first year there that she met a man I would describe as a traveller - Douglas. Their relationship was brief, and after Dolly discovered she was pregnant, Douglas abandoned her. He later resurfaced in Israel and eventually in Australia, where he had two children. Allegedly, he fathered more children in Israel, leaving a trail of unanswered questions about his life.

The year was 1958, and the culture of nursing schools mirrored that of the military, marked by strict discipline, matrons, and rigid expectations. Having a child during training was challenging enough, but being pregnant out of wedlock brought added stigma and isolation. For Dolly, the experience must have been profoundly difficult, evoking memories of her time in the orphanage and compounding her sense of vulnerability. The judgment from her peers and senior staff would have been relentless, and the emotional toll immense.

In such circumstances, society often imposed harsh "solutions." Women in Dolly's position were pressured to consider abortion or give birth only to have their newborns taken away and placed for anonymous adoption. These decisions were frequently made on behalf of the women, framed as being "in their best interest," but in reality, they were acts of emotional blackmail and institutional cruelty. Such practices, unimaginable to today's generation in the UK and other developed nations, were all too common at the time.

During this tumultuous period, my grandfather, Papa, made perhaps his most significant contribution as a father. In an act that may have gone some way toward redeeming his earlier abandonment of Dolly and her siblings, he intervened to prevent Dolly's child from being permanently taken away. Instead, he took the baby to France, ensuring that she remained within the family. The baby's name was Charlotte—my half-sister.

This intervention by Papa, while imperfect, provided a glimmer of humanity in an otherwise harsh and unforgiving situation. It was a moment that may have offered Dolly some measure of solace amid her heartbreak.

Dolly, my mother, was allowed to continue her studies but was punished for her pregnancy by being set back a year in her training to become a State Registered Nurse. Despite this setback, she persevered, navigating a profession that was both demanding and significantly understaffed at the time. To address the chronic shortages, Britain turned to its Commonwealth countries, inviting citizens to fill critical roles, particularly in healthcare and public services.

Much like the transport industry, nursing became a field enriched by the arrival of the Windrush generation and migrants from former British colonies, including Rhodesia, South Africa, Trinidad and Tobago, Jamaica, India, Fiji, and British Guiana. My father, born in British Guiana, had already settled in Brixton, a burgeoning hub for Caribbean immigrants.

The Guianese, known for their love of celebration, formed a vibrant community in London, hosting parties that were as much about cultural preservation as they were about social connection. It was at one such party, organised by a Guianese nursing colleague, that Dolly was introduced to this lively world. The Guianese community, which was also flourishing in cities like New York and Toronto, had begun to establish its unique identity - a blend of Indian and West Indian influences where food, music, and warmth brought people together.

At this party, Dolly met my father who was navigating the end of a challenging relationship with his first wife, a marriage that was likely arranged or one of convenience. Despite the cultural differences, the Guianese community welcomed Dolly with open arms. Their generosity and warmth, expressed through food and camaraderie, helped bridge the gap between her French roots and their deeply embedded Indian and African traditions. However, cross-cultural relationships, while less unusual for men at the time, still posed challenges, especially when it involved a blond, blue-eyed woman standing out among her Guianese peers of Indian and African descent.

Perhaps my father was influenced by his cousin's encouragement to pursue a "white" woman as his companion. He may have drawn inspiration from the marriage of Cheddi Jagan, a prominent Indo-Guyanese political leader to Janet Rosenberg. Janet, a white Jewish woman born in Chicago in 1920 to Romanian and Hungarian immigrant parents, met Cheddi while working as a student nurse at Cook County Hospital. Cheddi, a Hindu studying dentistry, married Janet despite their vastly different backgrounds, proving that love could transcend cultural and religious barriers.

The Jagans moved to British Guiana, where Janet worked as a nurse in Cheddi's dental practice. But her contributions extended far beyond healthcare. She co-founded the Women's Political and Economic Organisation and the Political Affairs Committee, becoming an influential political figure in her own right. Janet supported Cheddi's political ambitions, serving as First Lady during his presidency and later as President of Guyana herself after Cheddi died, before retiring in 1999. Her pioneering role as a leader and activist undoubtedly served as an example of what cross-cultural unions could achieve.

Dolly's entry into the Guianese community mirrored this spirit of connection, resilience, and acceptance. Her journey was a testament to the transformative power of love and the strength it took to defy societal expectations in pursuit of her own path.

Charlotte was placed into the care of her Aunt Nancy, Dolly's younger sister, and the two formed a strong and enduring bond. Initially, Charlotte was raised in Le Havre, France, where Aunt Nancy became her de facto mother while Dolly pursued her nursing studies. The typical maternal bond between Dolly and Charlotte never truly developed, leaving Charlotte with a lifelong sense of closeness to Nancy, who had cared for her until the age of three.

Nancy, however, had her own family to manage. With one child already and three more soon to follow, the arrangement became increasingly strained. Sensing the need for change, Papa stepped in. By this time, Dolly had moved to Brixton to live with her partner, Abraham, and was forging a new life. Papa decided that the time had come for Charlotte to be reunited with her biological mother.

By then, Dolly had completed her State Registered Nursing certificate and was working as a practicing staff nurse. Her new life with Abraham included the desire to bring his children from a previous marriage—Kumari and Mark—into their home. However, Kumari and Mark, having found stability and care in a Salvation Army home and with foster families, were reluctant. Mark, in particular, had formed a strong attachment to his foster carer, whom he regarded as a true parent, providing the love and security he craved.

Meanwhile, Papa and Nancy who was now caring for her own son James and struggling with financial pressures, concluded that Charlotte's return to Dolly was the best option. At three years old, Charlotte arrived in London and moved into Dolly and Abraham's home on Beechdale Road. Mark recalls seeing the shy young girl standing at the front door of the house who could only speak in French. Charlotte had pale white skin that blushed easily and dark ginger blonde hair that would later turn a light mousy brown. Her skin was probably more from her father rather than my mother who whilst blonde had a more Celtic tone that would tan rather than burn. Despite having some features resembling Dolly, Charlotte bore a stronger likeness to her grandmother Denise and perhaps her biological father, Douglas.

Tensions simmered between Dolly and Nancy over the situation. Nancy resented Dolly's perceived indifference to her daughter, and the memory of Charlotte's uncertain early days—when her future was in doubt, or she might have been given away permanently—cast a long shadow.

Papa, now remarried and expecting a child, moved with his wife and eldest son into the downstairs portion of the house.

The shared living arrangements did little to ease the fraught dynamics. Charlotte, meanwhile, began adapting to her new life, though the scars of displacement lingered. Later in life, her search for her biological father's family would yield connections that illuminated her heritage. A striking resemblance between Charlotte's son, Alex, and her half-sister Denise, living in Australia, underscored the ties that time and distance could not erase. Charlotte's biological father was hidden from her until her early forties. In my mothers photo albums, I remember seeing an unfamiliar man but she would not say who he was. I presumed that his may have been Douglas. Maybe wanting Charlotte to grow up knowing both her and her new partner whom she would later marry was the only family she needed to know. It may also be that the trauma of what happened and Douglas abandoning her when she became pregnant was suffice to erase him from Charlotte's life.

Charlotte eventually had the courage to ask her mother about her father and went on a quest to find him. Charlotte would later say that names were given to deflect and appease rather than provide certainty on who was her biological father. It was not until she was in her forties that Chalotte discovered she had a number of half siblings the other side of the world in Australia and possibly in Israel. She has since formed a strong relationship with one of her half-siblings Denise whom she has visited on a number of occasions during her trips to Australia.

Crossing Lines

In January 1998, I began a year-long assignment in Afghanistan, working as a surgical nurse with the International Red Cross. Initially stationed at the surgical hospital in Kandahar, I helped treat men, women, and children injured by the conflict. Before long, I was redeployed as a Medical and Health Delegate to Jalalabad and had a more polyvalent and roving field role. Perhaps due to my gender, I was frequently tasked with accompanying protection and detention delegates as the health representative on missions to other regions and visiting various hospitals and prisoners of war. These assignments took me to places like Bamiyan, the Kunar Valley, and the Panjshir Valley - regions steeped in history, beauty, but also war.

By then, the Taliban had consolidated significant control across Afghanistan. Opposition mujahideen factions were either in retreat or exile, leaving the Northern Alliance as the last credible force resisting the Taliban's expansion.

In areas dominated by non-Pashtun ethnic groups, the Taliban's hold on power relied on a precarious strategy: convincing former mujahideen fighters from other ethnicities to switch allegiances. This practice of "turn-cloaking" was as old as conflict itself in the region. Yet, these alliances were fragile. After seizing new territories with their majority

Pashtun forces, the Taliban would often redeploy these loyal troops elsewhere, leaving turncloak soldiers behind to maintain control. This arrangement allowed local communities to be governed by their own ethnic leaders but under the rigid doctrine of Talibanism—a semblance of autonomy masking a deeper subjugation.

Standing in the way of this relentless expansion was the Northern Alliance, a coalition of ethnic groups united under the leadership of Ahmad Shah Massoud, an ethnic Tajik known as the "Lion of Panjshir." A veteran of the Soviet-Afghan War, Massoud had built his stronghold in the Panjshir Valley, a bastion of resistance that had withstood countless assaults. The only other credible opposition had been Uzbek warlord Abdul Rashid Dostum in Mazar-i-Sharif, but after his defeat at the hands of the Taliban, the Northern Alliance stood alone in its defiance.

For Massoud, who spoke fluent French having studied at the Lycée Esteqlal in Kabul, it was not just a military struggle but a moral one, symbolising hope for those unwilling to bow to the Taliban's rule. My time in Afghanistan brought me into the orbit of this resistance, illuminating the complex interplay of loyalty, betrayal, and survival that defined life in a land crossed by so many lines—ethnic, ideological, and personal.

A frontline had emerged between the Taliban and the Northern Alliance. The Red Cross and Red Crescent Movement operated under strict principles of neutrality, impartiality, and independence - values that allowed us to navigate even the most volatile regions. In Afghanistan, the International Red Cross maintained a presence in all major areas, including those outside Taliban control. One such location was the Panjshir Valley, our next destination.

The delegation in Panjshir operated independently from the Kabul-based mission. Staffed primarily by ethnic Tajiks, they had their own vehicles, buildings, and logistical support infrastructure. Unlike Kabul, the Panjshir office had no permanent international staff, which added a layer of complexity to our visit. To reach the valley, we would have to cross the active frontline.

Leading the mission was my colleague, a young Belgian delegate with an impressive blend of ambition and aptitude - qualities that marked him as a future leader in the organisation. Alongside us were two experienced drivers and senior field officers tasked with liaising directly with frontline commanders to negotiate our passage. Much of the groundwork had already been laid by our headquarters team, who coordinated with interlocutors from both sides to ensure our safety. As per protocol, we travelled in two vehicles - a critical risk mitigation in such missions.

Packing for Panjshir was slightly different from my usual preparations. My standard emergency evacuation pack was minimal, under 10 kilograms, but for this mission, I packed additional items. Given the uncertain duration of our stay, I included formal clothing for meetings, essential toiletries, my trusty Swiss Army Knife, snacks, water and communication equipment. We also carried supplies and upgraded communication equipment for the Panjshir office, a critical logistical component of our mission.

My feelings before departure were complex. Being selected for such a high-risk mission followed careful deliberation among senior management. My previous success in Bamiyan likely played a role, signalling that my contributions were being recognised beyond the usual considerations of gender.

In a field where most health staff were women, the added security risks could sometimes overshadow one's qualifications. This time, I felt honoured—and my excitement largely masked any underlying anxiety or fear. Dangerous as it was, I relished the opportunity, trusting that the Red Cross would never send a team where the risks outweighed the mission's objectives.

The journey to the frontline took four hours. The terrain gradually transformed, growing rockier and more barren as we ascended toward the crossing point. Narrow passes wound through the jagged hills, each bend revealing signs of life—clusters of local traders and women gathered near what we assumed was the crossing. This was where the Taliban and Northern Alliance forces faced off for the battle for Panjshir.

Our convoy came to a halt. The field officers disembarked, initiating a series of radio communications and conversations with what appeared to be a Taliban liaison officer. We remained in the vehicles, aware that a similar negotiation was happening on the other side of the frontline with Northern Alliance commanders. The question loomed: would these two warring factions temporarily cease fire to allow a pair of Red Cross delegates to cross?

Yet, the importance of our mission and the reputation of the International Red Cross seemed to carry sufficient weight. The negotiations—though tense—highlighted the delicate respect our neutrality commanded in even the most fractious circumstances. It was possible that the Northern Alliance's interest in our visit stemmed from the large number of Taliban soldiers they were holding as prisoners of war, whom we were likely to visit. This factor may have been pivotal in securing a temporary ceasefire for our crossing.

One significant hurdle, however, was that we couldn't cross in our vehicles or with our Afghan staff, who were Pashtun and thus could not accompany us into Northern Alliance territory. As these discussions unfolded, two mules arrived. Our luggage and communication equipment were carefully strapped to them, signalling a surprising twist to our journey: we would be crossing the frontline on foot.

As the agreed halt in firing took effect, the women and traders who had gathered at the crossing seized their chance to traverse the front line alongside us. Together, we walked over rocky terrain and along a gravel road, guiding the mules laden with supplies. The scene was surreal, a choreographed crossing that underscored the precision and coordination between the Red Cross field officers and their respective interlocutors on both sides. It felt like stepping into a narrative plucked from a film or novel—a moment where diplomacy, logistics, and human perseverance intersected. As per custom a few delicacies from Switzerland were in our packs ready to share with our new colleagues we would soon meet.

The path to the Northern Alliance's front line took about an hour. On a hilltop ahead, we saw two familiar Red Cross Land Cruisers and two field officers waiting to greet us. Their eagerness was palpable; it had likely been some time since they had seen anyone from the international team. Their movements were limited to Northern Alliance-controlled areas, which had dwindled significantly in size. For them, as for us, this encounter symbolised a rare connection across lines of conflict, a reminder of the larger mission we all served.

We were greeted like long-lost friends. The older senior field officer, who doubled as the head of the office, a younger colleague, and their driver welcomed us with broad smiles. The warmth of their reception was a striking contrast to the tense and uncertain atmosphere we had left behind just a few kilometres earlier. It was remarkable how drastically the mood and circumstances could change within such a short distance, as though we had crossed not just a frontline but a boundary between two distinct worlds.

The difference extended beyond ideology; it felt as if we had stepped across decades. I would experience a similar sensation a few years later in another conflict zone, though never quite the same - a sudden shift that felt like traversing a civilisation gap spanning 50 to 100 years. Here, the transformation was immediate, and it left a lasting impression.

Gone were the strict dress codes and austere appearances dictated by life in Taliban-controlled areas. The field officers here presented themselves with a sense of ease and individuality that mirrored their environment. The head of the office, whom I instinctively thought of as "the older one," wasn't old at all—just more experienced. Likely in his late twenties or early thirties, he carried himself with quiet authority. His neatly cut dark hair and well-groomed beard complemented a vest worn over his traditional shalwar kameez and wearing his International Red Cross badge and emblem, adding to his air of professionalism.

One subtle but fascinating detail I noticed was the variation in the styles of their shalwar kameez. Much like how men in the Gulf States—Saudi Arabia, the Emirates, Oman, Bahrain, and Qatar—distinguish themselves by the way they wear their ghutra headscarves, the men here seemed to incorporate elements of quality and fashion into their traditional attire.

Their shalwar kameez featured distinct details that set them apart. Some had pleats and a V-pattern on the back and a longer curved hem, subtly enhancing the appearance of broader shoulders and long torso. Others included small tassels at the front collar, adding a touch of flair. Most of the garments were pristine white, looking as though they had just come out of a washing machine, dried, and ironed to perfection—almost as if they were part of an advertising campaign for laundry detergent! The meticulous care they put into their appearance spoke to a sense of pride, even in such challenging surroundings.

His younger colleague, by contrast, was a study in contrasts. Slender and fair-skinned, with ginger hair, he stood out in a way that was almost disarming. He had the beginnings of a beard, lighter in colour, and a smattering of freckles that gave him an almost boyish actor Eddie Redmayne charm. If not for his shalwar kameez, you might mistake him for someone from the northern reaches of Europe. In fact, I couldn't help but imagine him in the Scottish Highlands, clad in a kilt and playing a Highland bagpipe - it was an amusing mental image that seemed to momentarily bridge the disparate worlds we had been traversing. We were told that several men who served under Alexander the Great who travelled through this region during his conquests, married and settled here rather than return to Greece.

Once our safe arrival was assured and confirmed via radio back to Kabul, we began our descent into the Panjshir Valley.

The view before us was breathtaking. A river snaked its way through the valley, flanked by scattered settlements and bordered by rocky hills on both sides. The gorge-like landscape was narrow yet punctuated by open spaces, where rows of dark green military vehicles—both armed and transport—were neatly arranged, a clear display of the valley's strategic importance. It was immediately evident why this valley had been deemed impenetrable, a lesson the Soviets learned the hard way.

Amid the rows of operational vehicles, a graveyard of rusted relics lay scattered: tanks, troop carriers, jeeps, and fuel tankers, left behind as stark reminders of past battles. These decaying hulks stood as a silent testimony to the resilience of the Panjshiris and the immense challenges the might of the Soviet Union faced here.

Our Afghan colleagues shared stories that further underscored the valley's legendary status. Thanks to its unique topography, any invading fighter jets were forced to navigate the narrow corridor, making them easy targets for the soldiers hidden in the hills. One tale stood out above the rest: the story of four brothers, celebrated as heroes, who were said to have single-handedly defended the valley with shoulder-fired missiles, bringing down every Soviet plane or helicopter that dared to enter Panjshir. Whether the tale was fact or folklore, it spoke volumes about the indomitable spirit of the people who called this valley home.

Staying in Panjshir for several days offered a much-needed respite. If not for the war, it could have been the perfect retreat - its refreshingly beautiful landscape, gentle rivers, wildflowers, and stone fruit trees nearing the end of their harvest painted a picture of serenity. Bees darted among the wildflowers along the grassy riverbanks, gathering the last nectar to sustain their hives through the harsh winter months. The shallow, gravel-lined river provided an ideal spot to rinse down our vehicles and cool our feet in its refreshing, clear water.

The International Red Cross office, where we stayed, doubled as our accommodation. Some of its rooms had been converted into makeshift bedrooms, while an underground cellar served as both a storage space and a "safe room" in case of emergencies. A small loft housed additional supplies. Its low ceilings and whitewashed walls, paired with uneven stonework, evoked the charm of a Cornish fisherman's cottage or a remote home on the Isle of Skye, perched on a hill overlooking the sea. Afghan cushions and vibrant carpets adorned every corner, transporting us far from the grim reality of the war just a short distance away.

With only five of us - my Belgian colleague, two Tajik field officers, our driver, and me - we operated as a close-knit team, sharing meals and responsibilities in the Afghan tradition. A chowkidar, a local guard, kept a watchful eye on our safety. Earlier that day, I had wandered through the bustling local markets brimming with fresh fruits, jars of honey, local yoghurts, cheeses, meats, and colourful displays of *shalwar kameez*. Eager to immerse myself in the local culture, I purchased a white *shalwar kameez* cut in the distinct "Panjshir" style.

That evening, I joined the team in preparing dinner over a stone fire pit in a small, separate building adjacent to the office. The fire pit's chimney drew the smoky air upward as we worked, baking bread, simmering hearty stews, and cooking beans. Afghan-style meat *shashlik*, reminiscent of kebabs, sizzled over the glowing embers, releasing mouthwatering aromas that filled the room.

We contributed our Swiss gifts - cured meats, Swiss cheese, and, later, a touch of sweetness with Swiss chocolate - to the meal. Once everything was ready, the five of us sat cross-legged in a circle, eating with only our right hands as was customary. The food was delicious, but it was the atmosphere that made the evening special. We shared stories about the region, local folklore, and snippets from our own histories and families. In that moment, amidst the simple yet meaningful exchange of culture and connection, it felt as though the boundaries of nationality and background melted away, leaving only the shared human experience.

These moments of camaraderie were often the most rewarding parts of any deployment. Sitting together, we stripped away the labels of war -good versus bad, wealth versus poverty, literacy versus illiteracy - and saw each other as simply human. Roles could easily reverse one day; history had shown us that much. For now, we cherished this time of shared humanity, a fleeting but vital reprieve from the divisions imposed by the world outside.

After a peaceful night's rest, I made my way back to the river, drawn by its gentle allure. The softly trickling water sounded more like a brook, its murmur harmonising with the stillness of the morning. The low sun bathed the scene in a golden glow, while the milky blue sky, streaked with white clouds, created an ethereal backdrop - like a dream you never wanted to wake from.

Before long, one of my Afghan colleagues joined me. The younger, fair-skinned man with a smattering of freckles came and sat cross-legged beside me, a flask of tea cradled in his hands. The distinct aroma of ginger wafted through the air as he poured the tea into a small glass, the warmth seeping into my palms as I clasped it gently, savouring each sip. His friendly smile, framed by striking grey blue eyes, had an effortless charm, and in another time or place, he might have been mistaken for a model.

He wore a *shalwar kameez*, its flowing design perfectly suited to movement and comfort, whether walking or sitting. Much like a school uniform, which strips away markers of wealth or status to place everyone on equal footing, the *shalwar kameez* did the same. Its simplicity highlighted an individual's inner beauty, radiating authenticity rather than relying on the embellishment of attire.

After a breakfast of Afghan bread, milk, cheese, honey, freshly cut pomegranates, apricots, and another round of tea, we gathered for a team briefing. The agenda centred on our upcoming meetings and activities for the next few days. Our first and arguably most critical task was to meet the local authorities. This introduction was essential to present ourselves, outline our objectives, and, crucially, secure the necessary permissions to proceed. Nothing in our work was undertaken without full consent and cooperation - this was the ethos of the Red Cross. Our mission was not to denounce or openly criticise but to support, as invited guests, always respecting the sovereignty of the Afghan people.

As we made our way to the Governor's residence, we passed a sleek, black 4WD that exuded an air of importance. One of our field officers pointed out that the vehicle belonged to Ahmad Shah Massoud, the renowned leader of the Northern Alliance. We would soon be meeting his advisor, Abdullah - a medical doctor who would later rise to prominence as the Minister of Foreign Affairs in the Karzai government. It was a stark reminder of the complex web of leadership and power that framed our work here, a delicate balance of diplomacy, respect, and purpose.

The soldiers of the Northern Alliance, with their dark green camouflage jackets, trousers, and patrol caps reminiscent of French military attire, presented a sharp contrast to the indistinguishable fighters in many modern conflicts. Their uniforms and command structure aligned them more closely with the Geneva Conventions' definition of combatants - individuals who can be identified as soldiers and operate under a clear chain of command. Yet, as I stood among them, I was struck by the growing challenge these principles face in today's warfare. The distinction between combatants and non-combatants, once as clear as a uniform, now blurs amidst tribal and factional conflicts where fighters often blend into civilian populations. Under the Geneva Conventions, protection is afforded not only to civilians but also to those no longer able to fight - combatants injured on the battlefield or those who have laid down their arms - and to individuals providing medical care or spiritual support to the wounded or dying. The uniforms of the Northern Alliance symbolised not just an identity but also a fading clarity in the rules of war, a reminder of the fragile line between order and chaos on the battlefield.

Serendipity – 'Fights and Bikes'

Many of us have encountered moments of unexplained intervention - instances that saved us from harm, redirected our path, or sparked a sudden epiphany. Perhaps it was a random delay in traffic that caused you to arrive late at an intersection, narrowly avoiding an accident. Or maybe it was meeting a stranger whose words planted a seed that ultimately changed the course of your life. Sometimes, it might be a gut instinct prompting you to take a different route, one you later realise was crucial.

In an age increasingly reliant on science to validate experiences, we risk losing touch with our innate senses and the unseen forces that may guide us. Our dependence on technology - such as alarms that sever us from the natural rhythm of waking with the dawn or GPS systems that replace our observational skills—further distances us from the world around us. By neglecting to engage with our surroundings, noting landmarks, landscapes, and the journey itself, we miss the mindful awareness that travel once required and the deeper connections it fostered.

Many have documented the remarkable behaviour of animals before impending disasters. One of the most notable examples occurred during the Boxing Day tsunami in 2004, triggered by a massive earthquake in the Indian Ocean. Elephants and other animals instinctively moved to higher ground, birds fled from estuaries and shallow waters, and dogs refused to venture outside. In stark contrast, the human death toll was devastating, highlighting our growing reliance on technology - such as tsunami warning systems - that failed to alert communities in time.

Unlike humans, animals appeared attuned to the subtle cues of nature, responding to signals we often overlook or disregard. The few animals that perished were primarily those confined to enclosures, such as domestic livestock, unable to move freely to safety. This tragic disparity underscores the consequences of our detachment from the natural world and the importance of reconnecting with the instincts and environmental awareness we once shared with other living beings.

Over the years, I have experienced interventions that I attribute to the presence of a guardian angel or spirit guide. These may appear in different forms such as mentor or random stranger, someone who drops into your life even if momentarily but in doing so left a profound impression upon you and shared their wisdom and knowledge. They can be non-human – such as pet or a wild animal. Some attribute spirit guides through specific assigned totems.

While I am not affiliated with any specific religion, I recognise how the place of one's birth and upbringing often orient individuals toward the dominant religious doctrine of their community. This influence is often reinforced through schools aligned with particular faiths, where religion becomes less a matter of choice and more a framework shaped by societal expectations—providing a sense of belonging, survival, and acceptance.

I consider myself someone who believes in God, the existence of the soul, and the presence of angels and spirit guides. However, I do not believe that any one religion holds a monopoly on faith or spiritual truth. To me, religion in its purest form is a path, a guide toward understanding and connection. Yet, in human hands, it can become a tool for exerting influence, creating divisions, and consolidating power by emphasising opposites and differences.

My beliefs evolved through a process: first accepting what I was told as truth, then defending and repeating it, and ultimately questioning it. This transformation often happens when we leave the "nest" of influence and begin to travel, encountering new perspectives. Myths and inherited stories gradually unravel, giving way to a journey of self-discovery. Away from the biases we were taught to accept as gospel, we start to discern our own truth - a truth unshackled by coercion or conformity.

I often wonder how many people marvel at paintings, sculptures, and architectural wonders yet overlook the more profound artistry that surrounds us every day—nature. Human creativity expressed through art, music, and monumental structures is admirable, even awe-inspiring at times. But it will always pale in comparison to the boundless, intricate, and ever-evolving masterpiece crafted by Mother Earth.

Consider the grand pilgrimages people undertake to visit structures built to immortalise power or love, such as the pyramids or the Taj Mahal. While I can appreciate the engineering feats and the stories behind these monuments, they do not stir the same sense of wonder in me as they seem to in others. The pyramids, for instance, provoke more questions than admiration. Who built them? Was it skilled labour, or were they erected by enslaved hands? And at what cost to human life and dignity? While they may have provided livelihoods to some, how many lives were lost or irreparably damaged during their construction? To me, the ethical weight of their creation overshadows their grandeur.

Similarly, the Taj Mahal - a mausoleum built by a Mughal emperor in memory of his wife—is often heralded as an eternal symbol of love. Yet, it too feels tainted by the immense privilege and power required to bring such a vision to life. Was it an act of devotion, or a demonstration of ego cloaked in romance? While it undoubtedly provided work to thousands of artisans, labourers, and merchants, I find it hard to marvel at its beauty without reflecting on its context. To me, the elegance of this structure cannot compare to the living poetry of nature: the sight of elephants, for instance, moving as a family across the Zambezi River. The matriarch leads, cautiously guarding the young from the strong currents, as they climb the far bank with quiet determination. This moment is a tapestry of instinct, connection, and survival that no human-built monument can replicate.

Even if a photographer or painter captures such a scene, the result is a mere echo—two-dimensional and incomplete. It lacks the scent of the riverbank, the soft rustle of leaves, the distant cry of a fish eagle, and the palpable weight of the elephants' movements. It is this multisensory, dynamic quality of nature that makes it divine—a sacred art form infinitely more powerful than any monument erected by human hands.

My first memories of feeling an unseen presence protecting me trace back to school. Jamie was a charismatic figure, the kind of boy everyone wanted to befriend or emulate. Popular, handsome, and effortlessly talented, he excelled in everything: sports, academics, leadership. Whatever he touched turned to gold. It was infuriating how he never seemed to study, yet always came out on top. Jamie was a force of nature, and over the 13 years we attended school together, from infants to secondary school, he remained untouchable in every arena.

We weren't just schoolmates, either. We joined the same Cubs and Scout groups, the 6th Croydon. He'd often drop in to our home and invite me to kick a ball at our local park and sometimes on the way to school I'd knock on his door and we'd walk to school together. Thanks to Jamie, we often clinched victories in competitions. He was the golden boy, the glue that held the team together. Jamie's parents, both teachers, lived modestly in a small terrace house on Brighton Road, opposite the bus garage. There was a magnetism about him - a quality that made everyone like him, or at least want to be near him.

But Jamie had a darker side. A cruel streak. Beneath the charm and wit, he had an uncanny ability to manipulate people for his own amusement. He delighted in stirring the pot, orchestrating petty dramas that pitted friends against one another. Sometimes it was subtle - he'd spread a rumour to provoke confrontation. Other times, it was outright malicious. One day, he set his sights on me.

Jamie told a group of classmates who had a formed a "secret JR Tolkien club" that I had challenged them all to fight. It was absurd! I was one of the smallest in our class, hardly a contender in physical confrontations, especially against some of the club's bigger, rugby-playing members. But Jamie's word was gospel. Before I even knew what was happening, whispers of a fight circulated through the school.

The home-time bell had barely rung when a crowd began to gather in the corridor. A group of classmates ushered me to a widening area of the corridor where Paul, my first opponent, was waiting. Paul wasn't a typical adversary. We'd been friends once, mock-fighting and wrestling during breaks, where I'd surprise him with my speed and knack for pinning his arm behind his back. But today, Paul wasn't playing.

"Fight! Fight! Fight!" The chant erupted as we were pushed toward each other. In the chaos, I caught sight of Jamie in the crowd, his face lit with twisted glee. I never knew what lies he fed the club to make them all turn against me, but there was no time for explanations.

Paul came at me with fists flying. At first, I defended myself, dodging and blocking. But soon I had no choice but to retaliate. Paul was prepared, keeping his arms out of reach to avoid them being caught and then being tackled to the ground - my one advantage. He kept pressing forward, landing blows, his knuckles turning red. Blood dripped from some small cuts on my face, but I held my ground.

Then it happened. A loud crack split the air. Paul recoiled, clutching his eye as he staggered backward. For a moment, time froze. I hadn't hit him - of that, I was certain. But something, or someone, had intervened.

Taking the opportunity, I grabbed my bag and slipped through the stunned crowd. My shirt was bloodied, my body bruised, but I made it to the bus. At home, nothing was said.

The next day at school, I was met with a mix of wary and curious stares which was probably due to some cuts and bruises on my face and arms. Paul walked into the classroom sporting a massive shiner. Despite the fight, there was no animosity between us. If anything, it was as if we shared a silent understanding. Paul also couldn't' understand considering how we were now grappling and wrestling on the ground rather than throwing punches how I suddenly punched him in the face, which was enough to end the fight. Jamie may have orchestrated our clash, but Paul seemed to see something in me after that day - a depth he hadn't noticed before.

The uneasy peace didn't last. Another club member soon approached me, declaring it was his "turn" to fight me after school. This time, I refused. I swallowed my pride and let go of whatever small honour there was in standing my ground. Enough was enough.

The "mystery hand" that had intervened during my fight with Paul made its presence known at least two more times. Not in a brawl, but in moments equally baffling. One such occasion occurred during a school trip to Europe.

We were lining up to enter a canteen when a fellow student - an overconfident lad with a black belt in karate - decided to show off his skills. Without warning, he began practicing flying kicks, his movements swift and calculated. As the line shuffled forward, he suddenly launched himself into the air, aiming a kick directly at me.

I turned instinctively, trying to swerve out of the way, but before I could react fully, something extraordinary happened. His legs, mid-flight, were abruptly yanked backward as if an invisible hand had grabbed them. The force sent him somersaulting through the air before he landed flat on his back, stunned.

For a moment, I and those around me stood frozen, unsure of what we'd just witnessed. At first, I thought it was some sort of elaborate trick—perhaps a choreographed move where he mimicked the kick and acted out an exaggerated response. But the shock on his face told me otherwise.

"Where did you learn to do that?" he asked, his voice a mix of confusion and awe.

"I didn't," I replied honestly, as bewildered as he was. Whatever had intervened that day, it wasn't me.

I was 17 years old when I got my first set of "wheels." At that age, you could hold a provisional license allowing you to ride a motorbike up to 125cc without taking a test, provided you displayed an "L" plate above or below the number plate. Being one of the youngest in my year due to my August birthday, I wouldn't turn 18 until the end of the Upper Sixth (Year 12). If I had been born a few weeks later, I'd have been in the year below. I digress, but this quirk of timing meant many of my peers had already turned 18 and were driving to school in their cars—often a status symbol of their family's wealth.

For me, a motorbike - or rather, a moped - was all I could afford. It wasn't glamorous, but it was freedom, and I cherished it. My moped was paid for with earnings from my evening job at a local pub, a job I landed in a stroke of irony. Too young to legally drink or drive a car, I managed to bluff my way into a role pulling pints for my schoolmates and locals, many of whom showed up in their cars. Even more amusing was the fact that I turned up in my school uniform to ask for the job, told them I was 18 and was hired on the spot, despite being underage.

My brother Adam, just 13 months older, worked with me at the same pub. Technically, this meant he had to pass as 19. Adam often worked in the upstairs night bar and disco that came to life after last orders, while I poured pints in the main bar, a hub for live bands and grumpy locals who inspected every pint for its perfect head. It didn't take long for me to master the art of prioritising patrons and keeping the peace in the bustling pub.

By my last year of school, I'd formed a close friendship with four lads from Purley. Our little group often gathered at Phil's large detached house on Foxley Lane, not far from where a legendary member of Status Quo lived, or at my house when my parents worked night shifts. Initially, we travelled to each other's homes by bus or train, but once we all acquired mopeds, life took a thrilling turn. Each of us had a different Japanese make and between us we rode a Honda, a Suzuki, a Kawasaki, and myself - a Yamaha. The other Nick stood out with his Italian Malaguti trail bike.

We spent our weekends riding through the country lanes of Surrey, exploring charming villages like Chaldon, Chipstead and Banstead. On warm balmy summer evenings, we'd sit in beer gardens, soaking up the twilight in the countryside's calm. The pubs, with their rustic charm and hearty meals, became our sanctuaries - places for laughter, conversation, and shared plans.

One summer's day, just Phil, Nick, and I decided to take a ride. I was still getting used to my bike, and this was the perfect opportunity to gain confidence. We rode through winding country roads, surrounded by fields and dotted with picturesque cottages. After about ten miles, we stopped on a quiet lane. I turned off my engine while we discussed heading back.

When it was time to leave, my bike refused to start. Despite my frantic efforts, the engine wouldn't fire. Phil had already started back on his bike without looking back but Nick turned back noticing I hadn't started to follow. Nick tried his hand at starting it, but after several failed attempts, he decided to ride ahead and let my mum know I'd be late. He didn't seem very concerned. As his bike disappeared down the lane, I found myself alone, sweating under the weight of my leather jacket and helmet, pushing my bike in the general direction of home.

Hunger gnawed at me as I trudged along, thoughts of my favourite egg, salad cream, and cress white bread sandwiches consuming my mind. Just as despair began to creep in, I stumbled upon a bus stop near a cottage with a red brick fence. There, improbably, was a sandwich wrapped in plastic film, perched on the post next to the gate. Without hesitation, I took it as I instinctively knew it was for me. To my astonishment, it was egg and cress - close enough to my dream snack. Nourished and recharged, I pushed on toward Phil's house.

By the time I arrived at Phil's house, the sky was painted with the dusky hues of twilight. I pushed the bike into the driveway to the open garage which also served as a workshop. Phil, in his usual navy dungarees, had his Honda hoisted above the work bench in his father's garage. He greeted me with a knowing grin his hands and clothing covered in grease. He jumped on my bike, gave the kickstart one swift motion, and the engine roared to life effortlessly. I stood there, equal parts bemused and sheepish.

That day, I learned more than how to ride a moped. It was a lesson in resilience, camaraderie, and the mysterious kindness of the universe - a reminder that even when you're stranded, you're never truly alone.

Nick hadn't told my mum and I didn't see him for a few days.

Our group at the time was very close – all very different in our nature yet there was something that brought us together. All later successful in our chosen professions in Engineering, Plumbing, Accounting and myself in Health. Whilst we have little connection today, much of our lives were formed in those early years.

I often find that I am usually the only Nick in a group or class but in our close nit group, we were four Nicks. Phil's mum called me 'Sensible' Nick and knew if I was in the group heading out she didn't have to worry. Phil's older brother was 'Moody' Nick which was very apt. The Nick who rode with us and introduced me to Phil, I spent a lot of time with ferreting and having philosophical conversations who later earned his wings as a paratrooper, played guitar in a band, became a plumber and activist. Nick was always up for a dare and challenged convention. Barred several times by Facebook due to his anti-vax rhetoric, we knew Nick as 'Silly Nick". There was another Nick – who during night fishing and camping trips did not speak for hours when getting up in the morning, was 'Handsome Nick" or Johno!

Serendipity – "Rocks and Knives"

These unusual events of "intervention" - moments some would call coincidence, others luck - seem to occur randomly, often when least expected. They have likely happened to all of us: instances of inexplicable grace, of narrowly avoiding disaster. Perhaps what we call coincidence is something more - an unseen force or a guardian angel steering us away from harm.

In today's world, our ability to listen to the whispers of the universe is increasingly drowned out by the relentless noise and distractions around us. These interruptions sever our connection to the natural rhythms and harmony that bind us to the cosmos. The scientific pursuit of evidence and explanation often leaves little room to consider alternative perspectives. It insists that every phenomenon must fit neatly into the framework of logic and reason.

Anything beyond our understanding - beyond what conforms to established societal, religious, or scientific order - challenges us. These outliers disrupt the categories and constructs we rely on to make sense of the world. Once, perhaps, humanity was unified in thought and spirit, undivided by labels and systems. Over time, these divisions have multiplied, fragmenting us further and further from a sense of collective oneness.

During my assignment in Afghanistan, the high security risks and limited social interaction outside of our accommodations and office meant that every three months, we were granted a six-day rest and recuperation period. Depending on the situation, if you worked continuously for seven days, or even back-to-back weeks, you might be eligible for a long weekend every six weeks. This was more than just a chance to relax in a safer environment; it was an opportunity to shop, visit local markets, explore places of interest, get a haircut, stock up on toiletries, dine at restaurants, or even go for a hike.

Our delegation organised these trips and accommodations. Depending on your chosen destination, you would need approval from both the head of delegation at your duty station and the head of delegation of your destination. Pakistan was the only destination allowed for rest and recuperation, as technically, you remained on duty and continued to represent the organisation. It was also the closest and easiest place to return from if the need arose.

During my second R&R, I decided to visit Hunza Valley in Gilgit, taking a road trip along the Karakoram Highway that connects Pakistan with China.

The Hunza Valley was a stark contrast to everything I had experienced thus far. It was a serene oasis, often described as "heaven on earth." The people reminded me of the mythical Middle Earth from Tolkien's stories – deeply connected to the land, working it diligently and sustainably, living self-sufficiently with a diet focused on fruits and vegetables and limited meat. At 165 cm tall, I felt I was above the median height in this community. Historically, the people of Hunza were Buddhist, as evidenced by the remnants of shrines and temples scattered across the valley. When Islam arrived, the Hunza people adopted the Ismaili sect, which is less strict than the Sunni Islam practiced by most of Pakistan.

The schools were co-educational, with children singing songs and participating in activities reminiscent of English schools, with playgrounds, uniforms, flag-raising ceremonies, and orderly queues.

Men and women worked side by side in the fields, with narrow irrigation channels separating paddocks where food was grown and harvested. Apricot trees were abundant, along with other fruits that thrived at high altitudes, blooming only after a frost had passed.

The people of Hunza looked strikingly different from the Pakistanis I had encountered in Peshawar, Lahore, Karachi, and Islamabad. They were a distinctive mix of Chinese and Indian features, with lighter skin and short in height with a well-proportioned physique that that was testimony to their effortless working ethic and exercise. Many Pakistanis came to Hunza for holidays, as it was a popular tourist destination, and in many ways, they stood out just as much as any Western visitor. Hunza was also a popular hiking destination for Europeans and Americans in the 1970s and 1980s. I could have easily blended in had I worn the same attire, especially with the traditional Pakol woollen cap worn by the men, often adorned with a peacock feather to signify honour and dignity.

With only a six-day break, including travel time, I could only stay a couple of nights in this beautiful valley. It was a place I could have stayed for much longer.

I was amazed by the engineering feats of the Hunza people, particularly their irrigation channels. The cool, silty water flowed smoothly along the channels, nourishing the vegetation and ensuring that the paddocks were well-supplied with water and minerals. The people were industrious, carrying gardening tools to maintain the paddocks, with women picking produce, weeding, and contributing to the community's sustenance. It was a perfect example of the "Paddock to Plate" concept. Their work ethic reminded me of the scenes from *Snow White and the Seven Dwarfs*—the Hunza men toiling in the fields, working industriously, and then heading home in unison to feast and spend time with their families and communities.

There are many reports that the people of Hunza are among the longest-living and healthiest communities in the world, and from my own observations, I wouldn't dispute this claim.

It was on this trip that something quite out of the ordinary occurred. Gilgit was the main district town – a very different feel to Hunza – a bustling market town and traditions more familiar with the wider Pakistan that I knew.

I organised a driver to take me along the Karakoram Highway that had ancient ties to the legendary Silk Road. I would be heading towards Kashgar at the Chinese border passing Sost, Nagar and stopping at Khunjerab Pass. Time and security requirements wouldn't allow me to travel further towards the border crossing with China at Kashgar.

My driver hailed from Gilgit, a hub for adventurers seeking to explore the northern reaches of Pakistan. The town hosted an array of individuals and small companies offering tourists the chance to rent vehicles with local drivers, typically rugged, open-top Jeep replicas designed for the region's challenging terrain. Arrangements were made for a driver and his Jeep to collect me early the next morning from my hostel.

The night before our departure, I lay awake, listening to the steady rhythm of rainfall outside, apprehensive about the conditions we might face. However, at dawn, the sky greeted me with an unblemished expanse of blue, and the air carried a freshness that only follows a heavy downpour. To my surprise—given the region's relaxed approach to time—my driver was already waiting in the hostel's courtyard, leaning against his freshly washed, black Jeep. The vehicle looked sturdy, capable, and oddly elegant but rugged for the adventure ahead. There were blankets that could be wrapped over your legs if you needed – almost a glamping version of a road trip! Hanging from the rear view mirror were Islamic prayer beads called a Subha.

Armed with basic provisions and snacks hastily gathered from the hostel, I slid into the front passenger seat, settling into the excitement of what felt like a true road trip. My driver, a charismatic young man in his mid-twenties, stood out in Gilgit's sea of traditional *shalwar kameez*. Sporting long, wavy hair under a baseball cap, wearing sunglasses, a black polo shirt, neckless metal chain, jeans, and sockless deck shoes, he had the casual air of someone more at home in a European city than in the rugged mountains.

He was eager to talk, switching between English and Urdu, and seemed proud of his knowledge of Western culture - likely fine-tuned from years of chauffeuring European and American travellers or watching a lot of BBC TV programs!

His target clientele sought not the chaos of the cities but the unspoiled beauty of Pakistan's countryside, rivers, and mountains. His enthusiasm for the journey was infectious, and his stories mostly about his family made the initial leg of the drive pass quickly.

We were soon cruising along the Karakoram Highway, now a well-paved road—a far cry from the treacherous gravel paths it had once been. As the Jeep ascended, the landscape unfolded with breathtaking grandeur: roaring turquoise rivers thundered below, and the highway weaved through narrow passes, hemmed in by towering rock faces on one side and precipitous drops on the other. I noticed the occasional rock on the side of the road and sitting on the edge which may have fallen overnight during the rain. Rock and mudslides were quite common along the highway. Overnight rain had transformed the cliffs into a series of gentle cascading streams that spilled across the road before trickling over the edge into the valleys below.

Our first stop came quickly: the Hussaini Hanging Bridge. Suspended high above the fast-moving Hunza River, its frail, weathered planks were spaced unevenly apart, swaying ominously in the wind. It seemed more like an artifact than a functioning bridge. It reminded me of those TV reality show challenges where contestants attempt to cross similar structures, encouraged (or hindered) by opponents shaking the ropes. In those cases, a misstep meant a short drop into calm waters with safety crews standing by. Here, falling meant plunging over 50 meters into the icy, tumultuous river, its surface concealing jagged rocks and unseen currents.

Even from the riverbank, the sight of the bridge made my pulse quicken. My driver chuckled at my apprehension, assuring me that a sturdier suspension bridge awaited us further along the highway at Passu. According to him, it was still in use and, unlike Hussaini, safe enough to cross.

Tourists were a rarity in this region. The ongoing conflict in neighbouring Afghanistan kept many away, leaving the breathtaking rivers, snow-capped peaks, glaciers, and forests to those of us who worked nearby and sought reprieve in the natural splendour. When we arrived at Passu, I stood gazing at the suspension bridge, a sense of both awe and respect settled over me - this wasn't just a bridge, but a lifeline for locals navigating a landscape both beautiful and unforgiving.

It was at the Passu suspension bridge that I encountered my first fellow tourists of the trip. Like me, they had hired a driver and Jeep. The two women, both in their late forties or early fifties, worked at the British Embassy in Islamabad. They were already gingerly stepping onto the bridge when we arrived. Despite the warped planks and missing boards, my driver reassured me that this bridge was far sturdier than the one at Hussaini. Their own driver stood on solid ground, camera in hand, ready to capture the moment. They ventured about 30 meters out—far enough for a triumphant photo - before retreating.

I was far less daring. Merely standing at the entrance of the bridge felt like an accomplishment. With a mix of encouragement from my driver and assurances from the embassy staff, I cautiously took a few steps onto the swaying structure. The first ten meters felt manageable, but the movement quickly became unsettling, and my instinct was to go on all fours which I resisted. The ground, solid and safe, soon beckoned me back.

We decided this was the perfect spot for a lunch break. Over tea and shared provisions, the women and I chatted about our respective jobs—mine in Afghanistan and theirs in Pakistan - while our drivers sat a short distance away, lighting cigarettes and exchanging stories in Urdu. The atmosphere was relaxed, but the looming curfew reminded us that we needed to be back in Gilgit by dusk. The embassy staff left first, hoping to make good time, while we lingered a little longer before setting off.

The return journey started uneventfully, and I allowed myself to relax, reflecting on the adventure and looking forward to a hearty meal and well-earned rest. That tranquillity shattered when our windscreen suddenly turned black, a viscous liquid oozing across the glass. The Jeep sputtered to a halt. My heart sank as the driver climbed out to investigate.

"It's oil," he muttered grimly, inspecting the engine. "Something's snapped."

My thoughts raced. We were still far from the nearest settlement, not even back to Hussaini. The driver, now visibly concerned, assured me this had never happened before. He quickly reached for the radio, calling for assistance. His confident demeanour returned as he explained that help would come, though it might take several hours.

"Sit in the car," he advised. "Everything will be okay."

He walked a short distance away, likely searching for better reception to relay the issue. I watched nervously, wondering if he had faced this problem before. When he returned, he shared the news: a mechanic would bring the necessary spare part, but a recent rockfall ahead had blocked the road. We decided to walk toward the rockfall to assess the situation.

The sight ahead was intimidating. Mud, rocks, and water cascaded down the cliffside, completely blocking the road. The previous night's rain had triggered a landslide, loosening debris that now spilled across the path. The Pakistan Army was already at work, deploying bulldozers and heavy machinery in a well-rehearsed operation to clear the way. This was clearly not an uncommon occurrence on these perilous mountain roads.

As we stood watching the progress, my driver received another radio call. The mechanic was on the far side of the rockfall, waiting to bring the part across once the road was safe. Meanwhile, I noticed a familiar vehicle on the other side - the embassy women's Jeep. They had managed to cross before the rock fall and mud slide and must have stopped to witness the clearing process before venturing back to Gilgit or were being held back in case there was another fall further down the road.

The army's efficiency was impressive. With the blocked section stabilised, the mechanic carefully navigated the rubble on foot to reach us. He was greeted like an old friend by my driver, who was visibly relieved. In no time, the issue—a ruptured pipe - was fixed, the oil replenished, and the Jeep ready to go.

When the convoy was finally allowed to proceed, we led the procession, guided by the army through a muddy, waterlogged path. The road remained treacherous, but the sight of heavy machinery working tirelessly offered reassurance. That night, the road would be closed again to secure the rockface fully.

As I caught up with the embassy women in Gilgit for dinner, their relief mirrored mine. They said the rock fall began just after they passed the area. Reflecting on the timing of the events, I couldn't help but feel a chill. Had we not been delayed by the oil leak, we might have been directly in the path of the rockfall. The black streak across our windscreen, which seemed like a setback, may well have saved our lives.

Was it divine intervention, mere coincidence, or just the fickle nature of fate? I couldn't say. But as I settled back in Gilgit that evening, I couldn't shake the feeling that something - or someone - had been watching over us.

Sometimes, we court danger through our own actions. Despite knowing the risks, human nature drives us to be curious, to take chances, and occasionally, to make regrettable decisions. In my younger days on deployment, I carried the confidence of a fitter, healthier body and the recklessness of youth. Caution was an underdeveloped instinct, overshadowed by a sense of invincibility. Age, and perhaps wisdom, tempers that outlook, instilling a keener awareness of limitations and a stronger inclination toward risk aversion.

One particular event, during my time stationed in Jerusalem as a medical delegate during the Second Intifada, stands out as a moment where fate—or perhaps something more—intervened. By all accounts, it could have ended much worse.

Jerusalem, despite being a focal point of the conflict between Israelis and Palestinians, felt at times like a cosmopolitan retreat. Unlike the overtly tense and dangerous settings of Gaza or the West Bank, Jerusalem and Tel Aviv offered a veneer of normalcy. There were vibrant nightlife scenes, bustling shopping districts, restaurants, gyms, resorts, beaches, and even classical concerts. One evening, I attended a performance by the Israeli Philharmonic Orchestra and chorus, conducted by the legendary Zubin Mehta. They played Carl Orff's famous oratorio *Carmina Burana*, and it was nothing short of breathtaking. The orchestra's rich sound, precise execution, and the superb vocals of the chorus resonated through the magnificent concert hall, creating a powerful and moving experience. It felt surreal to witness such artistic excellence amidst the backdrop of a region so fraught with division and strife.

A year earlier, I had experienced a similarly striking moment of artistic brilliance during a visit to Yerevan, the capital of Armenia. On a short R&R from my work in Nagorno-Karabakh, I attended a classical concert in a modest venue. The passionate string section swayed in unison, their music radiating warmth that defied the bitter cold of the unheated space. Audience members wrapped themselves in layers of clothing, relying on gas blow heaters more suited to warehouses to stave off the chill. The economic aftermath of the Armenia-Azerbaijan conflict over the disputed territory was palpable, yet the pride and resilience of the musicians shone through. Their performance paid homage to Armenia's rich musical heritage, including composers like Aram Khachaturian, whose *Spartacus* ballet theme is iconic. These concerts, both in Jerusalem and Yerevan, were poignant reminders of humanity's capacity to create beauty even in the most challenging of circumstances - a serendipitous testament to the enduring spirit of culture and art.

Even with the threat of a random civilian bomb attack on a bus carrying civilians which was common at the time, life went on as in defiance against those wanting to sow fear. It often felt more like an overseas work assignment than a deployment to a conflict zone. Yet, the illusion of safety was a fragile one, shattered each time I travelled to areas of active tension - Gaza, Hebron, or parts of the West Bank. The thin line separating peace and conflict was not geographical but psychological, a mere few kilometres apart in reality.

Living in East Jerusalem, within walking distance of the Old City's walled quarters, afforded me a unique perspective. The Christian, Jewish, Muslim, and Armenian Quarters felt like worlds within a world, steeped in history and divided by faith, yet interconnected by cobbled streets. Early mornings and late evenings, when the shops had closed and the streets were deserted except for a few stray cats and patrolling soldiers, were my favourite times to wander. The silence, punctuated only by my footsteps and the occasional nod to a soldier in a deep red beret, made the ancient stairways and narrow alleys feel timeless.

By day, the Old City transformed into a bustling marketplace. Pilgrims retraced the Stations of the Cross, while visitors explored holy sites, sampled kebabs, falafels, humous, pita bread and mint tea. Locals preferred to sit smoking a shisha- glass based waterpipe - with various flavours - in deep conversation or watching the milling crowd. The shisha provided a sweet aroma of apple, cherries and incense that filled the narrow lanes. Other visitors visited the many souvenir shops and open craft rooms of men making pottery and blowing glass.

The Greek Orthodox and Muslim Quarters teemed with life and commerce, while the Jewish Quarter retained a more solemn air, its square dedicated to worshippers. The Armenian Quarter, less touched by tourism, preserved its tranquil seminaries for priests of the Armenian Apostolic Church.

Despite the rich tapestry of history and faith, some of the sacred sites left me underwhelmed. On a visit to Bethlehem, my driver - a Palestinian field officer—offered to show me the grotto marking the Nativity. To my surprise, there were no queues. I ducked through the low entrance and stood before the modest site where Jesus was believed to have been born. The simplicity of the setting and the lack of grandeur struck me. For something so central to faiths and conflicts spanning two millennia, it seemed almost too ordinary.

Back in the old city of Jerusalem, my ability to blend in with locals gave me a chance to observe life beyond the tourist lens. I smiled at moments of unintended humour, like the solemn reenactment of Jesus carrying the cross juxtaposed with a vendor hawking leopard-print lingerie nearby. Even within the sacred Church of the Holy Sepulchre, where pilgrims reverently prostrated themselves before the Stone of Unction, life's innocence peeked through. I watched as a young mother stood horrified while her two sons, blissfully unaware of the stone's religious significance, paraded their Teletubbies toys across it as though it were a play table.

Moments like these reminded me of the innocence of children, untainted by the divisions of belief and culture that adults often impose. In their simplicity, they brought a poignant clarity to the complexity of human faith, history, and conflict - a reminder that beneath it all, we are all just human.

One evening, I decided to take a shortcut through a park. The edges of the park were lined with restaurants and cafés, their lights reflecting faintly on the walking paths. The park itself was a mix of open grass fields and bushy areas dotted with trees. Couples strolled leisurely along the paths, giving it an air of safety.

I headed toward my accommodation on the far side of the park, away from the bright shopfronts. The path ahead was dimly lit, flanked by shadows from the trees and dense bushes. It was quieter here, the occasional rustle in the undergrowth accompanying my steps.

Partway through, I was approached by a young man. He asked me for the time. His tracksuit pants, polo top, and beard suggested he might be of Arabic descent, though I couldn't tell whether he was Israeli or Palestinian Arab. He was friendly and chatty, and I instinctively mirrored his demeanour, as I often did in these situations. When a few exchanged words revealed he spoke Arabic, I took the opportunity to respond in kind.

He quickly realised I was not a local and began asking where I was from and why I was there. I gave vague answers, saying I was doing some project work at the university. His curiosity shifted from me to my wristwatch, and he asked to take a closer look. Politely but firmly, I declined, mentioning I needed to get home.

Then his eyes landed on my Motorola mobile phone. Unlike a regular mobile, it doubled as a push-to-talk radio—a silver flip device issued specifically for our work. It was unique, designed for seamless communication in critical situations, and likely not something he'd seen before. His interest sharpened. He asked to see the phone, becoming increasingly insistent despite my repeated refusals. My voice must have betrayed my unease, as he reached for the phone, grabbing my wrist when I pulled it back.

Alarmed, I shouted loudly to draw attention, struggling against his grip. In the dim light, I noticed my metal watch strap loosening as his hold tightened. Then, to my horror, he pulled out a knife and demanded the phone. My heart raced. I tried to stay calm but felt panic rising.

Suddenly, the Motorola emitted a piercing alarm. The sound startled me as much as it did him. He hesitated for a crucial moment, loosening his grip. Seizing the opportunity, I broke free, turned, and ran. My shouts echoed through the park as I sprinted away, his footsteps conspicuously absent behind me.

When I reached the park's edge, my pace slowed to a brisk walk. My breathing was ragged, but I forced myself to steady it, my heart still pounding. Only then did I realise I'd lost my watch in the scuffle. There was no going back to retrieve it.

Back at my accommodation, I sat down, shaken but unharmed. I stared at the Motorola, wondering how it had activated an alarm sound I hadn't heard before. Was it a hidden feature, an automatic response to sudden movement or sound? Or was it something else entirely - a guardian angel watching over me?

Whatever it was, it had saved from something that could have potentially been very harmful not just to me but the organisation. And for that, I was profoundly grateful.

The Package

Working in the Kingdom of Saudi Arabia opened doors to incredible travel opportunities. Its location, at the crossroads of Africa and Asia, served as a gateway to countries I might never have visited had I remained in the grind of the National Health System in the UK. Back then, I couldn't imagine affording more than a modest one-bedroom apartment on the outskirts of London, let alone embarking on the kind of adventures Saudi Arabia made possible.

The job in Riyadh came about during the first Gulf War, a time of geopolitical upheaval. As Iraq invaded Kuwait, tensions spread across the Gulf States, including Saudi Arabia, causing many expatriates to leave. Around this time, I had been contemplating a move to Florida, USA, to work as a nurse and had attended several recruiting forums. However, one advertisement caught my eye—it was seeking nurses for the Armed Forces Hospital in Riyadh.

A former colleague, who had worked in Saudi Arabia, shared his experience of financial security after just two years. While the lucrative salaries and benefits he enjoyed were no longer on offer by the time I applied, the package was still more attractive than anything back home. For me, however, the real allure was the opportunity to travel.

Arriving in Riyadh amidst the Gulf War, I gained firsthand experience in managing war injuries, including burns, and developed a growing interest in policy development, combat medicine, and community health. My responsibilities soon expanded to include writing and coordinating nursing policies and procedures - roles that sharpened my organisational skills and broadened my understanding of healthcare systems.

The job came with exceptionally generous travel benefits. With up to six weeks of vacation annually and airfare allowances equivalent to a round-trip to my home country every six months, the world opened up to me. An in-house travel and government relations team made planning trips seamless, enabling me to explore destinations far beyond the typical European holiday hotspots of Spain, Portugal, and Yugoslavia.

Spain, once a favourite for British travellers, was losing its charm, with places like Benidorm becoming overrun by the "Barmy Army" and hooligans. Southern Spain, particularly areas around Málaga, still had its appeal, and I had friends who had settled into serene communities there. The Algarve in Portugal held a special place in my heart during my early twenties, though I've yet to return. Yugoslavia, meanwhile, was emerging from its socialist past, enticing tourists with its stunning coastline and rich cultural history.

But my time in Saudi Arabia encouraged me to look further afield - to places I had only dreamed of visiting. It was in this chapter of my life that Africa beckoned, and during my first safari experience in Kenya – a trip that would forever shape my understanding of the continent's beauty, complexity, and resilience.

Ever since I was a child, I was captivated by wildlife. Zoology or becoming a veterinarian was my dream and should have been my career. Although I had gained a place to read Zoology at Liverpool University, unfortunately, certain situations and teenage setbacks derailed that path. The next best option was to care for the two-legged animal - humans.

My passion for animals started early, running the animal club at school and bringing home exotic creatures during the holidays with my mum's support. Over the years, I had my own menageries, including rats, ferrets, axolotls, and stick insects. For long stretches, however, work assignments and constant travel meant I couldn't have pets. Despite that, my love for wildlife never wavered. The best way to connect with these amazing creatures was to see them in the wild and in their natural habitats.

Africa, particularly the southern and eastern regions, became my top priority for holidays once I was closer and could afford the travel. Kenya would be my first stop to embrace my passion and where the 'Big Five' roamed free, and the landscapes felt like stepping into a living documentary. I began planning a three-week safari and scuba diving trip to Kenya, eagerly anticipating the adventure of a lifetime.

Kenya would become the first of many journeys and a stepping stone to exploring Southern Africa. Over the years, I travelled to Zimbabwe, Botswana, Namibia, Malawi, Mozambique, Zambia, and South Africa - each destination offering its own unique beauty and challenges. Botswana, Zimbabwe, and South Africa became frequent stops, with multiple visits that deepened my connection to the region. In 2010, I spent an entire year in Southern Africa, coordinating the H1N1 response for the International Red Cross - a mission that remains one of the most impactful periods of my career.

Every time I stepped off the plane at an African destination, I felt something indescribable in the air. Perhaps it was the breeze, carrying with it distant fragrances and echoes of the past. Maybe it was the warmth of the sun, the clarity of the light, or something far deeper - something that connected me to this part of the world in ways I couldn't fully articulate. Whatever it was, it was intoxicating and always felt like I was coming home.

I planned my Kenya trip through the travel department at the Military Hospital where I was working at the time. The department, predominantly staffed by Eritreans, was efficient and knowledgeable - a perfect resource for crafting my adventure. With their help, I drafted a suggested itinerary that included a few days in Nairobi and visits to some of Kenya's most iconic National Parks and reserves: Tsavo, Amboseli, Samburu National Reserve, and Lake Nakuru.

The journey would begin with arriving in Nairobi and being picked up by a travel company that would take me to Amboseli National Park – what better way to start your African adventure than at a famed Safari camp! I would then return to Nairobi to immerse myself in the city's vibrant atmosphere before embarking on a series of road trips to other National Parks. Each park stay was planned for two to three nights, allowing for multiple safari excursions and the chance to fully absorb the incredible wildlife and landscapes. After these adventures, I would fly to Mombasa to break up the trip, relax at a resort. There, I planned to indulge in scuba diving trips in the turquoise waters of the Indian Ocean.

To wrap up the trip, I planned to return to Nairobi by the famous overnight train from Mombasa, savouring the romantic nostalgia of railway travel. Back in Nairobi, I would embark on another round of safari visits including Lake Nakuru before concluding the trip and flying back to Riyadh via Jeddah.

Whilst this would be the first of many safari and work trips to Southern and Eastern Africa, this journey isn't remembered so much for its incredible wildlife and safari experiences but for what happened later on the overnight train.

Planning for my trip to Kenya commenced with talking to friends who had been to Kenya, researching the Loney Planet travel guide for Kenya and sending an outline of places and things I would like to do to hospital's travel department. The travel team meticulously converted my outline into an itinerary, organised flights, accommodation, connections, and train bookings. Packing for the trip was an exercise in balancing practicality and anticipation - essentials included a good camera, ample mosquito repellent, clothing that blended into the safari surroundings, and more relaxed attire for the resort. At the time, I didn't own a backpack, so a friend lent me one along with a waterproof camera for scuba diving just below the surface. The backpack was well-worn, seemingly holding stories and adventures of its own.

My flights began at Riyadh's King Khalid International Airport. From the domestic terminal, I flew to Jeddah, where I checked in for the international flight to Nairobi. While waiting in the check-in hall, a tall Sudanese man in traditional attire approached me. He asked if I was flying to Nairobi, and when I confirmed, he requested that I ensure his young daughter, traveling alone, arrived safely. Glancing over, I saw the girl, perhaps eight or nine years old, standing shyly near the check-in counter. I suggested he speak to either the check-in desk crew or cabin crew about unaccompanied minors, as it was typically their responsibility. The man thanked me and walked away. I didn't see him or his daughter again, either in the check-in hall or on the flight.

I thought little of the encounter at the time, but the memory would resurface two weeks later under very different circumstances.

Upon arriving at Nairobi's Jomo Kenyatta International Airport, the building's dated appearance stood out. The terminal was in need of renovation, with luggage carousels that chugged along rather than operating smoothly. At the luggage pickup area, I noticed a baggage handler had set aside several pieces of luggage. Nearby, a few currency exchange counters lined the space, so I decided to exchange some Saudi Riyals for Kenyan Shillings while keeping an eye on the carousel. When I returned, I saw the handler pulling my backpack off the conveyor belt and place it with other luggage taken off the carousel. I quickly approached him, claiming the bag as mine. As he handed it over, the worn zipper gave way, spilling my belongings onto the floor.

Gathering my scattered items, I stuffed them back into the backpack and headed to the customs desk. The setup was simple: a lone customs officer sat behind a small moving belt. I placed both my backpack and smaller hand luggage on the belt for inspection. Surprisingly, the officer seemed uninterested in the larger bag, focusing only on the smaller one. After a brief glance, she waved me through without further scrutiny.

In hindsight, I was incredibly fortunate she didn't inspect the larger bag. The reason why would only become clear later, and it would change how I remembered this trip forever.

I had arranged for a safari company to pick me up from the airport and take me to my first lodge in Amboseli. The prospect of my first safari filled me with excitement. While zoos and open-range enclosures had made strides in becoming more animal-friendly - focusing on breeding endangered species and replicating natural habitats - there was no comparison to observing wildlife in its true environment. Here, we humans would be the intruders, the ones being watched, and that thought promised to transport me into this parallel world.

As I exited the airport, I noticed a man of Indian heritage holding a sign with my name on it. His welcoming smile reassured me immediately. Many citizens of Kenya trace their ancestry to Indian migrants who had come as indentured workers during the British colonial period, much like in British Guiana. Over time, they had established themselves in various sectors, including the flourishing travel industry.

After my luggage was loaded into the waiting mini-bus, I climbed in to find a couple already seated. With everyone on board, we were ready to begin our journey. The man who had greeted me turned out to be both our tour guide and the organiser, sitting beside his driver as we set off.

Following the long flights and the minor mishaps - like the unexpected request from the Sudanese man and the spectacle of my belongings spilling out onto the baggage carousel - I was simply relieved to sit back in the comfort of the minibus. The journey to Amboseli would take two to three hours, and I welcomed the chance to unwind.

As we left behind the chaos of Nairobi, the city's traffic slowly dissolved into open stretches of road. The landscape shifted to reveal scattered trees, shrubs, and patches of farmland. Small roadside huts sold trinkets and souvenirs, while herds of domestic livestock - cows, goats, donkeys, and chickens - wandered lazily in the fields or along the shoulders of the road. Occasionally, I caught sight of large marabou storks that portrayed an image of 'death' and other opportunistic animals such as stray dogs, foraging amid piles of rubbish left for domestic animals or carelessly discarded by passersby.

With my head resting against the window, I watched the scenery glide past, a moving tapestry of rural life. The rhythmic hum of the road soon lulled me into a light doze, broken only by the occasional jolt when the bus slowed or stopped. Each time I opened my eyes, I was greeted by a new scene, a different slice of this captivating landscape. Despite the fatigue of travel, I felt completely relaxed and unexpectedly safe, cocooned in the anticipation of what lay ahead.

The climate grew drier as we drove, and the roadside transitioned from patches of tarmac to stretches of loose sand. Soon, clouds of dust rose in the wake of the bus and passing vehicles - evidence that we were nearing the heart of the action. Our journey paused at a roadside tea stop, a well-trodden waypoint dotted with souvenir stalls catering to tourists along this popular route. The brightly coloured stands showcased their wares: woven baskets, soapstone carvings, tribal masks, intricate beadwork, vividly patterned tablecloths, stick figures, and wooden animal sculptures.

I was intrigued by the small soapstone hippopotami - each uniquely painted and polished, ranging in size and colour. Though I wasn't ready to start collecting just yet, those hippos would later become a hallmark of my travels. Over time, I've amassed a small herd of them, now numbering around twenty.

We reached the safari lodge at Amboseli National Park in the late afternoon. Staff in smart uniforms (I expected safari attire) welcomed us with chilled fruit drinks, their hospitality a refreshing contrast to the dusty journey. After check-in, porters delivered our luggage to the rustic accommodations - two-room ensuite lodges adorned with safari-themed decor. The furnishings, tribal artwork, and depictions of savannah wildlife created a cozy, authentic charm.

With a few nights ahead of me, I decided to unpack properly. The evening safari was set to begin at 6 p.m., and dinner would be ready upon our return. As I emptied my backpack, I double-checked for any losses or damages from the earlier flight fiasco. Thankfully, nothing seemed to be missing - instead something appeared to have been added!

A green plastic Marks & Spencer bag peeked out from the depths of my backpack. Confused, I pulled it out and felt the unmistakable weight of a package. Wrapped in several layers of British newspaper, the parcel seemed deliberately hidden. My pulse quickened. A sense of foreboding overtook me as I began unwrapping it.

There, beneath the layers of newsprint, was a tightly compressed block of shredded leaves almost like a pack of refill mixed herbs from the supermarket. The realisation hit me like a thunderbolt - was this something illicit or contraband? My mind raced. Who had planted it? Was this why my backpack had been unzipped at the airport? Had the customs officer been aware of it and chosen not to check further?

I stood frozen between panic and fury. Fear gripped me as I imagined the consequences if the package was discovered. Reporting it to the lodge staff seemed logical, but what if it led to questions and accusations I couldn't answer? Every scenario that played out in my mind made my chest tighten.

It was almost time for the evening safari - an adventure I'd dreamed about since childhood. I took a deep breath, determined to think rationally. Carefully, I rewrapped the package and returned it to my backpack and put my bag under the bed. I resolved not to act immediately. Nothing would change in the next few hours, and I needed time to think.

For now, I would focus on the safari. This was the moment I had long awaited—the chance to witness the untamed beauty of Africa. The package could wait. My dreams could not.

The safari was a great distraction from the earlier events. The khaki-coloured jeep with its soft top set the scene perfectly. The driver, who doubled as our guide, was incredibly knowledgeable about the wildlife and shared tips on how best to spot them. With the sun beginning to set, it was the perfect time to see some of the larger game, including lions.

We encountered several elephants, mostly in small herds led by a matriarch. These herds included young calves, juvenile elephants, and young bulls, as well as other cows who supported the matriarch in protecting the group. A short distance away, we saw a small pride of lions — primarily lionesses with a few younger lions. One of them, with the beginnings of a mane, stood out as a young male.

The plains were teeming with antelopes such as gazelles, impalas, and countless wildebeest, interspersed with zebra and giraffe. As we approached a large waterhole, we saw more elephants arrive, displacing zebras and other wildlife that had gathered for an evening drink in the cooler air. In the distance, buffalo steadily made their way toward the waterhole. Birds of various species filled the air, perched in trees, and moved across the ground, each seemingly content in its ecological niche. I was particularly hoping to see a hippo or a rhinoceros.

A distinct smell of decay wafted through the air as we ventured further into the bush. It likely explained the vultures circling overhead. Our driver decided to follow a track deeper into the bush, hoping to catch a glimpse of smaller mammals and possibly a hyena. At one point, we thought we saw a serval — a striking, slim cat — disappearing into the undergrowth. The driver explained that servals are relatively common in Kenya and primarily feed on small mammals, birds, reptiles, and insects when necessary.

With the elephants and lions, we had already checked off two of the Big Five!

As we made our way back to the lodge, the driver used a handheld spotlight to scan the bushes. He explained that the first sign of an animal would often be the reflection of its eyes. We caught a glimpse of some porcupines with their spines raised as we passed by — a defence mechanism that even lions prefer to avoid. While we didn't spot much else that evening, the anticipation, cool air, and the distinct, earthy smells of the bush made the experience memorable. It was the perfect way to end the day.

When we returned to the lodge, a warm meal awaited us. Tables with crisp white tablecloths and linen were set outdoors, with a large fire pit burning brightly nearby. Other guests, already seated, were helping themselves to the buffet laid out on trestle tables. Large bowls and warmers held an assortment of dishes, while pots were being stirred by attentive staff. Waiters helped serve rolls, salads, and other accompaniments, with desserts and beverages also available. I opted for the local beer in a bottle – 'Tusker' to accompany my meal and as a reward after the day's adventures. I also had with me a traditional pipe which I had bought in Saudi Arabia – I loved the smell of Tobacco, particularly a brand called 'Captain Black'. I had always imagined sitting on a large deck overlooking a water hole holding a pipe to warm my hands in the evening dusk as the wildlife appeared from the horizon to drink before they rested for the night. Now was my chance!

The safari schedule for the next day was presented to us. Those interested were encouraged to sign up or inform reception before the evening concluded so that the number of vehicles, guides, and drivers could be arranged. My plan was simple: I would go on as many safaris as possible. Rising at 5 a.m. was a small price to pay for the chance to experience more of this breathtaking wilderness.

While the safari provided a much-needed distraction, the matter of the package lingered at the back of my mind. However, I felt far more at ease now, the weight of earlier anxieties momentarily lifted by the magic of the Kenyan bush.

I left the evening meal with a sense of keen determination. Back in my room, I retrieved the package from my backpack, which I had stashed under the bed earlier. Carefully, I removed it from the green plastic bag and unwrapped the newspaper to reveal the plastic-wrapped bundle of what looked like crushed leaves resembling a large bag of mixed herbs that you would buy from the supermarket.

Curious but resolute, I carried the packet to the bathroom. Tearing it open, I began pouring the contents into the toilet and flushing. The lightweight material swirled and disappeared into the pipes, but some stubbornly floated back to the surface. Undeterred, I repeated the process—pour, flush, wait for the cistern to refill—until, after several attempts, every last bit was gone.

I was left with the plastic carry bag and newspaper wrapping, which I decided could wait until morning for disposal. Standing in the now-quiet bathroom, I wondered what the occupants of the adjoining room might have thought of my constant flushing. Perhaps they imagined I was battling an unfortunate case of food poisoning.

Satisfied with my course of action, I returned to my room feeling relieved and at ease. I could finally sleep with a clear conscience.

Mombasa

To break up the safari trips - which included early morning, evening, and occasional night drives - I planned a five-day retreat at a resort in Mombasa. This interlude would offer me a chance to scuba dive, relax, swim, sunbathe, and, with any luck, connect with like-minded travellers. It promised to be a striking contrast to the rugged natural world of the Animal Kingdom although with the scuba diving I would encounter the Animal and Plant Kingdoms of the Oceans! After my stay, I had arranged to take the famous overnight train from Mombasa to Nairobi, where I'd complete two short safaris before returning to Riyadh.

I was in good shape and loved being in the water. The resort attracted a mix of visitors - some drawn to its amenities and vibrant entertainment, honeymooners, and others, like myself, using it as a base between adventures. It also served as a layover for several airline crews, adding an international flair to the atmosphere.

During my time in Saudi Arabia, I had trained to instruct high-impact aerobics classes, crafting energetic routines set to dance music. For many expats working at the hospital, these classes were a rare and welcome opportunity to exercise and dance in an otherwise restrictive environment. Music, dancing, and mingling with the opposite sex to whom you were not married were either frowned upon or outright prohibited, but within the compounds, expatriates were granted more freedom—provided locals were not involved.

At the resort, a Kenyan instructor was leading water aerobics sessions by the pool, blending fitness with a touch of theatrical entertainment. He was looking for volunteers to demonstrate moves to the audience and spotted me in the crowd and waved for me to join him. Without hesitation, I jumped into the pool and became his assistant for the session. It was impromptu, but we synced surprisingly well. The audience applauded enthusiastically, and the instructor gave me a warm thanks before I returned to my poolside lounger.

After drying off and spending some time sunbathing and reading, I noticed two young men with British accents settling near me. One of them turned to me and asked, "Were you the guy in the pool just now?" I confirmed with a nod, and the conversation shifted to the diving watch I was wearing. The watch, designed to measure depth and pressure underwater, caught their interest as I explained my plans to dive into a nearby reef in the Indian Ocean the next day.

When I asked about their visit, they explained that they were cabin crew for a British airline and often stayed at the resort during layovers. Our conversation drifted easily from their work to my safari itinerary and the upcoming train journey to Nairobi. They knew the route well, having taken it themselves, and for a moment, I wondered if I might have chosen the wrong career. Later that afternoon, one of the crew invited himself to my room. It seemed that one of the perks of their job was meeting strangers and indulging in a little no-strings-attached fun. I wasn't unfamiliar with such pleasures, especially when travelling, and the attention of a handsome cabin crew member was certainly tempting. Yet, the day had already given me a sense of contentment I didn't wish to disturb. I politely declined the offer.

We decided to meet for dinner that evening, a delightful way to conclude the day. Over a shared meal, we exchanged stories and laughter and as I was amongst fellow nationals and that they worked for airline, I felt confident to tell them about the package I found in my bag and how I disposed of it. All this was done surrounded by the soothing rhythm of ocean waves and the soft glow of resort lights. The balmy air carried the faint scent of salt and tropical blooms, creating a perfect backdrop for our conversation.

As the evening wore on, I excused myself around 9 p.m., mindful of the early start needed to catch the dive boat the next morning. With the promise of another adventure awaiting me, I retreated to my room, content and ready for the next chapter of this incredible journey.

The next morning was charged with anticipation for the diving trip. I had completed my PADI Open Water and Advanced certifications in the warm, pristine waters of the Red Sea off Saudi Arabia's west coast. Untouched by mass tourism, the Red Sea was a diver's paradise, and its underwater beauty had spoiled me. This would be my first dive in the Indian Ocean—a thrilling milestone before future dives on the Great Barrier Reef.

The resort had arranged the diving trip, and a shuttle bus picked me up to take me to the boat. My diving buddy for the day was a young Japanese woman, likely in her early twenties. She introduced herself as Mika, and while we exchanged pleasantries, it was clear we were both slightly nervous. That apprehension was familiar—diving always stirred a mix of excitement and anxiety - but I knew the post-dive euphoria would make it all worthwhile.

The dive site was a sheltered enclave flanked by land on either side. I wasn't a fan of the backward roll entry from the boat, so I opted for a long stride entry instead. After donning our borrowed wetsuits, masks, regulators, and tanks, Mika and I stepped confidently into the water. It always took a moment to adjust—regulating breathing, clearing the mask, and calming the nerves. After a few deep breaths, we signalled to each other, released air from our buoyancy compensators (BCDs), and began a controlled descent feet first.

Descending was always the most nerve-wracking part for me. Timing the release of air, keeping my mask clear, and maintaining balance required focus. An initial burst of rapid breathing was common but used up precious oxygen, so I worked to calm myself, regulate my breathing, and find my rhythm. Mika mirrored the process, and we quickly established a supportive dynamic, signalling to each other to ensure everything was in order.

Underwater, it's the subtle teamwork with a buddy that builds trust. We'd checked each other's equipment before entering the water, but now we relied on gestures and mutual awareness. I didn't know Mika's experience level, but she seemed confident and attentive, making her an excellent partner for the dive.

Once we began moving, the nervous tension melted away. The steady kick of our fins propelled us through the water, our hands managing BCDs to adjust buoyancy. As a naturally negatively buoyant diver, I carried minimal weight on my belt, making the descent easier. Mika, like many women, required additional weight to counteract natural buoyancy, but she handled it gracefully.

At times, I achieved perfect buoyancy, hovering mid-water in a meditative pose, a meter above the seabed. Most dives stayed under 30 meters, though my advanced certification had taken me deeper. At shallower depths, the reef teemed with vibrant life. The colours were at their most vivid here; as you descended, the spectrum dimmed, with reds disappearing first, followed by orange and yellow. By the time you reached deeper depths, only shades of blue remained visible, lending a surreal quality to the underwater world.

The dive itself was enjoyable. Although visibility wasn't ideal, we encountered a variety of coral and marine life, capturing some of it with an underwater camera borrowed from a friend. Encased in a waterproof housing, the camera allowed me to snap photos between two meters and the surface, where the light enhanced the colours.

After completing the dive, we enjoyed refreshments on the boat before switching to snorkelling. Free from the constraints of tanks and vests, snorkelling felt liberating, and the shallow waters revealed just as much beauty as the dive itself.

By lunchtime, we were back at the resort. Although Mika returned with me on the shuttle, I didn't see her again. The afternoon stretched out lazily, offering time to sunbathe, read, and soak up the resort's tranquil ambiance. The evening brought the soothing sounds of waves, distant voices, and birdlife - a symphony that made sleep come easily.

The next day was set aside for exploration. Though warnings had been issued about venturing too far due to disturbances linked to Somali Islamist groups in the Lamu region north of

Mombasa, I planned to stay close to the resort. Feeling refreshed and reenergized, I knew it was time to return to the safari trail—the true purpose of my journey to Kenya.

The iconic overnight train from Mombasa to Nairobi awaited. Scheduled for an early evening departure, the narrow-gauge train - built by British colonialists between 1898 and 1901 - would take twelve leisurely hours to reach Nairobi. Today, the historic train has been replaced by the Chinese-built Madaraka Express, which completes the same journey in under six hours. But for me, the romance of the slower, nostalgic journey held far greater appeal.

Mombasa to Nairobi

Arriving at the train station in Mombasa felt like stepping into a time capsule. The platform buzzed with activity as passengers milled about, luggage in tow, beneath the warm glow of station lights. The train itself was a marvel—a seemingly endless line of carriages marked with class distinctions and reservation details. Each cabin had a name card neatly displayed in a small window pocket, an old-fashioned touch that both charmed and puzzled me. Why would they make passengers' names so visible?

I walked along the length of the train, scanning the cards until I found my allocated carriage, marked with the letter *C* which was almost the last carriage. Sure enough, there was my name, printed on a card tucked into the display pocket of a window. This would be my home for the night—a semi-private cabin that promised both adventure and rest.

Boarding at the nearest entrance between two carriages, there was steward or guardsman - I couldn't tell which - standing at his post, overseeing boarding of passengers as well as freight. Turning right led to a large metal cage that served as storage for parcels and luggage. Turning left led to the carriages with overnight sleeping cabins. My carriage was conveniently connected to the restaurant car, with its inviting promise of a warm meal and lively conversation. Further down the train, I glimpsed rows of regular seating, where passengers sat facing one another in an arrangement that seemed both sociable and practical for the long journey ahead.

I was soon met by a uniformed train steward who escorted me to my room. The cabin a throwback in time was compact but functional. A double seat ran along one wall, with another seat above folded against the wall. The two seats could be converted in a bunk bed. On the opposite side, in the corner was a small basin, a fan mounted above it, and a narrow built-in wardrobe for storage.

The atmosphere was alive with anticipation. This journey, spanning more than twelve hours, would take me from the coastal charm of Mombasa to the heart of Kenya's capital, Nairobi. The historic train, a relic of British colonial ambition, had been built to connect Uganda to the Indian Ocean over a century ago. For me, however, it represented more than just a mode of transport—it was a window into the past and an opportunity to savour the romance of slow travel.

The departure was imminent. Outside, the sounds of doors slamming shut and sharp whistle blows filled the air, signalling the train's readiness. Excitement bubbled through the carriages, the chatter of friends and fellow travellers weaving into a tapestry of anticipation. I sat alone in my cabin, a quiet contrast to the buzz outside, reflecting on the past few days, the journey ahead, and the promise of the safaris waiting for me in Nairobi.

My collection of souvenirs thus far were neatly tucked away—a small collection of soapstone items bought from local stalls and shops, intended as gifts. I had packed them separately in a bag, keeping them safe from the clutter of my backpack. My essentials - passport, wallet, and important documents—remained securely stowed in a waist belt pocket, discreetly tucked under my shirt.

I began reorganising my belongings, pulling out what I'd need for the journey: a fresh shirt for dinner, my toiletry bag, and shoes. The rest stayed packed away in my backpack. The inbuilt wardrobe with mirrored doors, seemed more decorative than practical, and I decided against unpacking everything.

As the train pulled out of Mombasa, I leaned against the window, gazing at the passing scenery. The sky was a masterpiece of colour - deep red and burnt orange streaks melting into the darkening blue horizon. The rhythmic motion of the train and the hypnotic landscapes lulled me into a light nap.

A gentle knock on the door stirred me awake. A train inspector in a sharp uniform and cap entered, checking my ticket with practiced efficiency. He was followed by the same steward who escorted me to my room earlier, who handed me a menu and informed me that my dinner setting would be at 7:30 p.m. Dinner for the earlier 6:30 p.m. seating was already being served.

Before leaving the steward began transforming the cabin into a sleeping compartment. The seamless process fascinated me. He pulled down the foldable upper bed, revealing a snug replica of the lower seat, complete with safety rails. Bit by bit, the seating area metamorphosed into a cozy sleeping space. A crisp white package was placed on the seat, which he unfolded with care—starched sheets, a doona, and a pillow emerged, arranged neatly with an almost ritualistic precision.

He asked whether I preferred the upper or lower bed, and without hesitation, I chose the top. The steward pointed to a small ladder secured to the side of the bunk. For a moment, nostalgia washed over me, memories of the bunk bed I'd shared with my brother Adam during our childhood in Brixton and Croydon. Back then, I always claimed the bottom bunk, but tonight, on this journey, I decided to embrace a new perspective and sleep up top.

The steward gave a polite nod and left the room, leaving me alone with the hum of the train and the faint glow of the setting sun beyond the window. The promise of the evening ahead filled me with quiet anticipation, as the train rocked gently onward into the night.

It was soon my turn for the dinner setting, and I made my way to the next carriage, which housed the dining car. As I entered, I took in the neatly arranged rows of rectangular tables on one side, paired with single chairs along the other.

It was dimly lit with lamps rather than strip lighting giving the carriage a tone of elegancy and romance. Each table was set for four, with crisp white tablecloths, metal cutlery, and neatly folded napkins. The carriage had an understated charm, though it was quieter than I expected.

I had anticipated a bustling dining car filled with chatter and laughter, but the subdued atmosphere suited me. While I enjoyed meeting fellow travellers on other occasions, this trip was more about unwinding and reflecting. There were other times when I gravitated toward busier carriages, where people mingled freely, played games, or visited the buffet bar for snacks and drinks. Tonight, though, I welcomed the quiet.

A waiter dressed in a white suit and typical Masai multi coloured belt greeted me and guided me to a table, soon inviting another traveller to join me. The man, a Kenyan national dressed in a checked short sleeve short and light chino trousers of a similar age to mine, introduced himself as a teacher. Polite and articulate, he engaged in light conversation about his life in Nairobi, his work, and his impressions of the journey. His presence added a pleasant note to the evening, though the conversation remained casual and unintrusive.

The menu itself escapes my memory, as it was the occasion, more than the content, that left an impression. I ordered a Coca-Cola, which arrived shortly on a tray. The drink came in a classic glass bottle, its metal cap already loosened but still resting on the bottle's mouth - a considerate touch, presumably to avoid any spillage on the pristine tablecloth. The waiter deftly removed the cap and poured the fizzy drink into a glass with an effortless grace.

I declined the offer of ice, a habit ingrained over years of travel and later reinforced during my humanitarian aid work. I'd learned to avoid ice unless I was certain it had been made with bottled water. Similarly, I avoided unpeeled fruit, raw vegetables, and fresh salads, opting instead for well-cooked meals. While this often meant sacrificing some of the nutrients and freshness of the food, it was a small price to pay for avoiding the common gastro-related illnesses that plagued travellers.

The evening unfolded at a leisurely pace, the train's rhythmic sway creating a gentle backdrop to our meal. By the time I finished, I felt a quiet satisfaction, not just from the food but from the ambiance - the unique experience of dining while the train carried us steadily onward through the African night.

Feeling relaxed after dinner, I decided to return to my cabin and get a good night's sleep. Tomorrow, I'd be stepping back into the hustle, bustle, and noise of Nairobi, and I wanted to be well-rested. On my way back, I nodded goodnight to the guard stationed in the corridor near my cabin. He seemed poised and watchful, and I assumed he'd be there all night, providing an added sense of safety for travellers.

Inside my cabin, I changed into a pair of shorts and a T-shirt, then brushed my teeth at the small ceramic basin. I felt very relaxed and a sense of peace came over me - the bed becoming more and more inviting calling out to me as I yawned. Climbing into the top bunk, I kept on my waist belt pocket as well as my watch on my wrist. The train swayed gently, lulling me to sleep almost immediately. Though the train made several stops during the night, I slept so soundly that I didn't register a single one.

When I woke, it was early morning, and I felt surprisingly well-rested and calm. The fan above the sink was still spinning slowly, a faint, rhythmic sound accompanying the train's motion. Pulling up the window blind, I saw a soft, peachy dawn breaking over the horizon. The scenery outside had shifted; instead of open savannahs, small villages and farmland dotted the landscape. Civilization was approaching.

Still half-asleep, I glanced around the cabin. Something felt different, though I couldn't immediately place it. My room seemed strangely bare. Peering down from the top bunk, I noticed that my luggage, which I'd placed near the mirrored wardrobe, was gone. Initially, I dismissed the thought of theft - perhaps the porter had come in during the night and reorganised the room. Yet as my mind cleared, unease began to creep in.

Then I realised I wasn't wearing my watch. Checking the bed linen and floor yielded nothing. My confusion deepened. I distinctly remembered locking the door from the inside before falling asleep. If I hadn't been disturbed during the night, how could things have been moved or taken?

Trying to keep calm, I opened the door and saw the same guard I'd greeted the night before. "Do you know where my luggage is?" I asked, my voice tinged with growing panic. His blank expression sent a chill through me. "No," he replied.

I hurriedly checked my waist belt pocket. My passport and airline tickets were still there, but my wallet—with all my cash and credit cards - was gone. A wave of fear and helplessness swept over me. My thighs, wrists and upper arms ached faintly, and when I looked closer, I saw faint bruises. My mind raced: **What the hell had happened last night?**

I sat down heavily on the lower seat, my head in my hands. The enormity of the situation hit me - I was alone in Kenya with no money, no clothes, except what I was wearing and the pair of cargo trousers I wore for dinner and a cap. Also, my boots, sandals and sneakers were gone! I couldn't understand how my wallet, which had been with me in the bed inside my waist pocket belt, was gone, yet my passport and airline tickets had been left untouched.

Pulling myself together, I stepped back into the corridor. "I've been robbed while I was asleep," I told the guard. He seemed genuinely concerned and offered to fetch the train's police officer, who he said always travelled on board. I clung to the faint hope that my luggage was still somewhere on the train. After all, where else could it be?

The officer arrived shortly, holding a blue cloth bag - the one in which I'd packed my souvenirs. He explained that he'd found it abandoned in the corridor. It also contained a towel that I had used to protect some of the souvenirs. Seeing it restored a glimmer of hope; perhaps my other belongings were still nearby. The officer asked me to list what was inside, and I described everything I could remember.

As I explained, I asked why he wasn't searching the rest of the train. To my dismay, he said, "This has happened before." He recounted a strange story about a thief who supposedly hid inside cabins, spraying some kind of gas to render the occupant deeply asleep before stealing their belongings. He suggested the thief might have jumped off the slow-moving train with my luggage, making a search futile.

The explanation unsettled me. If this thief had been caught before, as the officer claimed, why hadn't more precautions been taken? And why did the officer seem resigned rather than proactive? Despite his assurances, I couldn't shake the feeling that my belongings were still on the train.

I decided to search the carriages myself but was quickly barred from moving along the carriages. The officer insisted I stay in my cabin, leaving me to stew in frustration and disbelief. I switched between despair, anger and crying. As we approached Nairobi, the train slowed, and I could see passengers from the front carriages gathering their belonging ready to disembark. Some of the carriage doors were already being opened by the passengers ready to dash to the exit gates to avoid the crowds and to get on the waiting buses and taxis outside the station. I remained in my cabin, now grappling with the dawning realisation that I might never recover my stolen belongings. I was convinced that one of the disembarking passengers from the front carriages was already exiting the station with my luggage and there was no one there to stop them!

The officer finished his report, but it offered little comfort. Why wasn't he doing more? Why weren't the passengers or carriages being checked? The sense of vulnerability, combined with the officer's inaction, was overwhelming. Nairobi loomed closer, but the promise of its vibrant streets felt distant. I had arrived, but not in the way I had imagined.

The police officer kept me on the train until everyone had disembarked. He explained I would be taken to the transport police hut along the platform. Barefoot, wearing what clothes I had left, and clutching my souvenir bag, I followed him. The wooden hut was modest, its interior starkly lit. A sergeant wearing stripes sat behind a desk, while a junior officer stood nearby. Outside, a police guard with a rifle kept watch. It felt humiliating - more like being treated as a criminal than as a victim of theft.

The sergeant seemed uninterested in investigating the crime. His priority was simply to list the stolen items and file a report – it was just a process that seemed rehearsed. I mentioned that a driver was likely waiting for me to continue my safari and asked if a message could be relayed. The sergeant agreed, but I could tell the report was more for insurance purposes than any real attempt at justice. Ironically, I realised I had foolishly failed to take out insurance - something I had always done in the past and certainly would in the future.

I asked to use the toilet, which was a small shed adjacent to the hut. The door had to remain ajar, and the armed guard stood outside. When I returned, the sergeant handed me a typed report on a yellow piece of lined paper. That was it. I was free to go.

Barefoot, clutching my meagre belongings and a cap that mercifully hadn't been taken, I made my way to the station's exit. There, to my immense relief, I found the owner of the safari company waiting. My message had reached him, and he had waited patiently. Ushering me into his minibus, he drove me to the lodge I'd pre-booked in Nairobi. Having prepaid for accommodations and most meals, I felt some security despite the ordeal.

With no cash or credit cards, I asked the lodge owner for a twenty dollar loan. It was enough to buy a pair of cheap shoes, a T-shirt, track pants, socks and underwear. My beard trimmer was gone, so I resigned myself to letting it grow. Souvenirs, I thought bitterly, held little value in their country of origin.

That first day back at the lodge, I was too stunned to process what had happened. I oscillated between anger and despair. Someone, somewhere had orchestrated this. Everyone I encountered during my journey now seemed suspect. Faces I had smiled at and shared conversations with - could any of them have been involved? My name had been displayed on the train carriage cabin window for all to see. I trusted no one. Polite conversations, friendly gestures - they all seemed potentially sinister in hindsight.

Had I been drugged during dinner? I remembered the teacher I'd spoken to, the pre-opened Coca-Cola bottle handed to me. And the bruises on my arms and thighs - had I struggled against someone? The explanation about an intruder in my cabin felt implausible. No one could have hidden there unnoticed, nor exited through the window. It seemed more likely the culprits were connected to the package I'd been asked to carry earlier in my travels.

The package! What had I unwittingly carried? Were the thieves searching for it? Was this some elaborate plan stretching back to the Sudanese man in Jeddah or the travel department in Riyadh that helped me with my itinerary and made all my bookings? My trust in the British airline crew felt misplaced; I recalled their interest in my diving watch and the unusually serious expressions when I joked about flushing the leaves down the toilet. Were they part of it? Was this entire ordeal linked to that moment?

The next morning, I reported the incident to the British High Commission. They were supportive, arranging funds I could repay once back in Riyadh and helping me cancel my stolen cards. I later found out that nearly 500 pounds had been spent using my credit card. I also informed my senior nursing officer, who was empathetic and urged me to return safely. I'd be traveling light, with only memories and a few remaining souvenirs.

On my final safari, I found solace in the savannah's vastness. With no camera to focus my attention, my senses sharpened. I observed the intricate connections within the ecosystem - the ripple effects of movement, the interplay of predator and prey. Without a lens narrowing my perspective, I saw the full panorama. My mind became the camera, capturing a story no photograph could match. While a painting or photograph might convey a thousand words, my mind painted thousands more.

The theft had taken much from me, but it also left me with something unexpected: a deeper awareness of the interconnectedness of life, a profound story that only I could carry.

About nine months later, during a trip to England, I found myself at a nightclub in southeast London. As I danced, I noticed a familiar face nearby - a member of the cabin crew from Mombasa, dancing with his male companion. His friend seemed to take an interest in me, offering frequent smiles before heading to the bar for a drink. The memories of that harrowing train robbery and the events at the airport, the package during my trip to Kenya came rushing back.

Seizing the moment, I approached the cabin crew member and introduced myself. He appeared intrigued but didn't seem to recognise me. Perhaps it was the winter setting, my more sombre demeanour, or the fact that I was bundled in heavier clothing compared to the carefree days of my holiday. The dim lighting in the club didn't help either.

With a deliberate seriousness in my voice, I asked if he remembered me, hoping to jog his memory. Something seemed to click. Perhaps the sheer unlikelihood of seeing me there - especially as I was still based in Saudi Arabia - unsettled him. As his friend returned from the bar, the cabin crew member quickly walked over to him and whispered in his ear. Without a word, they both left the nightclub in a hurry. Did he have concerns I was there for another reason and had purposely tracked him down?

In that instant, my lingering doubts evaporated. The connection between them and the package, the drugging, and the robbery was no longer just a suspicion - it was now quite likely they at some point, were connected to what happened.

The Art of Blending

Have you ever considered whether the behaviour of those around you is shaped by who they perceive you to be, or influenced by your own expectations of the world as you know it?

Imagine stepping into a world entirely different from the one you identify with - where customs, language, clothing, and traditions diverge from your own. Would your reception in that world shift if your outward appearance seamlessly blended with its people?

When you travel to a foreign country, do you wonder if what you're seeing is a curated version of reality - crafted for tourism or tailored to match your cultural expectations? If you could strip away that carefully constructed image to glimpse the unvarnished truth of life in this new environment, free from the influence of your own moral compass or societal norms, how would it feel? Would you embrace the contrast, or recoil from the discomfort of an unfamiliar world?

Our physical appearance often serves as a marker of our nationality, yet for many of us with mixed heritage, those boundaries blur. Without language or other cultural cues, I could be mistaken for someone from Southern or Eastern Europe, North Africa, South Asia, Central Asia, the Caucasus, or the Middle East. It's my voice, language or accent that anchors me - shaping assumptions about where I belong.

My accent reveals my connection to England, narrowing further to London, then shrinking again to specific communities within my birthplace. Even within professional circles, certain words and phrases signal membership to a distinct group, identifying me as one of "them." This malleability of identity can be an advantage - allowing me to adapt to new environments—but it can also leave me vulnerable when others seek to define, exclude, or exploit difference.

We can often bridge or imitate difference by learning a language, adopting an accent, and adapting behaviours to minimise what sets us apart. The remaining distinctions may be so subtle that only the keenest observer - or an unintentional misstep—could reveal them.

Now, imagine stepping fully into the identity of "the other." What if, for just a moment, you became one of *them* - seeing the world through their eyes, living within their reality? Consider, for instance, not the persecuted, but the Nazi soldier. What would it mean to infiltrate their ranks - not out of agreement, but to grasp the roots of their moral compass, to understand the conviction behind their belief that they consider is right and that you are wrong? Surely it is our belief that we are better, what we believe is better, our culture is better and so on? Maybe others believe you are better and they want to be like you and prefer to escape their culture and embrace yours and become even more you than you? "More British than the British" was a phrase I would often hear for migrants who came to the UK during the British Nationality Act in 1948 to attract migrants from

Commonwealth countries to fill the shortage of workers after the second world war.

As the Health Coordinator for Former Yugoslavian Republic of Macedonia (FYRM), working closely with the Protection team and Head of Delegation, I visited Serbian POWs and several Mobile Army Surgical Hospitals (MASH) facilities. These visits were critical for inspecting conditions, disseminating knowledge about the International Red Cross's neutral role, and ensuring compliance with the Geneva Conventions regarding the treatment of POWs in medical facilities. Some of the MASH units were modern prefab structures, while others reflected the more temporary setups seen in the iconic *MASH** TV series, albeit with contemporary infrastructure.

I met with counterparts and nursing officers, many of whom were well-versed in Red Cross principles. The American Red Cross filled many specialist roles within the International Red Cross teams, and their professionalism was evident. Some of these MASH units treated captured Serbian soldiers, whose safety and eventual release under the Geneva Conventions were paramount. Registering these individuals with the Red Cross ensured that their families knew they were alive and cared for.

Meanwhile, Serbia's actions during the conflict—seen by much of the world as the aggressors—had left deep scars, destroying buildings and shattering lives. Yet Serbia retained staunch allies, most notably Russia, which sought to assert its presence in Kosovo after the war's conclusion in 1999. The British, aiming to secure control of Pristina Airport for KFOR, faced a tense standoff with Russian forces, who projected an aggressive stance. Britain's Paratroopers, seasoned in guerrilla warfare from years of experience in Northern Ireland, were a natural choice for this high-stakes operation.

My first somewhat official experience of "blending in" came at the request of my Head of Mission. Following an evacuation from Pristina to Belgrade, I was redeployed to Montenegro and then to the Former Yugoslav Republic of Macedonia (FYRM), now known as North Macedonia. The task was to gauge the true sentiments of the Macedonian people about their country serving as the primary staging ground for KFOR (Kosovo Force), NATO's peacekeeping and military operation against Serbia. Understanding these sentiments was vital, as Macedonia's role was politically sensitive and culturally complex.

Macedonia, once part of Yugoslavia, had navigated its own path to independence after the dissolution of the union under Tito. Its two dominant ethnic groups—Macedonian Slavs, who shared cultural and religious ties with Serbia, and Macedonian Albanians, aligned more closely with Kosovo and Islam—presented a complex backdrop. Publicly, Macedonia supported KFOR, with the promise of accelerated membership in the European Union. Yet, the question remained: Was this hospitality genuine, or was it a transactional arrangement driven by economic and political aspirations? Understanding this dynamic was crucial for KFOR's mission, as well as for fostering communication and collaboration within local communities.

To try and get a sense of the hidden feelings towards the International presence including the hundreds of humanitarian organisations, some newly formed to take advantage of the funds being thrown at the crisis by the

International community, I was tasked with going to local cafes in Skopje, the capital of Macedonia. It was often in cafes and similar settings where locals gathered, let their guard down and shared their true sentiments. This was valuable information to help develop our communication and dissemination strategies as well as identify any threats to our organisation. Your relationship with your local community was your first pillar of protection and defence if a security threat manifested often due to the actions of a third party. This connection to community was crucial in a previous deployment in Afghanistan. My presence at a café outside of my work was mostly to observe and listen rather than engage.

A similar experience but on my own terms was to attend a rally in Podgorica, the capital of Montenegro. Culturally, Montenegro was closely tied to Serbia and was considered to be supporting them during the war. Montenegrins were mostly Slavic and shared the same heritage as Serbians, as well as being economically and ethnically tied to Russia.

Although advised not to be visible outside of the workplace and residence due to potential security risks, I often went to the main town square during the late afternoon, which was within walking distance of my accommodation in an apartment I shared with the Head of the Sub-delegate. I knew that he did the same, if not only to pick up several bars of German-made Richter Marzipan chocolate. I had grown very partial to them as well and still seek them out when I can in Australia.

Late afternoon and early evening were the times when locals gathered to meet their friends, have a drink, and socialise. Like many Eastern European countries at the time, tradition still required most women to stay at home, cook and look after the children, while the men worked and socialised together. It was a very 'macho' society. Dressing local, casually but smart, was key - Montenegrins, like Serbians, were quite fashionable. As a slim and fit race, men often wore stylish jeans, slim-fit t-shirts, polos, and checked shirts. I already had the complexion to blend in. It was also important not to speak. I always had a backup in case - I would pretend I was mute and use simple sign language.

Rallies were mostly in support of Serbia, and due to its ties, Montenegro was gradually being drawn into the conflict through ethnic association. Rallies would become loud but not aggressive. There were speeches, rallying calls, and defiance against KFOR and the International 'aggressive' stance and labelling by the wider International Community in support of Kosovars. The Serbians and Montenegrins were grieving too and felt that the world was against them, including the supposedly neutral and impartial humanitarian organisations. As in most wars, there were casualties on both sides, particularly among civilians who took no part in the conflict. The vast majority of the world supported the victims—the Kosovars. But the Serbians had their own story to tell and were also victims. While the international community responded to the 'effect,' the cause was centuries old. History from the 12th and 13th centuries, particularly the legacy of the Ottoman Empire, still resonated strongly. In the eyes of the Serbians and wider Slavic nations, the world was ignoring atrocities committed by the Kosovo Liberation Army (KLA). The Serbians felt aggrieved that their support for the Allied forces during the First and Second World Wars was not recognised. Many paramilitary groups supporting Serbia during the conflict were formed or found refuge in Montenegro, including the infamous Arkan's White Tigers.

It was not our role to decide who was right or wrong. Our role was to provide assistance to those affected by armed conflict and to remind the respective authorities involved in the conflict of their obligations as signatories to the Geneva Conventions, particularly regarding the protection of civilians and prisoners of war (POWs). Very few international organisations worked in Serbia or Montenegro; the majority operated in neighbouring countries such as Macedonia and Albania, which hosted thousands of refugees fleeing Kosovo. Some humanitarian organisations, often linked with religious or human rights groups, made clear their allegiance to one side or the other. While we may have had personal opinions, these did not impact our work. Maintaining neutrality and the impartial distribution of aid based on need was paramount.

What I saw and witnessed at the border crossings from Kosovo to Macedonia was enough to demonstrate how historical events from centuries ago are often manipulated to justify present-day conflict. These narratives are frequently used as a cover to commit crimes against humanity and to stir nationalistic fervour. Only children, untouched by prejudice, see people as one until adults infiltrate their minds with stories creating division and bias.

Years earlier, I had the privilege of visiting the former Yugoslavia as a tourist around 1984, and I still treasure a few pieces of its now-defunct currency. As a keen supporter of British Athletics, one of my most vivid memories was the 1990 European Athletics Championships in Split. It was a remarkable event: Great Britain triumphed in every men's track event from the 100 meters to the 800 meters, as well as the 110 and 400-meter hurdles. Meanwhile, East Germany dominated the equivalent women's events, except for the hurdles. It was a time when sports and politics often intertwined, a reflection of the broader tensions that would soon unravel the region.

I often mimicked the accents and mannerisms of others. Spending even a short period in a community different from my own - or visiting another English-speaking country where accents clearly marked one's birthplace - left a lasting impression. After living in South Africa for a relatively short time, whenever I returned to Australia or visited family in the UK, they would often comment on my newly acquired South African accent. Sometimes, I leaned into this and exaggerated it for effect. Similarly, despite living in Australia for over 25 years, non-Australians often identify my accent as distinctly Australian, while Australians immediately hear the British - and, more specifically, London - undertones in my voice.

Most English accents familiar to the world hail from Northern England, often harsher or more pronounced, whereas my accent, from the South, is more neutral. While studying in Liverpool, I fell in love with the Liverpudlian or "Scouse" accent, even attempting to imitate it. These playful adaptations of speech and mannerisms allowed me to blend in on the surface, but I soon realised there was more to assimilation than outward appearances.

Blending in, like an iceberg, only scratches the surface of identity. The greater part lies beneath - unseen and harder to emulate. While one can mimic language, clothing, and even cultural behaviours, the unseen depths of our true selves are far more difficult to replicate. These nuances, shaped by values, beliefs, and lived experiences, can only be fully understood through years immersed in a different culture.

Nevertheless, my ability to adapt provided fleeting opportunities to see the world through others' eyes, offering insights into their perspectives. On a professional level, this skill allowed me to better understand unspoken emotions and underlying tensions. Often, what is said aloud can mask true feelings. Words can conceal, guide, or even manipulate behaviour, especially in situations where religious or cultural doctrine dictates actions - such as treating one's enemy as a friend or offering them sanctuary.

In many cultures, including Arabic and Spanish-speaking ones, there is a common phrase: *"Bayti baytak"* - "My home is your home." Yet, the weight of this hospitality can shift depending on who it is extended to. Offering one's home to someone perceived as undesirable or even a threat challenges the boundaries of this generosity and tests cultural and personal values.

The complex interplay of national interests, ethnic loyalties, and individual experiences in these regions underscored how blending in - on any level - requires more than surface adaptation. It demands an understanding of the underlying currents that shape identities, relationships, and decisions. For me, these moments offered not just a glimpse into another world but also a deeper appreciation of the unseen forces that bind and divide us all.

Living and working in Saudi Arabia for nearly seven years equipped me with cultural and religious understanding, adaptive skills, and linguistic fluency that became invaluable in my humanitarian career. These skills were especially beneficial during my work in Afghanistan under Taliban rule and in other Arabic-speaking regions, such as Jordan, Lebanon, Israel, and the Palestinian Territories, as well as Islamic states like Pakistan.

It wasn't until my third year, when I moved out of the expatriate compound and into the local community, that I truly began to immerse myself in Saudi culture. Expat compounds often maintained a parallel existence, detached from the host country's traditions and daily life. Living in a local neighbourhood with Saudi neighbours allowed me to experience a deeper, more authentic connection to Arabic culture. As a nurse working with primarily Arabic-speaking patients and colleagues, I developed a medium proficiency in spoken Arabic, including Gulf-specific accents and colloquialisms. Even today, when I converse with Gulf Arabs, they often ask if I am from Saudi Arabia due to the regional words and pronunciations I use. However, when I was deployed to Lebanon during the Syrian Crisis in 2013, I discovered that my Gulf-influenced Arabic was less effective, as Lebanese Arabic has its own unique cadence and vocabulary.

This experience reaffirmed a universal truth I've often encountered in my travels: speaking even a few words of the local language, showing curiosity about the culture, and asking thoughtful questions immediately dismantle barriers and foster mutual respect and collaboration.

My immersion deepened further through my best friend, who sought to marry a Bahraini woman. Her father requested that he convert to Islam, a requirement not imposed if the situation had been reversed - if he had been

Muslim and she non-Muslim. My friend, deeply committed to this union, embraced the journey wholeheartedly, studying the tenets of Islam, attending five daily prayers, and receiving guidance from an Imam. Sadly, the union didn't happen for reasons not shared with me. My friend was deeply saddened and remained committed to converting to Islam. He later married an Iraqi girl and now has four children.

As his closest companion, I shared parts of this journey out of curiosity and a desire to broaden my understanding of the faith. I had always been drawn to studying religious practices, having read the New and Old Testaments multiple times, the Quran, and other sacred texts in their entirety. While some passages are complex, the Quran's poetic cadence imbues its recitation with a profound sense of spirituality. I also came to appreciate how the Hadiths complement the Quran, offering practical guidance on behaviour and faith in everyday contexts.

I found it fascinating how much overlap exists between Islam, Christianity, and Judaism, all Abrahamic faiths. Names may change across languages, but the connections remain: Mary and Jesus feature prominently in the Quran, though Jesus is revered as a prophet rather than the Son of God. The Archangel Gabriel of the Bible is Jibril in the Quran, and Abraham becomes Ibrahim.

During my time in Saudi Arabia, I attended several calls to prayer (Salah) in the hospital and local mosques. While not participating, I was allowed to sit at the back and observe. Outside prayer times, mosques provided a tranquil space for quiet reflection. Their simplicity, adorned with geometric art rather than figurative imagery, fostered a unique spiritual focus on Allah.

The early morning prayer, held just before dawn, was my favourite. Walking to the mosque amidst a quiet procession of worshippers, the world still untouched by the day's demands, felt deeply meditative. This ritual emptied the mind, preparing it to be replenished with clarity and purpose. The prayer's conclusion brought a profound sense of peace, setting the tone for the day ahead.

After prayers, worshippers often lingered to share tea or cardamon spiced Arabic coffee, fostering a sense of community and equality. These daily prayers—five moments of collective pause - elevated spiritual priorities above worldly tasks. They also included the ritual washing, a practice rooted in both spiritual purity and public health. In times when sanitation standards were lower, such rituals protected not only physical well-being but also reinforced spiritual discipline.

Many of these traditions, from using the right hand for eating to communal meals after prayers, reflect Islam's holistic integration of spiritual and physical health. As a public health professional, I came to appreciate how these customs doubled as some of the earliest forms of preventive healthcare, rooted in religious practices yet deeply practical for human health.

I've had similar transformative experiences attending churches and retreats led by Buddhist and Christian monks. One place holds a particularly special place in my heart: *The Abbey* in Jamberoo, nestled in the serene Southern Highlands of New South Wales. This unique retreat, run by the Benedictine order of female monks, became a sanctuary I would return to regularly. It offered me the space to immerse myself in prayer, reflection, and quietude - a much-needed reprieve after the intensity of working in war zones and the challenges of readjusting to "home."

The Abbey's cedar wood interiors, beautifully crafted stained-glass windows, and the ethereal singing of the monks created an atmosphere of profound spiritual upliftment. It was a space where the sacredness of simplicity allowed for a deep connection to God and the self.

During my stays, I was often invited to share the midday meal with the monks - a humble but nourishing spread that embodied the spirit of the community. These meals, unadorned yet hearty, mirrored the quiet strength of the Abbey itself, reminding me that restoration often comes through life's simplest offerings.

The Abbey was more than a retreat; it was a place of grounding. In its stillness, I found the spiritual clarity and emotional healing I needed to carry forward, stronger and more centred, into the next chapter of my life and work.

For many, blending in is about fitting into societal expectations and gaining acceptance. It often requires sacrificing parts of your true self in favour of a constructed identity - one that aligns with the norms or ideals of the group you wish to join. This can be a strategic choice, driven by the desire for better opportunities in work, relationships, or even personal safety.

At times, the act of blending in is about survival: adopting behaviours, appearances, or attitudes to gain recognition, belong to a "gang," or find support within a community. Yet, there are moments when this conformity isn't a choice but an imposition, forced upon you by circumstance or necessity, leaving little room for authenticity.

Occasionally, the attempt to blend in and be part of something when you are technically an outsider can go awry. While in Gilgit, Pakistan—my staging post for a trip to the Hunza Valley—I decided to adopt a local appearance and wander the bustling streets. I dressed in a grey *shalwar kameez* similar in style to what men commonly wore in the region. Staying at a hotel frequented mostly by tourists, I managed to walk past the reception unnoticed. For a moment, I was simply another face in the crowd, observed as a local.

There was an exhilarating sense of freedom. No one stared at me in the way tourists often draw attention. I imitated the slower, shuffling pace of the locals instead of my usual purposeful stride. Stopping at a street stall for sweetened milk tea, I didn't need to speak; my order was assumed, and a steaming cup was handed over in exchange for some rupees. The streets buzzed with activity—vehicles, chatter, the aroma of street food mingling with dust. The atmosphere felt entirely different, unfiltered by the lens of tourism.

As I moved with the crowd, I realised we were all heading in the same direction—towards a polo match. It reminded me of walking to Selhurst Park to watch Crystal Palace play football. Back home, fans would march together in unison, singing and bantering, scarves fluttering in team colours. Here, however, the focus wasn't soccer but polo, a sport second only to cricket in Pakistan.

The scene was lively, with vendors selling snacks and drinks, and last-minute shoe shiners stationed along the curb. And that's when I was caught out. My shoes—or, more precisely, my sandals—betrayed me. A shoe shiner, with a knowing and mischievous smile, glanced down at my feet. I was wearing *Teva's*—a dead giveaway!

In that instant, I remembered how much footwear can signify status. While working in Saudi Arabia, I had learned to identify princesses and VIPs by the designer shoes they wore, the one exposed part of their otherwise modest attire. Even in school, shoes often revealed one's economic background—polished leather for the privileged and worn soles for those less fortunate.

Despite the revelation, nothing was said. The moment passed, and I joined the throng of spectators at the polo grounds. The match was unlike anything I'd experienced—a chaotic, almost violent game, both on and off the pitch. The crowd roared with excitement, and the players charged with relentless energy. Immersed in the celebration, I realised this was an experience I might never have had if I had remained visibly "different."

Evacuation – Jalalabad

Out of 23 deployments spanning from 1998 until 2022, there were three occasions when I was evacuated from my duty station, either as part of a team or individually. Two were due to major security events in active war zones, while the third, in 2022, was for health reasons. In every instance, I returned to complete my deployment.

The first of these evacuations occurred in 1998 during my assignment in Afghanistan. I began my deployment in Kandahar, but after three months, I was reassigned to Jalalabad. In this new role as a health delegate, I took on expanded public health responsibilities and acted as a representative for the International Red Cross in dealings with provincial authorities and government departments.

At the time, Afghanistan was in a state of rapid upheaval as the Taliban extended its control across the country. The fall of Mazar-i-Sharif, previously held by Uzbek warlord Abdul Rashid Dostum, marked a significant Taliban victory. The Northern Alliance, under the leadership of the Tajik commander Ahmad Shah Massoud— the "Lion of Panjshir" - remained the only force capable of mounting meaningful resistance.

In early August 1998, the global security landscape shifted dramatically. Al-Qaeda operatives carried out devastating attacks on two U.S. embassies in East Africa—one in Dar es Salaam, Tanzania, and the other in Nairobi, Kenya - resulting in over 200 fatalities. The United States responded swiftly and decisively. A few weeks later, Tomahawk missiles launched from Navy destroyers in the Red Sea struck targets in Sudan and Afghanistan. The strikes included a chemical plant in Sudan suspected of manufacturing chemical weapons, as well as Al-Qaeda bases in Khost, Afghanistan - a province bordering Pakistan in the country's southeast.

Khost lay just south of Nangarhar Province, where I was stationed in Jalalabad. While the missile strikes were targeted, the resulting tension was palpable, reverberating throughout the region. Afghanistan's decision to host Al-Qaeda operatives within its borders - specifically in Khost - reflected a complex relationship. Whether one views this through the Islamic and Arabic phrase *"Bayti baytak"* ("My home is your home"), Sun Tzu's adage "keep your friends close and your enemies closer," or the New Testament teaching to "love your enemies," the Taliban's actions suggested more than just religious solidarity. Their bond with Al-Qaeda, however tenuous in its origins, was ultimately reinforced by Wahhabism - a revivalist Sunni movement rooted in fundamentalist interpretations of Islam.

Yet, the relationship was not without its contradictions. The Taliban and Al-Qaeda were vastly different in ethnicity and culture: the Taliban were predominantly Afghan Pashtuns, while Al-Qaeda's leadership and ideology were largely Arab. These differences, however, seemed to matter little in the face of shared objectives and overlapping religious frameworks.

As events escalated, my role in Jalalabad became increasingly precarious. What began as a public health-focused mission was soon overshadowed by the realities of operating in a war zone. The strain of heightened security concerns, shifting alliances, and external military interventions set the stage for my first evacuation - a departure that, while unexpected, would not be my last.

While not internationally recognised, except by a handful of countries, the Taliban functioned as the de-facto government or 'authority', controlling nearly three-quarters of Afghanistan, including the capital, Kabul. As the ruling authority, they oversaw legal and administrative operations, managing various governmental ministries at state, provincial, and district levels across the territories under their control.

It was during one of our routine daily briefings that we received news of a missile strike by the US Navy in Khost province, where Al-Qaeda operatives had taken refuge among the rugged hills and caves. The operation was part of what the Americans called *Infinite Reach*, a calculated strike aimed at dismantling terrorist strongholds. While the missile detonations could reportedly be heard in Jalalabad, I did not hear them myself.

The repercussions of these strikes rippled quickly across the region. Though most Afghans were not supportive of Al-Qaeda's presence in their homeland, the attack was widely perceived as an assault on Muslims and Islam itself. Rather than sowing division, the operation seemed to strengthen ties between the Taliban and Al-Qaeda. What had previously been a loose arrangement - providing sanctuary to the group - hardened into a deeper alliance.

In response to the escalating risks, our security protocols were immediately tightened. Our movements were restricted to essential locations: our residence, the office, and any critical meetings with local counterparts. For me, that meant interactions with the District Minister for Health, a young but astute Talib whose demeanour often belied the complexities of his role.

Tensions within the local population were becoming increasingly evident. Instead of rallying behind foreign intervention, communities appeared to coalesce against what they viewed as an external threat to their faith and sovereignty. This growing solidarity manifested in subtle but undeniable ways: murmurs in the marketplace, sharp glances at foreign staff, and, eventually, overt threats against Westerners.

Humanitarian organisations began to react swiftly. Many were already withdrawing international staff, either relocating to neighbouring countries where operations could continue remotely or suspending programs entirely in preparation for a safer return. UN agencies and diplomatic missions followed suit, scaling back their teams and evacuating all non-essential personnel.

The International Red Cross was no exception. Contingency plans were drawn up across our network of offices throughout Afghanistan, including my duty station in Jalalabad. Evacuation procedures prioritised non-national and non-essential staff, with timelines growing tighter by the day as the situation deteriorated.

As Friday approached, the anticipation of **Salah al Jumu'ah**, the sacred Friday prayers, weighed heavily on us. This weekly gathering held profound significance in the Muslim world, often uniting communities through ritual washing, recitation of scripture, communal prayer, and, most critically, the **sermon**. The sermon, a powerful moment of reflection or call to action, had the potential to stir strong emotions among the congregation, especially in times of conflict. For men, attending was obligatory if physically able, while for women and children, it was optional. I understood the significance of these sermons and the weight of their potential impact in our already fragile environment.

Through the night, reports trickled in about various organisations abandoning their duty stations. The International Red Cross, with its deeply rooted reputation and direct dialogue with local authorities, was viewed as a bastion of relative safety. By midnight, our compound had become a refuge, drawing in other groups, including **Médecins Sans Frontières (MSF)**—Doctors Without Borders from their Ghazni base. They had been driving from late evening the day before arriving at our office.

My room, situated at the back of our compound, was separated by narrow gardens and winding paths. It provided some solitude but also left me isolated during unsettling moments. That night, the distant rumble of cars and loud voices pierced the stillness. My heart raced; I feared a local mob might be storming the compound. I instinctively ensured my door was locked - a precaution ingrained in all of us after a horrifying incident in 1996 where armed men had killed six International Red Cross staff in their rooms at the Red Cross hospital in Chechnya. Survivors of that attack owed their lives to locked doors.

My room had an ensuite bathroom that I could also secure, and it became my fallback. Standing in silence, I kept the room dark, staying away from the windows, and maintained radio silence. I clutched my small torch - vital for navigating the bathroom, where scorpions often found themselves stranded in the shower base, unable to escape the slippery surface. Walking barefoot was a habit I had long abandoned.

The muffled sounds of shuffling feet and voices grew louder, yet the language was indistinct. The cadence and tone suggested a local dialect, heightening my alarm. Then, amidst the chaos, I caught fragments of French. Relief washed over me as I realised it was our guards and drivers escorting the night arrival of MSF staff to their guest accommodations.

The tension slowly ebbed, and I returned to bed, though sleep was fleeting. Dawn brought a profound sense of relief. Gathering with my team that morning felt grounding, a necessary reassurance in a world teetering on the edge of chaos.

After a communal breakfast shared with our unexpected night arrivals, we were summoned to a briefing led by our head of sub-delegation. A decision had been made: all non-essential staff and those deemed at higher risk were to be evacuated. Among our international team, only the Administrator and the Head of Sub-Delegation would remain. With a large team under my supervision, including a capable local counterpart, I handed over my responsibilities, confident they could manage the work on the ground. Contingency plans were outlined to protect national staff should they face threats, as we were acutely aware of the dangers their association with international organisations might bring.

We were instructed to prepare our "evacuation packs," a 6kg bag of essential items and documents, and reconvene in the meeting room for further instructions. My priority was briefing my team, providing guidance, and ensuring they had everything they might need to continue operations. Though I could still offer remote support, the weight of leaving my team behind gnawed at me. The goal of every deployment was to build sustainable programs, and this sudden evacuation was an unexpected test of how much knowledge and skill we had successfully transferred.

Our radios remained tuned to designated channels, keeping us in constant communication with the delegation in Kabul and the logistics team overseeing our evacuation. The International Red Cross relied on two dedicated planes stationed in Peshawar, flown by highly skilled South African pilots adept at navigating terrain under radar. Their expertise was a lifeline, but the weight of the situation became more palpable as Friday prayers approached—a critical juncture.

As anticipated, the sermons were fiery, their tone escalating into loud denunciations of the international community. The rhetoric spilled into action as reports emerged of a mob gathering near the UN offices, a frequent target due to their strained relations with the local population. Our head of sub-delegation swiftly contacted the Taliban authorities. Cooperation agreements ensured our presence as guests in their country, and now was the moment for them to uphold their responsibility to protect us.

Soon, two Taliban pickup trucks arrived, armed soldiers stationed visibly outside our gates. Their presence was a stark contrast to the global image of the Taliban, but here, they were our protectors. It was surreal to witness. Despite the assurance, tension remained high as rumours of the mob attacking and destroying the UN offices spread.

The call to leave finally came. We climbed into two waiting Red Cross Land Cruisers, flanked by armed Taliban vehicles - one leading, one trailing. The sight of an armed escort, almost unheard of for the Red Cross, underscored the precariousness of our situation.

At Jalalabad airport, our anxiety lingered. The expected Red Cross plane would not be coming; instead, a UN aircraft already en route from Kabul would extract both UN and Red Cross staff. Without formalities like check-in or passport control, we headed directly to the runway. The small turbo-prop plane arrived, already loaded with passengers, luggage, and files crammed into every available space. The math was clear: adding six more passengers risked overloading the plane. But there was no alternative.

We boarded, squeezed into seats meant for two, with some of us bracing ourselves against the seatbacks in front. As the plane taxied, its engines strained under the weight. The runway stretched long before us, but doubt clawed at our minds: could it lift off in time? The engines roared louder, and finally, the plane lumbered into the air. Its climb was agonisingly slow, the engines screaming as the pilot fought to gain enough altitude to stabilise. Eventually, the aircraft settled into a low but steady flight toward Peshawar.

Relief washed over us upon landing, but the ordeal wasn't over. We waited for a bus to transport us—not to the main terminal, but through a circuitous route that seems to take forever to exit the airport and then the freeway to Islamabad International Airport. Dusk was now occurring at it would be another three hours until we would arrive in Islamabad. Somehow, I felt safer back in Afghanistan as looking through the window due to the glares given to us by people we passed.

We arrived at Islamabad International Airport around 10 p.m., a collective sense of relief sweeping over us. Yet, the ordeal was far from over. Members of the Afghanistan delegation who had been evacuated earlier were already there, including colleagues from Kabul, Herat, and Kandahar. Despite the brief reunion, our minds were preoccupied with the next step: evacuation to our regional headquarters in Bangkok, where we would remain on standby until the situation stabilised.

Tensions in Pakistan were as palpable as in Afghanistan, if not more so. Each hour brought an increasing sense of unease, the atmosphere heavy with anger and unrest. Adding to the pressure, several international airlines had temporarily suspended flights, reducing available seats. With no pre-booked tickets, our team had to rely on negotiations with Thai Airways to secure passage.

Only standby tickets were available, and there was no guarantee we would all get seats. At the Thai Airways check-in counters, staffed by stern-faced Pakistani men, it became clear that securing boarding passes would require more than polite requests. Enter Michele, one of our colleagues - a British-Swiss woman in her early thirties, with dark, shoulder-length hair, wearing a crisp white blouse and skirt. She exuded an air of confidence and charm that could disarm even the most unyielding of gatekeepers.

Like a scene from a James Bond film, Michele approached the counter with poise, her blouse subtly undone just enough to command attention but still in good taste. In her polished accent and professional demeanour, she explained our situation to the two men handling ticketing. Whatever magic transpired in that exchange, it worked: moments later, we each held a boarding pass in our hands.

Boarding the Thai Airways jet was a moment of triumph. As we settled into our seats, an audible sigh of relief swept through the group. The hum of the engines was a comforting reassurance, and exhaustion quickly overcame us. Most of us fell asleep, knowing that Bangkok awaited us with the promise of rest and recovery.

Upon arrival, arrangements for our accommodation and transportation to the regional office had already been made. The next morning, we debriefed and discussed plans, learning that it would be at least a week before we could consider returning. In the end, it turned into a ten-day hiatus. While many of our team chose to enjoy Bangkok's vibrant city life or retreat to the islands, my friend Martin and I opted for something quieter- exploring Thailand's national parks and serene lakes, immersing ourselves in the country's natural beauty.

Returning to Afghanistan was bittersweet. The national staff had managed operations impressively in our absence, a testament to their resilience and dedication. Still, a pang of guilt lingered. As foreigners, we had the privilege of leaving when danger loomed, while they stayed behind, often risking their safety due to their association with us. This experience underscored the importance of empowering local teams. For the medical and health teams, it became a catalyst for accelerating the transition to local management - a step toward sustainable operations in an unpredictable environment.

Savuti – 'The Calling'

Savuti, nestled in the heart of Botswana, has become a name inseparable from my life and business. I christened my gardening and hobby farm *Savuti Gardening and Hobby Farm* and my fitness enterprise *Savuti Health and Fitness*. At first glance, it might seem like an unusual name for a gym and fitness club - or perhaps not.

Every business carries a story, a thread connecting its name to its essence. For me, Savuti symbolises an experience, a mystery, a miracle - something profound that defies simple explanation.

When David Livingstone, the first European explorer, ventured to Savuti in 1851, he found the channel flowing with life. But just thirty years later, it dried up, leaving behind desolate marshes. For nearly 80 years, the Savuti channel remained barren until the late 1950s when water returned, only to vanish again in the early 1980s. Then, as if guided by unseen forces, it began to flow once more in 2008, transforming into a deep, clear waterway.

Savuti holds an enigmatic duality. Known as a river that flows in both directions, it is a paradox of nature - a river that outwardly rushes for all to see, yet also retreats inward, concealed from the world. It reveals itself only on nature's terms, a phenomenon as unpredictable as it is breathtaking. The wildlife here adapts to this ever-changing mystery, thriving in a realm untouched by human hands, living as they have for millennia. To stand on the outskirts, to witness this world where humanity is merely an observer, is a privilege beyond words.

To experience Savuti even once is transformative, yet it never feels like enough. It is a place that imprints itself on your soul, a sanctuary of secrets and wonder. While I dream of returning, I have made a simple request: that when my time comes and I enter mortality, my ashes be scattered among the Savuti marshes. In that timeless expanse, I will find peace - forever a part of the mystery that is Savuti.

It wasn't by design that I found myself in Savuti for the first time. Life often takes us down unexpected paths, and this was no exception. I had heard whispers of its allure - stories of a place where nature's rhythms unfold in ways that defy explanation. But it was not until I set foot there that I began to grasp the truth behind the tales.

I first heard about Savuti staying at Safari camp close to the Botswana border in Zimbabwe. Not far from the Safari Camp was Kazungula and where four countries come within touching distance to each other – the eastern part of the Caprivi Strip. These four countries are Namibia, Botswana, Zambia and Zimbabwe. After my previous African experience visiting Kenya, I was reluctant to return due to the events that occurred on the train. My next trip to Africa would be to the south and I would be in charge of my itinerary and destiny.

I had good friends who had travelled to Zimbabwe which at the time was a stable country with a flourishing tourist trade and well managed safari camps maintained a balance between tourism and preserving the delicate flora and fauna. It was a relatively safe place. Previously, the southern half of Rhodesia, it still retained a strong connection to its former colonial power, Great Britain. The northern half of Rhodesia was now called Zambia. Unlike Zimbabwe the economy was in collapse and much of the land was being razed, turned into farmland and exploited. Wildlife was being decimated or forced like human refugees to seek safety in neighbouring countries. Zimbabwe became a haven for fleeing wildlife and its National parks were teeming with wildlife making Zimbabwe one of the best places to experience the big five. Combined with the awe of the Victoria Falls is became a magnet not just for the experience of the wildlife but also for thrill seekers and extreme sports including white water rafting, bungee jumping which in turns creates a space for clubs, bars and music bringing back-packers, tourists, wildlife enthusiasts, thrill seekers from all over the world together. Sometimes you were all. It was my first white water rafting experience.

My itinerary consisted of a trip to Kariba, the world's largest artificial lake. Dead and petrified tree trunks protruded from the waters, creating a stark and haunting contrast. If it weren't for the hippos and the teeming wildlife - including fish eagles - the landscape might resemble a post apocalyptic scene.

Following Kariba, I embarked on a three-day canoe safari on the Kafue River. The journey involved gentle paddling in pairs or solo, guided by a lead canoeist who skilfully navigated the waterways. We moved slowly, scanning the surroundings for hippos and the majestic sight of elephants crossing the river. As the largest tributary of the mighty Zambezi River, the Kafue offered both serenity and thrilling encounters.

Hippos, while seemingly docile from a distance, are responsible for more human injuries and deaths than any other large animal. The golden rule is never to come between a hippopotamus on land and its refuge in the water! Whenever we spotted hippos in the distance, we carefully adjusted our route to maintain a safe distance.

The true magic unfolded when elephants descended from the banks to graze knee deep in the water along the shoreline. Overhanging trees offered them a delicious treat, and we watched in awe as they waded into the river to cross over to the other side. When the water became too deep, their trunks acted as snorkels, particularly for calves and young adults. It was a mesmerising scene of adaptation and grace.

On one side of the river lay Zimbabwe, and on the other, Zambia. We camped on the shores or small islands in the middle of the river, immersed in the wilderness. The Zambian side of the landscape glowed with fiery light, the sky painted red from the burning of the land to prepare for crops. This method of razing the land provided only fleeting agricultural benefits. The fires destroyed essential minerals, leaving little for the next planting season. Any remaining nutrients were quickly depleted by the crops, leaving the soil barren.

It seemed that many people were living for the moment, without consideration for sustainable farming practices like crop rotation or planting nutrient-replenishing species. The constant movement of animals crossing the river throughout the night resembled refugees fleeing a war zone, seeking a place of safety. The atmosphere was alive with the rhythm of survival, a poignant reminder of nature's fragility and resilience.

The itinerary took me across different parts of Zimbabwe, each destination offering its own distinct character. I began with the capital, Harare—once known as Salisbury when is part of British Empire - a city alive with energy and contrasts. From there, I ventured to Bulawayo, renowned for its broad, tree-lined streets and as the gateway to Zimbabwe's largest national park, Hwange, a haven for wildlife.

For a complete change of scenery, I set my sights on Mutare, nestled in the Eastern Highlands near the Mozambique border. Unlike the iconic safari landscapes, this region offered a dramatically different climate, with lush vegetation and unique fauna and flora. True to my preference for authentic experiences, I chose to travel from Harare to Mutare by local bus.

The journey was a vibrant immersion into the everyday lives of Zimbabweans. The bus was alive with activity - laden with wares, pots, pans, and fresh produce from the markets. Foreigners were a rarity on this route; I didn't spot another among the passengers. As the bus climbed into the cool highlands, I noticed curious glances from my fellow travellers, particularly the women with their children on their laps. Their expressions were not of suspicion but of warm curiosity, often accompanied by shy smiles.

Mutare itself was enchanting, a gateway to the Eastern Highlands' misty allure. I explored the Chimanimani Mountains, one of the region's three prominent ranges. The Highlands earned their name for good reason - evoking the rugged beauty of the Scottish Highlands with their cool air, rolling mist, and tranquil, sparsely populated expanses. It was a place of serene beauty, a far cry from the bustling savannahs I had come to associate with African travel.

Returning to Harare the same way I had come, via local bus, felt like retracing a thread through the vibrant tapestry of Zimbabwean life. From there, I set my sights on Victoria Falls, a magnet for backpackers, thrill-seekers, and adventure lovers. The town unlike the safaris allowed you just walk around on foot visiting markets, the train Victorian era built train station, sip tea at the Victoria Falls Hotel, sit in parks – it buzzed with energy, offering campsites, and a nightlife that seemed to mirror the roar of the falls themselves.

Victoria Falls was a place to unwind, connect, and share stories with fellow travellers. Thrill-seekers could choose from helicopter flights over the majestic falls, hikes to the edge where the Zambezi River thundered into the gorge, bungee jumping, or white-water rafting. I indulged in a helicopter flight, treating myself to a breathtaking aerial view of the falls, their sheer scale and beauty laid out beneath me like a living canvas.

The next day, I joined a group of eight for a white-water rafting adventure through the Zambezi's rapids. The

190

experience was nothing short of exhilarating. The surging water, the thrill of navigating the rapids, and the collective rush of adrenaline bonded our group in ways only shared danger and exhilaration can.

Evenings were filled with camaraderie and music. At the local clubs, we gathered to relive the day's adventures, flipping through photos taken by the tour companies and swapping stories over drinks. The soundtrack to those moments remains vivid—Freddie Mercury's *"Living on My Own"* and 4 Non Blondes' *"What's Up"* played in the background, etching themselves into my memory as the anthems of that time.

After a few unforgettable days in Victoria Falls, it was time for the final leg of this journey - one that would two years later in 1996 lead me into the wild heart of Botswana, to Savuti!

The final leg of this second, and far more enjoyable, trip compared to my adventures in Kenya a few years earlier, took me to a safari camp called 'Imbabala'. Situated near the Zimbabwe border crossing into Kasane, Botswana, the camp was operated by a tour company called 'Wild Horizons'. It was here that I met Gavin and Shay, the owners and white Zimbabweans who welcomed guests with warmth and enthusiasm. Gavin, blonde and handsome in khaki shorts and shirt and an experienced safari guide, would lead guests on foot to observe elephants and other big game that roamed the area, including the tributary of the Zambezi River that bordered the camp.

Imbabala consisted of six accommodation huts, a hut for the rangers, a hut for local staff, a kitchen, and a large thatched gazebo. The gazebo served as the social hub, with a bar, tables, lounge chairs, coffee tables, a library, and decorations featuring local African artifacts, paintings, and ornaments. It was here that we gathered for breakfast and relaxed in the evenings, recounting the day's adventures over drinks and immersing ourselves in the safari experience by watching wildlife videos.

My private hut was a charming round thatched, whitewashed mud-and-stone room with a unique layout - the shower and toilet tucked behind an interior wall for privacy. The decor featured African art and rugs that adorned the stone floor. Above my bed, a mosquito net hung gracefully, and a ceiling fan rotated slowly - an effective deterrent against mosquitoes, which dislike moving air. The huts were surrounded by a lawn that seemingly blended into the surrounding bushland, trees, and the river. It meant there was no boundary between you and the wildlife, and at night, you could hear animals walking and exploring around your accommodation - even the grunts of hippos foraging on land, a safer activity for them at night compared to the day when they retreated to the water, where they moved with grace as their name suggests: River Horses.

The next three days, which soon extended to five, became a transformative experience. Traveling alone, I quickly bonded with the hosts Gavin, Shay, the rangers and local team, who embraced me as part of their family. Shay was particular interested in my best mates girlfriend who was often referred to as Bahraini princess. She was fascinated how this cultural divide would happen. She was hoping one day, they would visit as a couple and often asked me on future trips about them. I would eventually return with Graham – but on his own without his Bahraini bride in the making – the relationship was forbidden by her father.

My love for zoology and my ability to quickly identify various bird species and antelope breeds, combined with my eagerness to learn about animal behaviour and photography, made me feel like I had found my true calling. It was a bittersweet realisation; had I pursued my original plan to study zoology at Liverpool University, perhaps this might have been my life. My ability to classify mammal orders impressed the other guests, and the small group of visitors - mostly couples and friends - often mistook me for part of the team due to how seamlessly I integrated into camp life.

I joined the rangers on early morning, afternoon, evening, and night safaris. One night, I even slept on the pontoon by the riverbank with one of the younger rangers, surrounded by elephants that communicated softly among themselves as I lay still, mesmerised by their presence. On another occasion, I helped other guests board the camps own riverboat for a serene sunset cruise, identifying the animals and explaining what I had learned. The sense of connection with nature was unparalleled. I bonded well with the younger ranger who was from the Isle of Wight in England and was training to become a ranger. We would often take out the small motorboat after breakfast to go fishing or spot hippos in the river. One day, he got a bit too close to the edge of the bank when a hippo charged back into the water seeking safety after being startled by our presence. It was a reminder of never getting between a hippopotamus and the water. Well-marked paths emerging from the water onto the dry shore with flattened vegetation was a strong clue to keep your distance! We were lucky that day!

One particular adventure stood out. A ranger, a passionate zoologist, wanted to document the hatching of African Wattled Lapwing eggs. Knowing the hatching was imminent and had previously set up a makeshift hide in the middle of a marsh. I was asked if I bunker down in the hide and capture the moment the chicks emerged from the shells. I was taken there by a small motorised boat and was left there with my camera and tripod and some supplies to capture the event. The hide was basic but effective, made of hessian cloth and camouflaged among the grasses. I sat alone, watching over the clutch of eggs on the ground about 20-30 meters away, my Canon SLR and 300mm lens poised and ready.

The hours passed quietly, but I remained vigilant. The marshland was alive with possibility, and my mind wandered to the creatures that might be nearby—crocodiles in the river, lions, leopards, buffalo, cheetahs, Cape hunting dogs, monitor lizards, and snakes. I forced myself to focus on the task at hand, waiting for the first signs of life from the eggs.

Then it happened - the first crack. The parent birds hovered nearby, their watchful eyes fixed on the scene as more eggs began to crack open. I adjusted my camera settings carefully, mindful of conserving film. Back then, we relied on 35mm film, and each shot needed to count. Over the next few hours, I went through two rolls of 400 ISO, each with 36 exposures. Slowly but surely, the hatchlings emerged, with one of the parents gently assisting their chicks in breaking free from their shells. Time seemed to stand still as I witnessed this rare and beautiful moment of life beginning.

So absorbed was I in the experience that I didn't hear the small boat returning. The engine had been cut, and the rangers paddled silently toward me. When I noticed them, I carefully packed my camera and tripod, emerging from the hide to wade through the marshy ground to the boat. Excitement coursed through me as I shared what I had witnessed. Unlike today's digital age, the film needed to be developed, and this wouldn't happen until I returned to Saudi Arabia. The ranger asked me to send the photos to his university and the zoological museum where he taught, adding another layer of fulfillment to an already extraordinary day.

That evening, we dined outside, watching a herd of buffalo that would stop and stare at us and then turn back and continue their slow daily pilgrimage to the river to drink and bathe. The sunset filled the sky with a deepening red horizon as bats took to the air and evensong began. The evenings and early mornings were the best—cool, almost frost-like air enveloped the landscape as most wildlife came to life before retreating to rest during the heat of the day.

I have never enjoyed roller coasters or other fairground rides that spin, take you upside down, or propel you at great speed in a circular movement. For some, the adrenaline is the thrill to be wanting more. What would give a similar thrill was somewhat quite different – it came on one particular evening safari when our rangers took us out in two jeeps. A herd of elephants had been spotted. The rangers, familiar with their behaviours, were always mindful of our safety but wanted us to experience the thrill of getting close to nature. They knew these elephants, their temperaments, the female cows' oestrous cycles, and most importantly, when male bulls were in *musth*. Fortunately, this was the dry season, not the wet season, so we wouldn't be encountering herds during the mating period.

Large mating bulls often stayed away from the herd, leaving it led by a matriarch and her guard of adult females, baby and youth elephants, and young bulls. It was often the young bulls that posed more challenges, eager to exert their power and show off. Older and wiser elephants, including large bulls, understood we were no threat.

The herd spread out, grazing among the trees, and soon we found ourselves in the middle of them. With engines kept at a low rev, we were instructed to remain silent and still. The rangers moved the vehicles slowly to better viewing positions. The herd appeared unbothered, continuing to graze and interact, reaching high into the trees with their trunks. At one point, we were entirely surrounded, with no visible exit tracks. Dusk had succumbed to the early darkness with the elephants becoming more like moving shadows getting larger as they got closer. The rangers turned off the engines and whispered for us to remain motionless.

It was then that I felt a trunk behind my neck. It was sniffing me. Remarkably, I wasn't frightened. I trusted the ranger's expertise completely and knew he would act if needed. I had noticed before how he handled over curious elephants - a sharp tap on the side of the jeep and a firm, direct tone would send them on their way. True to form, the elephant withdrew after being allowed to complete it sniffing ritual at its own pace whilst I sat still. Maybe one day I could do the same in reverse!

I often tell those who love the thrill of adventure sports or fairground rides that my thrill comes from these moments. There is no greater exhilaration than being at the mercy of a creature that could easily trample or hurl you a fair distance.

Once the elephant decided it was time to move on, she gave us permission to leave as well.

This was one of several unforgettable experiences at Imbabala that would compel me to return on two more occasions. Among the highlights of this trip was an extraordinary moment made even more special by its rarity: being suddenly awoken by the ranger, who had spotted a pack of Cape hunting dogs - also known as African painted dog - tracking and pursuing a male kudu antelope, one of the larger antelope species.

Those of us who got up quickly dressed and jumped into the jeep with the ranger and driver, eager to witness the unfolding drama. We tracked the pack as they pursued their prey, whose fate was sealed the moment it was singled out. Cape hunting dogs are renowned for their remarkable hunting efficiency, boasting the highest success rate of any predator. Their strategy is as precise as it is relentless: like a finely tuned relay team, they take turns leading the chase, each dog falling back to allow another to take over. This coordinated effort exhausts their prey, leaving it vulnerable to the final strike.

From this experience, I learned a great deal. On my subsequent visits to Southern Africa, tracking on my own with my travel buddy, I could get up close to herds, understanding when to keep the car engine running and when to remain still.

On our first evening at the lodge, after dinner, we gathered in the gazebo. A National Geographic documentary played on the television. It was titled *Eternal Enemies* and narrated the fascinating rivalry between lions and hyenas in a place called Savuti, Botswana. Created by South African filmmakers Derek and Beverly Joubert, the documentary was more than just a study of wildlife - it was a powerful narrative of survival, loss, battles, scars, trauma, and love. Through the lens of their camera, Savuti came alive as a land of primal drama, where the unyielding laws of nature dictated life and death.

Savuti was synonymous with big game. Unlike most lion prides, where the lionesses primarily handled the hunting, here the large male lions often hunted big game—young bull elephants, buffalo, and giraffes - animals typically avoided by lionesses unless supported by numbers or maturing males. For the pride, such a kill was worth the risk, as an elephant could feed them for days.

Competing for these resources were the hyenas, creatures often dismissed for their haunting laughs and ungainly appearance. Yet, hyenas are closer relatives of felines than canines and possess a complex social structure. Their packs are matriarchal, with males subordinate to females. The hierarchy was rigid, with future matriarchs identified in early childhood, and the death of a matriarch could upend the pack's pecking order. A young hyena might rise to princess only to be relegated to servitude upon the loss of her protector.

The lion pride at the heart of the documentary was ruled by two imposing males, possibly brothers. *Mandevo* the older looking male bore the marks of countless battles, while the other, younger looking and more magnificent, was called *Ntwadumela* (pronounced En Twadumela) - "He Who Greets with Fire." His story was both poignant and fierce. During the filming, his female mate had been killed by hyenas in a pitched battle while the males were away. This loss came after a territorial fight with another pride, leaving the lions vulnerable to their eternal enemies.

The documentary opened with a haunting scene: a lioness leaving her pride to give birth in the rocky terrain surrounding the grasslands. Unknowingly, she chose a site inhabited by a spitting cobra. The venom sprayed on her and her cubs, leaving her near death. Though the lioness survived after days of suffering, her cubs did not. They fell victim to hyenas, their tiny bodies devoured. When the lioness instinctively returned to the place where she had given birth, she found only emptiness. Heartbroken, she rejoined her pride, who welcomed her as if they understood her pain.

Savuti's plains were a battleground for lions and hyenas. The hyenas, ever-opportunistic, often waited for the male lions to be away before taunting the pride. One unforgettable scene in the documentary captured the essence of their rivalry. The male lions had wandered off to mark their territory, leaving the pride vulnerable. Sensing an opportunity, the hyena pack, led by their matriarch, launched an assault to steal a kill made by the lionesses. The hyenas' numbers overwhelmed the pride, dragging away chunks of the carcass for their cubs hidden in underground warrens.

But then, something shifted. *Ntwadumela* sensing the commotion, turned back. The film captured his return in slow motion - his massive black mane flowing, his eyes locked on the matriarch. She saw him too late. The matriarch turned to flee, but *Ntwadumela* was relentless. Frame by frame, he closed the distance, his powerful stride unstoppable. In one swift motion, he clipped her hind leg, tripping her. Before she could recover, he launched himself onto her back, severing her spinal column as he demonstrated his art in wrestling to flip himself under her and dig his massive jaws closing around her throat to starve her of oxygen. With his ferocious grip, the life was gradually sucked out of her.

The hyena pack mourned the loss of their leader, their hierarchy thrown into disarray. The battle was over, but the war was eternal. The documentary reminded its audience that in Savuti, survival is a never-ending struggle, each victory temporary, each loss profound.

That night, as I lay in bed under the vast African sky, I couldn't help but feel a deeper connection to this land. The primal dance of predator and prey, of triumph and tragedy, mirrored the ebb and flow of life itself. Savuti had etched itself into my soul as a place of untamed beauty, eternal battles, and lessons in resilience.

Instead of returning the Harare for a few nights before heading back to Saudi Arabia, I slept in the rangers tents for another two nights.

It was sad to learn before my third and final trip to Imbabala with my partner Ian, that Gavin had a few years earlier been killed by a charging bull elephant whilst taking a group for guests out on the walking safari. Shay had sold the camp to new owners due to her loss of her life partner. I met her during my last visit sitting at a bar – a shadow of the person I once remembered – she was still mourning and devasted and never recovered. I later heard that she passed away – not sure if this was by a broken heart that led to other health conditions.

The Slap

It wasn't long after recovering from the effects of campylobacter infection that I was asked about my availability for deployment. I had previously declined a position in Tajikistan as my body was not quite ready. The new request seemed to accelerate my recovery, although my blood haemoglobin level was still below the required threshold. Foods rich in iron would take time to naturally elevate the levels, but with the help of a blood transfusion, I was deemed fit for deployment.

The war in the Balkans was spreading. Following the signing of the Dayton Agreement in December 1995, attention shifted to Kosovo, controlled by the Federal Republic of Yugoslavia (Serbia and Montenegro - FRY). The Kosovo Liberation Army (KLA) had formed in the early 1990s as a resistance force against the discrimination of ethnic Albanians and the erosion of their autonomy within Kosovo.

The Dayton Agreement ended the war between Serbian and Croatian forces, leading to the creation of a single sovereign state known as Bosnia and Herzegovina. However, the agreement failed to address the escalating tensions in the ethnically Albanian-dominated Kosovo region of FRY. After a series of sabotage attacks on Kosovo police stations by the KLA and the smuggling of large quantities of weapons from Albania, Serbian paramilitary and regular forces increased their presence in Kosovo. They initiated a campaign of retribution, targeting KLA sympathisers and political opponents. Thousands of Kosovar Albanians were displaced as a result.

In March 1999, the month of my arrival in Pristina, the capital of Kosovo province, Yugoslav forces escalated their campaign of repression and expulsion of Kosovar Albanians. This was compounded by the withdrawal of the OSCE Kosovo Verification Mission (KVM) and the failure of the Rambouillet Agreement. The KVM had been established to oversee the cessation of atrocities against ethnic Albanians and the withdrawal of Yugoslav and paramilitary forces. Without its presence, the situation deteriorated rapidly.

As was customary, my deployment began with briefings at the British Red Cross headquarters in London, followed by further preparations at the International Red Cross headquarters in Geneva. At the time, Kosovo was part of the Federal Republic of Yugoslavia (FRY), and the country's Red Cross headquarters was stationed in Belgrade, the capital. Outside of Afghanistan, the Red Cross operations in the FRY were among the largest and most complex and had increased its activities in 1998.

Belgrade, a city steeped in history, lies at the confluence of the Sava and Danube rivers. Yet, its charm was overshadowed by the tensions that engulfed not only Serbia and Kosovo but also the international community and the humanitarian organisations working within the region. The strife between Serbians and Kosovar Albanians was mirrored by fractures among aid agencies, where staff struggled with the emotional and ethical toll of their work.

By the time I arrived, many International Red Cross staff had been on the ground for months, bearing witness to the

Serbian forces' large-scale campaign of violence. The ruthlessness of paramilitary forces, in particular, was chilling, with widespread expulsions of Kosovar Albanians, including staff from humanitarian aid organisations. The disparity in safety between international staff and their national colleagues created a heavy burden of guilt. While expatriates could eventually return to safety, local staff often had no such option, with many fleeing to the Former Republic of Yugoslavia–Macedonia, home to a significant ethnic Albanian population.

The international teams were stretched thin, emotionally and physically. Gunfire was a constant backdrop, and security threats heightened daily. Many were on edge, including the medical doctor I was set to replace. Exhaustion, fear, and the moral weight of their roles had taken a toll.

The situation escalated as Serbian forces intensified their campaign in Kosovo. In response, NATO prepared to intervene with an aerial bombing campaign called Operation Allied Force targeting Kosovo and, later, Belgrade itself. My arrival coincided with this turning point in the conflict.

Driving from Belgrade to Pristina, the tension was palpable. Along the roadside, Serbian war planes sought refuge, gliding silently into the dense camouflage of the forests. Two MiG fighter jets descended gracefully, their silhouettes paralleling our Land Cruiser as we moved through the countryside. This eerie encounter underscored the gravity of the situation.

NATO's campaign marked its first full-scale military deployment and the largest military operation in Europe since the Second World War. My deployment began against the backdrop of an unfolding war - a war that would forever alter the region and the lives of those within it.

I arrived at the International Red Cross sub-delegation office in Pristina to an atmosphere heavy with exhaustion and relief. The staff, visibly tired, welcomed the arrival of new faces. For some, this marked the arrival of their relief team, signalling the end of their deployment. They could finally begin preparing handover notes, briefing their replacements, and looking forward to returning home - a distant sanctuary.

The pervasive stress of the conflict had left its mark on everyone. Heightened awareness was the norm, with staff constantly on edge. Communication was often hurried, abrupt, or tinged with impatience - a reflection of the pressure they endured.

Unlike my predecessors, I had not yet formed emotional bonds with the team. However, it was clear that deep connections had developed between the international staff and their local counterparts. These relationships were fraught with tension and heartbreak, as many international staff wrestled with feelings of guilt and helplessness. Unlike them, there were no plans to evacuate local staff, even as the security situation rapidly deteriorated.

This disparity - where evacuation privileges were reserved solely for international workers - left a bitter aftertaste. Local staff, who played critical roles as interpreters, field officers, drivers, and support personnel, were left behind. Their affiliation with the Red Cross, an organisation sometimes viewed as antagonistic by certain authorities, placed them at even greater risk.

This decision to evacuate only international teams sowed seeds of future grievances. For those left behind, the sense of abandonment was palpable. Their unwavering support and invaluable contributions to the mission were overshadowed by the harsh reality that, when the situation turned dire, they were deemed expendable.

My deployment began with a series of intense briefings, focusing on the security situation and its implications for our operations. Many programs had been suspended due to the escalating violence, but the health program remained active, necessitating my immediate involvement. I was introduced to my counterparts - the local administration for health services, the main hospital staff, our medical and supply warehouses, and partner organisations supported by the International Red Cross.

My predecessor, a German medical doctor, was eager to return home to his family, who were undoubtedly anxious as events unfolded. Even as I arrived, the signs of crisis were stark - an exodus of people leaving the town and sporadic gunfire echoing from streets and homes. There was little opportunity to acclimatise or familiarise myself with the town's layout, its shops, or its streets. On my fourth or fifth day, orders came for us to cease outdoor activities and operate solely from our residential accommodations.

My assigned residence was a single-story bungalow shared with three other delegates. Another staff house stood next door, and two others were nearby. Each residence had two Land Cruisers prepared and ready to depart at a moment's notice should the situation worsen. By night, the sound of gunfire - likely sniper fire - became a haunting constant, often emanating from nearby apartment buildings.

The head of our sub-delegation, an experienced and composed female delegate, exuded an air of confidence despite the escalating violence. Her poise set a tone of calm amidst the chaos. As a newcomer, without emotional entanglements to the ongoing crisis, I found my role evolving into one of quiet support - cooking meals, sharing stories, and playing music to help ease the stress. Maintaining a sense of routine - eating, writing, and staying in communication - became vital for our mental well-being.

Soon, stricter orders arrived: no one was to leave the houses, not even for provisions. We were to remain indoors, limit radio contact, and stay quiet, keeping low to the ground. Paramilitary forces began sweeping through neighbourhoods, going house to house. Our wooden shutter blinds remained closed, though occasionally we risked peering through to glimpse the outside. One day, soldiers -likely paramilitary, clad in camouflage and balaclavas - entered the neighbouring house where our colleagues lived. They escorted two of our logistics male team members out and drove away with them in their vehicle. Radio silence followed, leaving us in the dark about their fate.

Each day brought heightened uncertainty. Lights remained dim, voices hushed, and movements restricted. The following day, our colleagues were returned to their residence, dropped off without explanation. Unable to communicate with them, we could only speculate about what had transpired.

It was around midday, while I was alone in the kitchen, the head of the delegation knocked on the window. She was delivering the long-awaited order: it was time to leave. Permission had finally been granted by various authorities, and with the situation deteriorating rapidly, the risk to our staff had become too great to remain. As the Red Cross, we were often the last to leave, our neutral and impartial role affording us a level of trust, even with the Serbian authorities. Unlike many international organisations, we provided support not only to Kosovar Albanians but also to Serbians affected by the conflict. For the local population, our presence was vital - a protective force and a witness to what might unfold. Without us, who would be there to document the potential crimes against humanity that could arise? As an organisation, our departure during a conflict signalled that the situation had become critical, likely prompting even greater urgency among the population to flee. There were reports that a vehicle and two international staff from the aid agency Médecins Sans Frontières were in need of assistance to leave. They, similar, to some other organisations were more outspoken than the Red Cross and often responded to need without consent from the Government of the country. They had left it too late and didn't have the same relationship with the Serbian authorities. Arrangements were made for them to travel with us as passengers but to leave their vehicle behind as their vehicle might compromise our safety.

Behind the scenes, our logistics team had been preparing for days. The convoy would consolidate from eight vehicles to four, each stocked with provisions, spare tires, and water. Specific radio channels were designated, and each vehicle was assigned a driver. With my international driver's license, I was nominated as a relief driver.

The plan was clear: all vehicles would rendezvous at the Head of Sub-delegation's residence. Each vehicle would carry four to five occupants, with the lead vehicle hosting the head of the sub-delegation, an experienced Red Cross driver, and our senior field officer - a Serbian national. Due to the route leading to Belgrade and the inherent risks to their safety and ours, no Kosovar Albanian national staff would accompany us.

As we loaded the vehicles and finalised preparations, the gravity of the moment sank in. This was not just an evacuation; it was an acknowledgment of the fragility of our presence in a conflict spiralling out of control.

We boarded our vehicle with our luggage. Excess or non-essential items were left behind in the rented residences, to be retrieved if and when we returned. Our vehicle and that of our neighbours departed together, heading towards the residence of our head of sub-delegation. On arrival, we remained in our vehicle. The convoy was to maintain strict order - no overtaking and driving in single file. We were the second vehicle. Vehicle radios were kept on, while personal VHF radios were switched off to ensure commands were clear and uninterrupted. Instructions were straightforward: maintain a steady pace, adjust speed as directed -slower, then quicker, and so on. All vehicles were required to maintain a distance sufficient to prevent any other vehicle from coming between us. Our destination was Belgrade—or so we believed.

Plans changed constantly, with new instructions arriving from the head office in Serbia and headquarters in Geneva. Both were also in communication with their respective interlocutors. A decision was made to proceed only as far as the Pristina Hotel and remain there until further notice. This caused considerable anxiety, as NATO's aerial bombing campaign had begun, and Serbian commanders and forces were growing increasingly agitated by the perceived threat of NATO's superior firepower. We were all regarded as potential enemies of NATO - even neutral countries like Switzerland were not spared such suspicions.

We arrived at the Pristina Hotel to find the lobby bustling with activity. Men dressed in Serbian army uniforms were moving about, clearly officers and high-ranking officials. We couldn't help but wonder why we had been brought to this particular hotel. The reason soon became apparent: with Kosovo under attack by NATO, our presence as international aid workers offered a degree of safety for the senior Serbian military personnel. NATO would be unlikely to bomb a location housing international civilians. But did NATO even know we were staying here?

We were assigned rooms on the seventh and eighth floors, likely out of the ten floors the hotel had in total. After checking in, we convened in a meeting room, where we were assured that the situation was under control and that we'd only be staying for one night. It seemed possible this arrangement had been pre-negotiated as part of ensuring our safe passage to Belgrade. Meanwhile, NATO's aerial bombing campaign was intensifying, targeting infrastructure to dismantle Serbian authority and command structures in Kosovo. For us, it was now a waiting game, and we could only hope that NATO was aware of our presence. Without such knowledge, the hotel, housing high-ranking Serbian officials, would be a justifiable target.

As night fell, we remained in our rooms, restricted to communicating via handheld radios strictly for safety checks and instructions. We were explicitly warned to stay away from the windows, as the bombings were concentrated around nearby ministerial and government buildings, including the police headquarters a legitimate target. Uncertain of NATO's awareness of our situation, we devised a plan to use the satellite phone to relay messages to our headquarters in Belgrade.

To secure a stronger signal, a colleague and I climbed to the top floor, where there was access to the roof. Rather than risk standing in the open due to the threat of aerial bombings and the danger of being seen in the light, we stayed in the stairwell near a window. I extended my hand through the opening, holding the flat aerial – which resembled a small solar panel – and rotated it to catch the satellite signal as it passed. My colleague sent the messages while I maintained the signal. The messages conveyed that we were safe and confirmed our location. We hoped this information would also reach NATO, ensuring the hotel was spared as a target.

As we returned to our rooms, a massive explosion shook the building. Despite the instructions not to look out of the windows, my colleague and I couldn't resist glancing through a corridor window. The building next to ours had been struck, the attack appearing precision-guided. In the darkness, the explosion resembled a lightning strike, its silver flashes illuminating the night. The building collapsed inward, imploding with chilling efficiency. It was the police headquarters!

We quickly retreated to the safety of our rooms. The bombings continued sporadically, interspersed with bursts of gunfire. The absence of sirens added an eerie edge to the chaos. By around 11 p.m., the city fell silent. Whether it was exhaustion or the calming absence of noise, I managed to fall asleep, my door double-locked and a wedge secured beneath it to prevent entry in case the lock failed.

In the morning, breakfast was served in a conference room on the sixth floor, exclusively arranged for us to avoid the bustling activity downstairs. The ground floor remained a hub of arrivals and departures, with men in military uniforms adorned with medals and insignia indicating their ranks.

Following breakfast, a briefing was held. Most of the staff were urging for an immediate evacuation, citing the escalating dangers after the night's bombing. The head of the sub-delegation explained that she was awaiting clearance from the Ministry of Interior Affairs to coordinate our departure from the hotel. Confusion arose over the decision to head toward Belgrade instead of Thessaloniki in Greece, which seemed safer. The directive to travel to Belgrade had come from the Head of Delegation. Yet, there was an undercurrent of disagreement; our head of sub-delegation, with her extensive local knowledge and strong relationships in Kosovo, appeared hesitant but obliged to follow orders. Could she have made a different decision if not bound by the chain of command?

After the briefing, we were instructed to check out and gather in the lobby. Two civilian officials in plain clothes engaged in discussion with senior team members and our Serbian field officer. Soon, we were ushered into our vehicles. The officials, now donning black leather jackets and sunglasses—likely intelligence agents linked to the Ministry of Interior Affairs   would escort us to the provincial border with Serbia in a light blue Yugo Zastava.

For safety, I was assigned to sit in the back seat, sandwiched between two colleagues. As a British passport holder, my nationality posed a higher risk due to the UK's involvement in the aerial bombing. The rest of the team, primarily from Switzerland and other non-bombing NATO countries, faced comparatively less hostility. I was instructed to present only my Red Cross identity card, which resembled a passport, and not my actual passport unless explicitly required.

We travelled in single file at a speed dictated by the lead vehicle. The civilian population, gripped by mobilisation efforts and conscription, viewed all foreigners not allied with Serbia as adversaries. Some regions, fraught with high emotions and tension, were deemed unsafe, necessitating a circuitous route.

In a remote area near a river, it was considered safe to pause for a break and a light snack. Bianca, our Serbian field officer, struck up a conversation with two young men in dark green army fatigues. Conscripts, as it turned out, they had been fishing and were on their way home. Their exchange appeared relaxed and jovial. Several colleagues who spoke Serbian joined the conversation, broadening the dialogue.

While some of us returned to our vehicles, the soldiers approached, not threateningly, but out of curiosity. Nervously attempting English greetings, they asked about our nationalities. When my turn came, I claimed to be Swiss French and spoke a few words in French, which they didn't understand. It was only after we resumed our journey that I learned the soldiers spoke German. My choice to claim Swiss French, rather than Swiss German, had been fortunate - any suspicion of British identity could have led to dire consequences.

We bid the soldiers goodbye and continued on. In towns we passed, the atmosphere grew hostile. Crowds gathered at fuel stations and shops, their anger and grief over NATO bombings palpable. We avoided stopping except at checkpoints, where the risk was unavoidable. At one point, onlookers - some in fatigues - began approaching, their movements slow and deliberate – almost zombie like - making throat-slitting gestures. Avoiding eye contact, I focused on remaining calm. Sensing the growing danger, our escort swiftly diverted us from the area.

Eventually, we arrived at a checkpoint manned by officials in camouflage uniforms and burgundy berets. They requested our documents, and as instructed, I presented only my Red Cross identity card. Bianca, our Serbian field officer, stepped out to engage with the guards. A heated exchange ensued, culminating in one of the guards slapping Bianca across the face. Despite this, he returned our documents and allowed us to proceed.

With our documents returned, we pressed on, relieved to be nearing the border crossing into Serbia. From there, we expected a more straightforward journey to Belgrade. Once we were safely away, we learned the reason for the guard's hostility. He had recently lost a family member in the bombings and accused Bianca of being a traitor.

At the border, our escort departed, leaving us to continue unaccompanied. By now, it was late afternoon. We carefully avoided towns known to harbour paramilitary forces or fervent nationalism. Meanwhile, NATO's air campaign had expanded, targeting Belgrade and other Serbian cities with military strongholds and airfields. The bombings had shifted the balance of power, with NATO achieving air superiority by striking aircraft that hadn't been hidden and rendering runways unusable.

Arriving at the Red Cross Headquarters in Belgrade was a relief. The welcome team had arranged accommodation at a local hotel. First, we attended a briefing with the Head of Delegation, who provided a situation update. We were assured there was no immediate threat to our safety. That night, we could rest, have a proper meal, and regroup at the office in the morning.

That evening, BBC World aired footage of the bombing, including scenes from Belgrade's outskirts. Knowing our families were likely watching the same images was unsettling. Unbeknown to us, the Health and Welfare team in Geneva had already contacted our designated next of kin, reassuring them of our safety.

For most of my colleagues, this marked the end of their deployment. Arrangements were being made for their return to Geneva for debriefings before heading home. My mission, however, had just begun. The next day, I departed by vehicle to my next duty station in Podgorica, Montenegro.

The British Red Cross expressed concern about my redeployment to a Serbian territory, considering my nationality. Although Montenegro was not actively involved in the war, its Slavic population maintained strong ties to Serbia. I remained there for two months until my replacement, a health delegate from New Zealand, arrived. From there, I was redeployed to the Former Yugoslav Republic of Macedonia, where I would spend the remainder of my assignment. To get to Macedonia I would have to travel by road through Croatia. I stayed in Dubrovnik for a few days rest witnessing the rebuilding of this ancient and magnificent terracotta coloured roofs and the wall surrounding the town that bore the brunt of the earlier war between Croatia and Serbia. Paintings and photographs of the destruction were on display at the museum.

In Macedonia, my work focused on supporting refugees arriving from Kosovo. Many crossed borders or trekked over mountains, seeking safety in villages before reaching one of the many refugee camps set up by international organisations such as UNHCR, the Turkish military, and various governments, including the UAE.

This was a European war with a unique distinction: near-instantaneous media coverage. For the first time, the conflict was being live-streamed to the world. Unlike past conflicts, it garnered significant global attention and unprecedented funding from governments. The influx of resources spurred the establishment of over 300 non-governmental organisations. Some seemed hastily assembled, offering minimal services under makeshift banners.

Countries began accepting quotas of refugees, with embassies conducting assessments to determine who would receive protection visas. The generosity exceeded demand, a stark contrast to responses in less developed, non-Western conflicts. Reports emerged of refugees from other nations, including Iraq, attempting to blend in for a chance at resettlement.

My role as country health coordinator included supporting protection teams and ensuring equitable access to healthcare. Discrimination in healthcare was rampant. Ethnic Albanians faced significant barriers to employment as medical staff in

Macedonian Serb-run facilities, and hospitals often showed bias in treatment. Despite the Hippocratic Oath, impartiality wasn't always upheld.

One of the biggest tasks for the Red Cross was documenting missing persons, registering refugees and gathering reports of abuse, including torture. Many refugees, both men and women had undergone abuse, including rape and torture.

Initially stationed in Tetovo, a predominantly Macedonian Albanian city near the Kosovo border, together with the protection team, I oversaw operations in surrounding villages. Each village was distinctly ethnic, marked by an Orthodox church or a towering mosque. Refugees often arrived through treacherous forest and mountain paths, guided by Macedonian Albanian scouts to safe villages for registration before reaching camps. Most of our local team were Kosovo or Macedonian Albanian whilst most of our staff in the Headquarters in the capital Skopje were Macedonian Serbs.

The Red Cross was usually the first to learn of incoming refugee groups, and the media often followed our leads. On one occasion, refugees mistakenly arrived in a Macedonian Serb town early in the morning. Our team rushed to the site, followed by CNN. The refugees had gathered in the church grounds, where local humanitarian organisations had set up a relief centre.

The presence of Kosovo Liberation Army (KLA) fighters among refugees wearing civilian clothing posed ethical dilemmas. Some international organisations offered treatment, tacitly aligning with one side of the conflict. For the Red Cross, neutrality was paramount. Our priority was protecting civilians. Suspected KLA fighters risked arrest by Macedonian police, who sympathised with Serbia. Our task was to count arrivals and ensure their safe transfer to camps for processing and before the arrival of the Macedonian police.

Mothers and children arrived carrying their possessions, often limited to what they could wear. To lighten their load, children wore multiple layers of clothing, which caused heat distress during the day. We distributed nutritional biscuits, knowing they had endured days of harsh mountain travel and had probably eaten very little during their journey. Some were severely dehydrated and intravenous fluid was set up within the hall.

Our days were consumed by visits to highland villages and border crossings. Refugees often abandoned their vehicles on the Kosovo side before crossing on foot. The Serbian border guards scrutinised young men for any association with the KLA, often detaining them.

As NATO's campaign progressed, the Serb border guards abandoned their posts, and Serbian flags were replaced by those of NATO countries. Each nation rotated control: the USA, Poland, Germany, and France. At one post, a Greek flag caused controversy among Macedonians, highlighting the region's deep-rooted tensions.

The war was drawing to a close. Gradually, Serbian forces were withdrawing from Kosovo, but their departure was far from peaceful. Reports indicated they were leaving behind booby traps, landmines, and other devices to make life perilous for anyone remaining or attempting to return. Even with the conflict ending, Kosovo was far from safe.

As the influx of refugees slowed, I was redeployed to Skopje. From there, I could operate at a national level, representing the Red Cross in meetings with UN agencies and other key stakeholders supporting the refugee crisis. Plans were already underway to assist refugees in returning to their towns and villages, many of which lay in ruins. These communities faced not only structural damage—broken sewage systems, fallen power lines, and crumbling walls—but also the deadly remnants of war, including unexploded ordnance (UXO), booby traps, and landmines. Refugees would be provided with rations of building supplies, sanitation kits, hygiene essentials, and kitchen sets to begin rebuilding their lives.

Despite these efforts, there were concerns about how controlled the return process could be. Agencies debated whether it would be possible to secure the areas before refugees flooded back to reclaim their homes - or, in some cases, the property of others. Safety was a major topic in sector meetings, as the urgency to prevent casualties from the hidden dangers of war grew. We knew this as the 'remnants of war'.

On 9 June 1999, the signing of a technical agreement officially ended the war.

The push for refugees to return began almost immediately, despite warnings and restrictions. Many feared losing their land to others, including Albanians from Albania, and rushed back to stake their claims. Overlooked in the frenzy were Kosovo's many ethnic minorities, including the Roma, Ashkali, and Turkish communities. Among these, the Roma were particularly vulnerable, regarded as traitors by both Serbian and Kosovar Albanian populations. Camps in Macedonia catered specifically to the Roma, who were well-organised, even forming their own political party to advocate for their needs.

As predicted, refugees began returning in large numbers, despite efforts by UNHCR and others to delay the process and secure the borders. Reports of injuries and fatalities soon emerged - landmines, unexploded ordnance, electrocution from fallen power lines, and debris claimed more casualties than the war itself. Relief teams responded by running landmine awareness campaigns, often using theatre to educate and entertain children in the camps.

On one occasion, I was tasked with surveying a potential return route with my field officer. The road seemed promising but was fraught with hazards. Every piece of debris was a potential booby trap. Along the way, we encountered anti-tank mines. Although our vehicle might withstand a standard landmine, these mines could easily destroy it. We turned back and reported our findings to the Head of Delegation, deeming the route unsafe for refugee return.

Once the technical agreement was signed, refugees could no longer be held back. Many returned at great personal risk, determined to reclaim their land. The scale of injuries and deaths underscored the urgency of landmine clearance efforts. On a trip back to Pristina, I drove through Tetovo and crossed the border, passing the fields where refugees had abandoned their vehicles during their flight. Hundreds of cars, trucks, and tractors were piled up, the area now cordoned off due to the potential for booby traps. I visited the area where our accommodation was when I arrived in Pristina in March. Our bungalow and neighbouring house which housed our team had been burned down.

Farmers were desperate to resume planting and prepare for the next season, but landmines scattered across their fields made this impossible. On one farm, we saw several dead cows that had triggered landmines. Whether these deaths were accidental or a deliberate attempt to clear the land was unclear. Landmine clearance teams were arriving en masse, racing against time to save lives as locals attempted to restart their shattered lives.

This deployment was among the most fulfilling of my career, but also the most terrifying - more so than my time in Afghanistan. Perhaps it was because this was Europe, where the veneer of modern civilisation could not mask a history of brutality. The ferocity and devastation of the First and Second World Wars, the Empire wars, and now this conflict served as stark reminders of just how violent humanity can be when provoked.

A slap, often delivered in anger or frustration, can leave a mark far deeper than the bruise it creates. As we departed Kosovo, I couldn't help but reflect on the slap our female field officer had endured. It wasn't just a physical act but a raw, unfiltered expression of pent-up anger, born out of frustration and loss. Though uncalculated, it left an indelible impression, one that lingered far longer than the moment itself.

Two more slaps stand out vividly in my memory, both from childhood. Growing up, slaps - delivered by a parent or teacher - were not uncommon, often seen as a necessary correction for minor misdemeanours. At school, corporal punishment was routine, meted out with a slipper or cane. While I was fortunate never to receive the cane or slipper, I understood the separation between punishment and love.

Punishment at the hands of someone who loves you feels different - though no less impactful.

At home, there were two slaps that still sting, not on the skin but in the memory. The first occurred when I was seven. My primary school encouraged children to open savings accounts. Each week, my parents gave my brother and me a shilling to deposit. By the end of term, we could withdraw our savings or continue saving. One term, I was tasked with collecting both my brother's savings and my own. My father's metal tobacco tins seemed the perfect container for the coins.

On my way home, I passed a pet shop near the bus garage, its window display teeming with animals - puppies, kittens, fish, and small creatures like guinea pigs. My mother often spoke fondly of a guinea pig she'd owned as a child, so well-trained it would only pee when taken out of her pocket. On impulse, I decided to use some of my savings to buy her a guinea pig. At seven, I didn't consider practicalities like a cage or food. I was certain she would be delighted.

With the guinea pig in a box and the tin of coins rattling in my pocket, I continued home. The sound drew the attention of two secondary school boys, who stopped me and asked to see the tin. Innocently, I opened it, not suspecting any ill intent. They snatched the money and ran.

An elderly man across the road, witnessing the incident, waved his walking stick at the thieves and came to my aid. He turned out to be a former mayor of the town and kindly escorted me home, explaining to my parents what had happened. But after he left, my mother slapped me across the face. It wasn't punishment, not really - more a reaction born of frustration and anger. In her eyes, perhaps I had been careless, too trusting. But to me, it felt like betrayal. I had already been punished by the thieves, and now I was being punished by the one I loved most, at a time when I needed comfort. My sister took the guinea pig back to the pet shop that same day.

The second slap wasn't on my face and wasn't delivered in the heat of emotion. It was calculated, deliberate - a punishment. I don't recall what I did to provoke it, but whatever it was gave my father the justification to hit me across the back of my legs with a hard plastic spade. For a week, I wasn't allowed to wear shorts or participate in physical education because of the raised red welts and bruises it left behind.

These moments linger in my mind, not because of the physical pain but because of what they represented. A slap can be a simple act, yet it carries weight far beyond the sting it leaves on the skin. It can fracture trust, blur the line between love and anger, and leave a mark that never fully fades.

Savuti – 'The Journey'

Graham and I meticulously planned our journey to Southern Africa. We had both previously visited Kenya and Zimbabwe. After my experiences in Kenya, the allure of East Africa had waned although I would later hold a Regional Health Coordinator for the International Red Cross based in Nairobi. The anticipation I once held for the Maasai Mara and the Serengeti had faded, their magic now confined to the pages of travel brochures and the lens of National Geographic documentaries. Although I appreciated their beauty, they had become crowded, almost too accessible. If I were to revisit East Africa, it would only be to experience the Ngorongoro Crater in Tanzania, where one is almost guaranteed to see the 'Big Five,' and perhaps to wander the spice-scented lanes of Zanzibar.

Nowadays, I prefer to explore closer to home, travelling within Australia - a land vast and diverse enough to feel like an entire world in one continent. Travelling locally also spares me the ordeal of long-haul flights.

My previous venture to Zimbabwe had exceeded all expectations, more than compensating for my underwhelming experience in Kenya. Zimbabwe offered a sense of authenticity that was missing elsewhere. The wildlife encounters felt raw and unscripted, as though the animals were still wary of humans. Patience was required, and the rewards of spotting them were richer for it. Unlike the busy convoys of safari jeeps in Kenya, where crowds jostled to glimpse a pride of lions as if they were exhibits, Zimbabwe felt untamed.

This time, however, the Zimbabwe I knew was beginning to unravel. The country was on the brink of crisis. Political unrest was brewing, and white farmers were having their land seized by supporters of President Robert Mugabe. The economy, once anchored by robust agricultural exports and tourism, was in free fall. The farms that had once fed much of Africa lay neglected, and tourism—the lifeblood of conservation efforts - was drying up. What had been a paradise for wildlife and a haven for travellers was rapidly deteriorating, not from natural disasters or climate change, but from within.

On this trip, our visit to Zimbabwe would be brief. We planned to see Victoria Falls and make a return trip to Imbabala, where I hoped Graham would meet owners Gavin and Shay, who had hosted me so warmly on my previous visit. This leg of the journey would come towards the end of our itinerary. We would cross into Zimbabwe via the Chobe region of Botswana, passing through the Kasane border at Kazungula, and then drive our hired vehicle to Imbabala.

This time, the journey was not just about visiting familiar places; it was about exploring new frontiers - Savuti among them.

The trip was six months in the making – developing our itinerary, booking flights, accommodation including camping spots, vehicle hire that would be able to manage the terrain, and wildlife permits. Due to some biosecurity measures, there were strict controls entering certain countries to protect against diseases that could easily spread via soil, fruit, and food. We also needed to ensure our required vaccinations were up to date, including Yellow Fever, with a mandatory Yellow Fever certificate required at customs.

Our journey began with a flight from Riyadh, Saudi Arabia to Johannesburg, followed by a connection to Cape Town, South Africa. In Cape Town, we stayed a few days in modest accommodation, giving us the opportunity to explore the city, ascend the iconic flat-topped Table Mountain via a walking trail, and travel to the Cape of Good Hope and Cape Point. These two 'Capes' mark the dramatic meeting point of the warm currents of the Indian Ocean with the cooler waters of the Atlantic. As our trip through Namibia and Botswana would be mostly camping at designated campsites and self-catering – we stocked up on provisions and cooking utensils as these would be easy to buy at the local markets, contributing to the local economy. At the end of our journey, we would be able to sell the enamel pots and pans.

On Table Mountain, we encountered the ubiquitous dassie, or rock hyrax. Despite their resemblance to large, earless rabbits with guinea pig-like faces, these creatures are not rodents. Remarkably, their closest living relatives are the land elephant and the manatee (sea cow), all of which share a common ancestor.

As we descended towards Cape Point, the flora gradually transformed into a striking landscape of shrubs and heathland. In the distance, several reddish-coloured steenbok antelopes grazed gracefully, adding a touch of life to the rugged terrain. I had hoped to catch a glimpse of an eland, the world's largest antelope, known to inhabit this area.

225

Weighing up to nearly 1,000 kilograms, the eland is an awe-inspiring creature, but it remained elusive on this occasion.

At the water's edge, the waves crashed against rocks coated in rust-coloured lichen, forming a frothing sea foam that surrounded the rock. You could pick up the foam which was formed by the churning sea, was a blend of particles -fats, algae, fish scales, and fragments of coral. With the wind and rain beginning to descend, the scene took on an almost Antarctic quality, the tempestuous weather lending an eerie beauty to the setting.

As we made our way back towards the visitor centre and restaurant, the weather shifted dramatically. High winds howled, and rain lashed the landscape, prompting most visitors to seek shelter or retreat entirely.

The storm unleashed its fury with flying debris and drenching rain, yet it also revealed the raw, untamed beauty of this unique place. Sheltering in rock crevices, we marvelled at the power of nature while others, including a group of tourists who appeared Asian, watched from the safety of their bus. They must have thought us two 'crazy Europeans' for braving the tempest.

As quickly as it had arrived, the storm subsided, giving way to cool breezes and the beginnings of a stunning sunset. With the sky painted in soft hues, we began our journey back to Cape Town, the experience etched into our memories as a testament to the Cape's ever-changing beauty.

The next day, we took a night coach from Cape Town, South Africa, to Windhoek, the capital of Namibia. Arriving early morning in Windhoek, we picked up our hired 4WD vehicle and after a one stay discovering the city we headed towards the quaint township of Swakopmund. We had room in our vehicle for a couple of British pack-backers who joined us paying some of the fuel costs for the trip. The German-built motorways, with their unlimited speed limits, seemed oddly out of place in the expansive African landscape. Travelling with minimal traffic was a breeze, and it felt liberating.

We stayed in Swakopmund for a few nights to explore the area and would make a trip to Walvis Bay, part of the Skeleton Coast. Swakopmund appeared more German than Germany itself, with its strong Bavarian traditions, cuisine, and residents dressed in Lederhosen and Dirndl. The streets came alive with dancing, and the oversized jugs and mugs of beer far exceeded anything I'd ever seen back home.

It was a quaint town, characterised by thatched-roof houses, well-tended gardens with vibrant landscaping, and streets lined with souvenir shops, cosy cafes, and inviting restaurants. From here, we drove to Walvis Bay, renowned for its large seal population. As we arrived, we were greeted by the pungent smell of thousands of Cape fur seals on the beach. The air was heavy with the odours of decaying afterbirth, excrement and the lifeless bodies of pups that hadn't survived their first days or had been abandoned by their mothers due to some defect.

Black-backed jackals weaved through the chaotic scene, darting among the seals and scavenging pieces of dead pups or afterbirth. Overhead, seagulls and other opportunistic carrion-eating birds added their cries to the cacophony of grunts and calls from the seals. Behind this bustling scene, the sea stretched out endlessly. In the surf breaks, bottlenose dolphins could be seen leaping gracefully. Walvis Bay was also famous for its pelicans and flamingos, and on rare occasions, the sighting of an elusive brown hyena added an extra layer of intrigue.

We then journeyed to Sossusvlei in the heart of the Namib Desert, a landscape dominated by towering red sand dunes with razor-sharp edges. These dunes could be climbed to reach breathtaking summits, offering panoramic views of the surrounding salt pans and unforgettable sunrises and sunsets. This region is also home to the majestic oryx antelope, a symbol of resilience in this arid environment. One of the rolls of film I lost contained photos of this striking creature. To capture the perfect shot, I had crawled along the ground, getting as close as possible. I believe I managed to take some magnificent photographs, as I had with several other animals. After finishing the film, I carefully placed it back into its plastic container. However, I suspect it was lost during my descent, likely sliding away as I navigated down one of the towering dunes.

The campground in the open desert provided a very different experience. I chose to sleep outside under the stars, waking up early to join a group of people gathered to witness the sunrise spilling over the dunes from the east. Before leaving, we searched for a Quiver tree – a tree named after the bushmen who used the quiver shaped leaves from the tree that looked upside down for their hunting arrows. The customary photograph which was to set up the tripod, set up the time and run to the tree in time took a few practices!

Our next journey led us towards Etosha National Park, the main reason I had wanted to visit Namibia. We bid farewell to the couple who had accompanied us and started heading northeast. Along the way, we stopped at the Okonjima

Nature Reserve, which ran a rehabilitation program for orphaned and injured cheetahs and leopards. Leopards often came into conflict with farmers as livestock was easy prey, far easier than chasing antelopes or other wild animals. To protect their stock, farmers would shoot predators. However, killing a dominant or 'king' leopard only created a vacuum for another to take its place, perpetuating the cycle of killing.

A program had been developed to deter leopards from acquiring a taste for livestock meat. Small electric nodes were placed under pieces of livestock meat, delivering a mild electric shock to any leopard attempting to eat it. Over time, this conditioning instilled an aversion to livestock, encouraging the leopards to hunt their natural prey instead. This initiative was a win-win situation for both farmers and leopards. Injured leopards or orphaned cubs, whose mothers had been shot, were brought to the reserve for rehabilitation in a natural setting devoid of livestock, allowing them to hone their hunting skills before being reintroduced into the wild.

The program also extended to cheetahs. Despite being the fastest land mammals, cheetahs' bursts of speed were short-lived, leaving them vulnerable in the open savannah compared to the more stealthy leopards who could climb trees. At the reserve, we had the unique opportunity to sit in a hide below a rocky outcrop, observing the program in action. This vantage point offered unprecedented views and photographic opportunities of a magnificent male 'king' leopard as well as a female leopard.

Back at the reserve camp, we learned more about the program. During lunch, a young female zoologist and researcher who managed the program called out to two adult cheetahs residing on the reserve. These cheetahs, injured as cubs, could not be rehabilitated for safe release into the wild due to their close bond with humans. The moment was extraordinary. Responding to her call, two cheetahs appeared out of nowhere, racing towards us like lightning. They purred like domestic cats and licked extended hands, their tongues rough to the touch. Observing these cheetahs up close revealed the intricate details of their markings, the tear-shaped streaks above their eyes, their elongated legs, and the posture that made them perfectly engineered for speed.

Our next stop was my highlight in Namibia – Etosha National Park. I had seen countless photos and coffee table books showcasing the magnificent wildlife inhabiting this vast park in the northeast of Namibia, near the Angola border. We stayed at an old German fort, Namutoni Camp, with its whitewashed walls and large wooden entrance doors. The fort evoked an image of French legionnaires but was originally built as a control post during the mad cow disease epidemic in 1897 and later reinforced by German colonial troops, the Schutztruppe, in the early 1900s. Subsequently, it served as a South African army base and is now a haven for tourists.

From the walls and lookouts of the fort, wildlife could be observed at a nearby waterhole, where animals took turns to drink, yielding to larger ones as they approached. It was here that I had one of my rare encounters with a black rhinoceros. We spent the next three nights exploring the park, following its well-mapped trails. Parking our vehicle close to, but hidden from, a waterhole provided a remarkable opportunity to witness wildlife behaving naturally, undisturbed by humans.

The sparse vegetation and flat, dusty terrain made for unique viewing. Animals were either out in the open or sheltering under the shade of a solitary acacia tree. Everything seemed larger here. It was also first encounters of seeing cheetahs and ostriches out in the open and easy to spot without the dense bush and long grass that usually provides cover. The giraffes appeared taller, and the elephants were enormous, their grey colouring stark against the dusty landscape. Unlike their counterparts in Tsavo, Kenya, and Hwange National Park, Zimbabwe, which were tinted red by the clay soil, these elephants stood like statues, majestic and imposing. One old bull elephant, the largest I had ever seen, approached cautiously but without threat. With only one very long tusk, he exuded a quiet dignity.

The waterholes were a magnet for wildlife, and a clear hierarchy was evident. Wildebeest and hartebeest lower on the social ladder, were displaced by zebra, which arrived in single file and lined up to drink in unison – a captivating sight for photography. Impala, with their striking horns, and kudu joined the zebras, creating a tableau of grace and symmetry. When giraffes arrived, others deferred, watching as they spread their long legs and bent their elegant necks to drink, always alert to potential danger. A sudden bolt by a zebra or antelope would signal the presence of a predator, triggering a mass exodus to confuse the threat.

Through binoculars, we spotted a lioness hiding behind a rock, another positioned across the waterhole. The scene was a carefully orchestrated ambush, with the lion on the far side poised to drive the panicked animals towards the waiting lioness. The tension was palpable.

But the spectacle was interrupted. On the horizon, a herd of elephants appeared, their sheer presence commanding the waterhole. They marched in, likely fatigued from traversing the sparse landscape in search of food. The younger elephants and calves, brimming with excitement, plunged into the water to play, while the adults drank deeply and rolled in the grey dirt before cooling off in the water. The lions retreated, as did most other animals, save for the giraffes, which turned their focus to the acacia trees. Watching the giraffes' dexterous tongues navigate between the thorns to pluck nutrient-rich leaves was a fascinating display of adaptation.

Etosha was everything I imagined and even more. A place I hope to one day return.

The next leg of our journey was the one I had been most anticipating and excited about: Botswana, and more specifically, Savuti!

We drove back to Windhoek, returned our hired 4WD, and flew to Gaborone, Botswana. There, we met with the travel agent who had helped arrange our permits, including access to the Savuti camping ground, which allowed only eight pitched tents. She also facilitated the pick-up of our 4WD vehicle. Botswana, an inland country, was lush with rivers, lakes, and sprawling deltas. It was by far the most stable of the Southern African nations, boasting a robust economy and low unemployment. The sense of pride and collectivism among the people was palpable, creating a relaxed and welcoming atmosphere. Perhaps because we were two male Westerners, we were greeted with many warm smiles from the Botswana ladies!

Meeting our travel agent Gladys felt like reuniting with an old friend. Many women from Botswana adopted old fashioned English names as well as their tribal name – names such as Vera, Agnes, Rose, Iris, Daisy were common and many names associated with as flower. After weeks of communication before our arrival, we had both formed vivid impressions of what she might look like—and we were spot on. Her casual and gentle manner was immediately disarming, making her someone you simply couldn't upset. She had an innate ability to deflect tension with ease. Our vehicle, however, wasn't quite what we had expected. It was noticeably older than the newer model we had used in Namibia, seemingly from a lesser-known car hire company. Despite its appearance, she assured us it was reliable and fully equipped for our journey. To be safe, we carried an extra jerry can so that we can have addition fuel when journeying through the flat and desert like terrain to Savuti.

If you have ever watched the television series, The No:1 Ladies 'Detective Agency' set in Gabarone, which I watched many years later , it would be pretty close to charms of the city and the charms of the people we met.

Botswana is a wildlife haven, offering not just an abundance of animals but also a variety of terrains that provide a complete wildlife adventure. From the lush, flooded grasslands and lagoons of the Okavango Delta to the Moremi Game Reserve, Chobe National Park, and of course, Savuti, it is a paradise for nature lovers.

At the Okavango Delta, we hired dugout canoes to gently navigate the meandering lagoons and dense forests. This brought us thrillingly close to hippos, crocodiles, and elephants. On dry land, we encountered lions, hyenas,

233

antelopes, buffalo, warthogs, and rhinos. Driving through the region's diverse terrains was an adventure in itself, but it came with challenges.

On one occasion, we misjudged our fuel reserves, only to discover that the fuel gauge was faulty. According to the fuel gauge, we had been running on empty for quite a while but it didn't seem to make sense based on our estimation of mileage covered and having a full tank when we left. We decided not drive too far out from civilisation in case we were actually close to being out of fuel. Luckily, we were near some local homes, but there were no fuel stations in sight. A kind local provided us with a piece of tubing to siphon fuel from their pickup truck into our tank. After some inevitable gagging and a lung full of fumes (a role assigned to Graham imagining this might be something he did in his wasted youth), it seemed we still had quite a bit a fuel in the tank – almost 50 litres.

This wasn't the first time a hired vehicle would let us down in a potentially precarious situation. On another occasions during a trip to Mozambique with my partner, Ian, our rented 4WD lost power on a sandy road cutting through maize fields as we headed towards a safari camp in Limpopo National Park, near its connection to South Africa's Kruger National Park. Just a few kilometres from the camp, the car's electrics failed completely. Stranded and uncertain of how far we were, we waved down another 4WD that happened to be travelling in the same direction.

The tourists inside kindly offered Ian a lift to the camp to seek help, leaving me with the vehicle. Alone, surrounded by curious locals emerging from the maize fields, I had to maintain a calm and assured demeanour. Mozambique has a history of kidnappings, especially in the north, but I made it clear that all was under control despite not speaking Portuguese and appearing somewhat vulnerable.

Relief came in the form of Ian, smiling broadly sitting atop a tractor heading my way. We arrived safely at the camp just before nightfall, where our vehicle was towed back. Repairs required spare parts, which the hire company arranged to deliver the following day.

The camp itself was idyllic, with wooden cabins, each featuring its own deck and hammock, set on a deserted beach. The stunning location felt all the more rewarding after the day's trials. It was a reminder that journeys that don't go as planned often turn out to be the most memorable.

One of the many highlights journeying through Botswana was visiting the Moremi Game Reserve, which held a special place in Graham's heart. He proclaimed it his favourite spot and vowed to return every ten years—if not with me, then with his future family. This magical place, called 'Third Bridge,' was an open campsite you accessed by crossing a wooden bridge. Solidly built with gum tree poles, the bridge dipped into shallow water before rising again to the entrance of the campsite. It was almost like crossing a moat into a castle through a lowered drawbridge.

The campsite's open design meant there were no fences separating us from the surrounding nature reserve. This added an exhilarating edge, as you could easily cross paths with lions or hyenas. True to form, the next morning as we set out on a safari drive, we found two lionesses lazily stretched out on the bridge, basking in the warm morning sun. We had no choice but to wait at their majesty's pleasure—a wait that proved worthwhile. Out of the bushes emerged two lion cubs, joining their mother and aunt. The cubs were greeted with affectionate licks and playful antics. Once they decided it was time, the lions casually made their way to the shade, crossing the bridge and disappearing into the forest. Watching this familial moment unfold in such a raw, natural setting was nothing short of magical.

Our next stop would be the climax of our trip and would hold a special place in my heart. It was a four-to-six-hour drive through terrain that changed and eventually become sandy and soft. Our experience driving in the deserts of Saudi Arabia prepared us well as we would adjust the tyre pressures accordingly and release the air form the tyres once we hit the soft sand. This would mean getting out of the vehicle in an area known to be inhabited by lions and leopards and we were easy prey. We managed this feat by keeping a look out and our backs as close to the vehicle while deflating the tyres and like any accomplished task there was always the aftermath feeling of satisfaction.

The journey was not an easy one. Reaching Savuti required navigating rough terrain, marshland and soft sand. It was taking us longer than we expected. It was time before GPS had been invented, so we trusted our map reading abilities.

The sun was beginning to set. We knew we were getting close as rocky escarpments appeared from the side of the road giving way to long grass, trees, bushes and riverbeds.

Savuti – 'The Arrival'

The sky was inky black as we approached the campsite, guided only by the faint signage we had been following for kilometres. Despite the proximity, there were no lights to be seen. The only visible structures were concrete blocks that, on closer inspection, appeared to be the remains of a toilet block and washrooms. Cracks and broken slabs littered the floor, the place bearing an air of abandonment. According to the map and signs, this was supposed to be the campsite - but it felt eerily deserted.

With no daylight left, the beam of our car's headlights was the only thing piercing the darkness. Beyond their reach, everything faded into an all-consuming blackness. As we strained to decipher our surroundings, a faint light appeared in the distance. It flickered, moving rhythmically up and down. Slowly, it became apparent there was a figure behind it, the light dancing like a beacon against the night.

We crept forward, the car's engine a low hum against the stillness, following the light as it led us along the path. When we drew closer, we realised the figure was holding a torch, waving us toward the relocated camp. A guard greeted us, confirming the recent misfortune: a herd of elephants, desperate for water, had raided the original campsite, destroying the facilities in the process. The site had since been moved to a safer spot nearby.

The check-in process was straightforward. Without leaving our vehicle, we presented our reservation and wildlife permits issued by the Botswana Tourism and Wildlife Parks Department. The guard then guided us to our camping spot, one of only eight in the area. Some were occupied by motorhomes and campervans, while others resembled our setup - a sturdy 4WD with a tent.

In the darkness, the camp was alive with muted voices and the occasional glow from lanterns or headlamps. Most campers were settling in for the night, their fires casting flickering shadows. Graham and I, however, were famished. Snacks had sustained us during the long drive, but they were no substitute for a proper meal. While Graham, familiar with his tent, set about assembling it, I focused on starting a small fire. A warm brew of tea and a simple meal were our immediate priorities.

From the snippets of conversation drifting through the night, it was clear most of our fellow campers were South Africans. They were seasoned safari-goers, accustomed to crossing the border into Botswana for adventures like this. One family stood out - parents trying to wrangle their mischievous children. The father's firm warning, delivered in an unmistakable Afrikaans accent, reached us: "If you don't stop misbehaving, I'll smack you on the *bee-hind!*" Graham and I couldn't help but chuckle, adopting the elongated vowels and repeating the phrase in jest for the rest of the trip.

Exhausted, dusty, and irritable from the long journey, tensions between us simmered. Graham was uncharacteristically terse, likely due to the anxiety of navigating unfamiliar terrain as night fell. I had probably pushed him too far with my nagging during the drive, although we had taken turns behind the wheel. His patience, while generally unwavering with me, had its limits—especially under pressure.

The journey reminded us of one of our earlier safaris when we experimented with riding on the roof of the car, climbing up through the rear passenger window rather than stepping outside. It was a practical lesson in wildlife perception: animals seemed to ignore vehicles and horseback riders, viewing them as part of a benign whole. The moment a human form was revealed, however, reactions shifted - they would flee, warn, or charge.

This behaviour was never more apparent than during a horseback safari in Victoria Falls National Park, where our mounts allowed us to approach zebras, buffalo, and even rhinoceroses without provoking alarm. For the animals, a fellow herbivore posed no immediate threat, a stark contrast to how they viewed the upright figure of a human.

Graham and I set about our respective tasks as though we had done this countless times before; it felt like second nature. I began collecting small pieces of dry kindling, twigs, and branches scattered along the edge of the campsite, while Graham focused on pitching the tent. Immersed in the rhythm of the work, I momentarily forgot we were deep in the wild - a domain teeming with opportunistic scavengers. Human presence might often deter predators, but it wasn't a guarantee of safety.

As I leaned forward to pick up a branch, my eyes suddenly locked with a pair of yellow, glinting ones peering from the underbrush. A spotted hyena. For an instant, we both froze, startled. The tension was palpable, the silence heavy. I stood about ten metres from the relative safety of our vehicle, but the distance felt immeasurable. Slowly, I began stepping backwards, keeping my movements deliberate and unhurried. The hyena mirrored my retreat, slinking back into the shadows of the bush as though reluctant to break the tenuous connection between us.

Reaching the safety of the car and the now-erected tent, I turned to Graham and said, "I think we should skip dinner, get into the tent, lock up the vehicle, and make sure nothing is left outside to attract night visitors - especially leather boots that might resemble carrion!"

That night, the sounds of the Savuti wilderness surrounded us: guttural grunts, eerie laughs, high-pitched squeaks, and distant yawns carried through the air. At one point, the unmistakable scraping and sniffing of an unseen animal resonated alarmingly close to the tent. We had heard cautionary tales of campers being dragged from their tents, usually when their feet extended beyond an unzipped closure. Thankfully, we were securely cocooned within, with anything remotely tempting to the nocturnal predators safely locked in the car.

Morning brought a palpable sense of relief and wonder. As the first light crept across the landscape, it unveiled the mysteries hidden by the cloak of darkness. The dense night had distorted our perception, amplifying every sound and movement, but daylight painted a new picture - one of beauty and tranquillity. The rocks and trees came into focus, revealing the gentle contours of the land. We spotted other campers nearby, their presence reassuring in this untamed expanse.

In the golden glow of the morning light, Savuti revealed itself as a place of breathtaking magic and fleeting safety - a haven, so long as you respected its boundaries and stayed within the sanctuary of the camp.

The light brought us a renewed energy. We organised our tent and the car's contents before preparing breakfast. We cooked over the fire and gas cooker, enjoying tea as the cool morning air carried the earthy scent of nature. From other campsites came hushed voices, mingling with the sounds of the bush. It was a perfect morning for exploring.

We set out in our vehicle, following marked trails that meandered through the long grass and shrubs. The landscape was strikingly similar to the *Eternal Enemies* National Geographic film I'd seen, as if we had entered the very spot where lions and hyenas raised their cubs and waged their unending rivalry.

Soon, the wildlife emerged. Giraffes towered over us, plucking leaves from the thorny branches of acacia trees. Their calves stayed close, their awkward movements endearing against the stillness of their towering mothers. Antelope were plentiful - Kudu, Waterbuck, a solitary Black Sable Antelope, and Impala moving with effortless grace.

In the distance, zebras grazed, their bold stripes mingling with the earthy tones of wildebeest. Together, they painted a living mosaic across the savannah. For every animal we spotted, many more were undoubtedly watching us. Vultures perched in the trees, their hunched forms stark against the sky, while baboons scrambled across the reddish-brown rocks, some foraging, others pausing to observe us with sharp, watchful eyes.

Morning and dusk were the prime times for predators to hunt. Those that were prey remained vigilant, with some acting as designated lookouts while others cautiously grazed or fed. As we drove along the trails, we occasionally saw side-striped jackals darting across our path, followed by the quick, curious movements of mongoose.

The birdlife was astounding, adding vivid colour and sound to the landscape. Among them, my favourite - the lilac-breasted roller—flashed its brilliant hues as it flitted between trees. Larger birds, like the imposing bustard and the elegant secretary bird, wandered through the grasslands, joined by various species of storks, each contributing to the rich tapestry of life.

The long grass provided the perfect cover for predators like leopards and lions, who moved with practiced stealth, inching as close as possible to their unsuspecting prey before launching their attack. Here in Savuti, life and death played out daily, a constant and unrelenting cycle.

For those who lived, every moment was a celebration of nature's abundance—a chance to take in all that this untamed world offered. But death was an inevitable companion, arriving in many forms: the slow decline of age, the consequences of injury, or the swift, predatory strike that ensured another's survival. It was the cycle of life and death, raw and unapologetic, at the very heart of this wild, breathtaking landscape.

Our mission was to find lions and hyenas. The latter had made an unexpected appearance the night before, when I caught a fleeting glimpse of one in the shadows. On several occasions during our safari, we had heard their unmistakable "laugh" echoing through the bush. Now, more than ever, I wanted to see them as a family, going about their daily lives.

Hyenas are most active at night, as well as during dusk and dawn, scavenging or stealing kills from other predators. Leopards, often the victims of their relentless harassment, resort to dragging their kills up trees to keep them out of reach. Cheetahs, while incredibly agile on the ground, lack this climbing ability and are often forced to abandon their kills, relying instead on their speed to escape what could be a dangerous encounter with a pack of hyenas.

By late morning, hyenas would typically retreat to their dens or linger over the bones of a carcass somewhere in the distance.

It was then that we spotted an open jeep heading towards us. The driver stood as he navigated the vehicle - a remarkable feat but clearly intentional. He had no passengers and was dressed in an olive-green safari shirt and shorts, his appearance rugged and purposeful. Pulling up beside us, he introduced himself as a ranger from a nearby luxury safari lodge.

He explained that he had been in contact with a spotter plane, which had witnessed a lion kill - a young elephant. The coordinates had been relayed, and he was now circling the area to locate the site. Rangers often went out early in the morning to identify key sightings for their lodge guests.

We were fortunate, not just to be early, but to cross paths with him. He informed us that the kill was nearby and suggested we follow him. "You can smell it—death," he said, sniffing the air. "It's faint, but it's there. Maybe a day or so old."

We mimicked him, sniffing the breeze. At first, I caught nothing, but with a sharpened focus, I detected the faint scent he mentioned - subtle yet distinct.

The ranger stood upright as he drove, his posture lending him a better view over the bush. As someone equally short, I appreciated the advantage it gave. We followed his lead, winding through trails and thick undergrowth until we emerged into a clearing.

And there, before us, were two male lions devouring and guarding the carcass of a young bull elephant, its tusks still intact. The air carried only a faint odour, suggesting the kill was fresh, confirming that is was likely no more than a day or two old. One lion, older judging by his scarred face and sparse mane, was smeared with blood after feasting on the elephant's open stomach. The other male, with a full, majestic mane, bore an uncanny resemblance to Ntwadumela—"He Who Greets with Fire" - from the documentary *Eternal Enemies*, which had inspired my journey to Savuti. These lions could have been descendants of that legendary pride or perhaps had taken it over since the documentary was filmed.

Our ranger explained that the elephant had likely been taken down by the lions, known here for their audacity in hunting large prey, even elephants. He speculated that the young bull may have wandered away from its herd, leaving it vulnerable, or perhaps it had been injured. It was just us and the ranger, with an unobstructed view of this extraordinary scene. In the nearby trees, vultures perched in anticipation, waiting for their turn at the remains. They would have to bide their time; the male lions would gorge themselves first, passing the carcass to the pride's females and cubs only when they were satiated. For now, the vultures kept their distance, knowing they would have to compete with hyenas and jackals when the feast finally dwindled.

This was a day when only the male lions would rule over such an immense prize. Not long after our arrival, other vehicles from our camp began to trickle in as word of the kill spread. It was a breathtaking morning, and we resolved to return at dusk, the following morning, and again at dusk for the next few days. In the intervals, we explored the reserve, marvelling at the abundance of wildlife that made Savuti so captivating. We came across a den of hyenas and spent time watching the young cubs play with the adults lying around lazily. They were probably acutely aware of the elephant kill knowing that this enormous feast would be enough to fill them for a long time. They would be patient as they would be no match for two adult males guarding the kill – they would wait and take their opportunity once the male lions had gone and take their risk engaging and harassing the female lions if the numbers favoured them.

As planned, we returned that evening. The lions were still resolutely guarding their kill, occasionally entering the carcass to feed, though now they seemed more intent on licking the meat than consuming it. Not long after, we noticed movement—female lions emerging from the bush, followed by several cubs. They approached cautiously, keeping a respectful distance. The females and cubs would have to wait for the males' permission to eat, knowing that any premature attempt could provoke a violent, even fatal, reaction.

Each night, we prepared meals from our own supplies, experimenting creatively with simple ingredients. These evenings, under the starlit sky, were some of the most magical moments - living close to nature, far removed from the noise and entrapments of city life and commercialism. I had never felt more at peace.

The next morning, the scent of death was more pronounced, making the path to the kill easy to trace. A white, lipid-like fluid had appeared on the surface of the elephant's thick, grey skin, a macabre testament to the ongoing process of decay. The carcass had grown more tattered as the lions began dismembering parts they deemed most nutritious and prized. They reserved the best for themselves and, once sated, would simply walk away, inviting the awaiting females, young males, and other pride members to feed. The cubs, still too young for the feast, were nourished through their mothers' milk.

For a while, we had this incredible spectacle entirely to ourselves, with no other vehicles in sight. It offered extraordinary photographic opportunities, particularly with the two male lions sitting majestically in front of their kill, guarding it. In a moment of daring - probably not my wisest decision - I wanted a close-up photo of one of the lions gazing directly at us. Graham was in the driver's seat while I sat in the passenger seat, nearest to the lions. I cracked the door open just a fraction. Instantly, the older male snarled and bristled, poised to charge. I slammed the door shut in a heartbeat. In that fleeting moment, he saw me as a human - an intruder. Inside the vehicle, I was merely part of the car. It was a reckless move, but it yielded some remarkable photos. Needless to say, I wouldn't recommend anyone try it!

The following morning was unforgettable. The pungent stench of decay now hung heavily in the air, detectable long before reaching the site. The male lions had finally abandoned the carcass, effectively inviting the pride to take their turn. Around six or seven lions - primarily females with a couple of young males—gathered around the remains. In the nearby bushes, we spotted cubs watching curiously, soon joining the feast by gnawing on discarded bones or scraps of flesh. Overhead, vultures were now joined by marabou storks, the large, ominous carrion-eating birds. Both scavenger species waited patiently, knowing their time would come, though they risked becoming prey themselves if they ventured too close too soon.

Even if these few days had been the entirety of my trip, it would have been enough - a memory etched in my mind forever. Everything else we experienced after this felt like an incredible bonus.

Our final visit to the kill was in the evening. By then, the elephant resembled a deflated balloon, its skin sagging and ribcage exposed. The odour was overwhelming, a visceral reminder of nature's cycle of life and death. These moments were unforgettable, imprinted on my soul for eternity.

The next morning, we packed up our tent and gear, ready to head towards the Zimbabwe border with an overnight stop planned at Chobe National Park. By now, our food supplies were running low, and there's only so much creativity you can muster with tins of beans. Any remaining food, which we couldn't take across the border, was shared with the curious mongoose that gathered around our campsite.

Chobe offered some final, spectacular wildlife encounters. We observed several lion prides, including cubs lounging on low tree branches. We also came across a rhinoceros and several antelope species. It was here that I saw my first eland - the largest of them all - a fitting end to a journey filled with awe and wonder.

Both feeling privileged and honoured to witness some spectacular moments we left Botswana with mixed emotions. It had left a mark that would be forever imprinted in me. A consolation on leaving is that we would return – at least for me -to Imbabala across the border to Zimbabwe. It would be my second visit and Grahams first where he would meet Gavin and Shay and also come away with some of the experiences I had during my first visit.

Savuti for me is not a place that merely exists; it breathes. The air carries a symphony of life - the distant roar of lions, the haunting calls of jackals, and the rustle of dry grass beneath the feet of elephants. The sheer abundance of wildlife was staggering, but it was the sense of timelessness that struck me most. This was a place untouched by the chaos of human civilization, where life unfolds as it has for centuries, governed only by the laws of nature.

The adventure that unfolded was one of discovery—of the land, its inhabitants, and myself.

Classification and Labels

Whilst I had a fondness for classifying objects by make, appearance, or model type, and liked a sense of order, I probably would have made a good librarian! In an age of writing with pen and ink, my mother kept A4 hardback notebooks meticulously cataloguing her plants and cacti. She listed their common and Latin scientific names, grouping them into orders, families, and species. Her handwriting was immaculate. I soon inherited this penchant for organisation, though not her handwriting skills—my scribbles looked like a spider's frantic dance, as my writing raced ahead of my mind.

Unlike my mother's devotion to plants, my focus turned to fauna, particularly vertebrates and, more specifically, mammals. At one point, I could recite the entire Carnivora order classification order by heart. In school, my fascination with genetics found an outlet in breeding pet rats. I meticulously charted their lineage, tracing the colours and patterns of their offspring from my first two rats, Nimbus and Cumulus - named after cloud types. Their progeny, with distinct patterns of black and cream or fawn, bore names like Nimbus Cumulus or Cumulus Nimbus, depending on the ratio of their markings and having white or black socks.

As head of the school's animal club, I brought home the school's critters during holidays. My mother would arrive in her Chrysler Alpine hatchback, and we'd load up cages and tanks of animals, transforming our lounge annex into a bustling menagerie. Later, my personal collection expanded to include ferrets. During the annual school fete, I turned the boat club into a mini zoo, borrowing exotic animals like bullfrogs, snakes, leaf insects, and snapping turtles from research centres.

I loved neat and orderly systems—even the buses lined up in the garage fascinated me. The logistical feat of returning 120 buses, washing them, changing destination blinds, and arranging them so the last one in was the first one out was awe-inspiring. My obsession extended to supermarket trolleys and community wheelbarrows at my father's allotment. I imagined them as buses, ensuring they were neatly aligned and ready for their "journeys." My matchbox collection of London Transport buses allowed me to mimic real bus routes, complete with homemade destination blinds and route numbers. The legs of a chair served as my bus garage.

I had a tendency to always have things facing forward which strangely enough was how we parked out vehicles when on assignments. By parking so that you could drive forward was essential for quick getaway in case of an emergency. I still park like this at home and have tendency to never have my back to a window or door when dining out or in a café.

One of the few bonds I shared with my father was our mutual fascination with London Transport, where he worked as a linesman and engineer for the Underground. Every six months, he'd bring home the latest bus network map, a foldable treasure detailing routes, garages, and stops. I spent hours pouring over these maps, noting changes, discontinued routes, and new additions. Armed with a discount travel card, I explored bus garages across the city and beyond, from

Peckham, Camberwell, Chalk Farm to Chelsham, Reigate and Godstone.

My love for classification brought order and understanding to my world. But it was also a double-edged sword. Applying labels or categories to classify people could limit them to the set characteristics, creating stereotypes that were difficult to escape. Breaking free from such imposed identities often required immense effort or led to the creation of dual personas.

Classification could be dangerous. In the hands of a despot, they became tools for oppression, used to differentiate and persecute people based on race, religion, gender, or sexual orientation. From a young age, while I cherished the classification of species and objects, I recoiled from labels that defined human identities and dictated what one could or could not do.

Having travelled extensively and worked in countries notorious for human rights abuses, I learned that freedom often lay in the absence of labels. Without a word to define a behaviour, it escaped judgment and prohibition. The moment something was named, it could be deemed sinful, illegal, or unacceptable, with religious texts or cultural norms weaponised to enforce those judgments.

Good and bad, like all opposites, exist in cultural and contextual frameworks. What one society deems virtuous, another may condemn. As a child, my actions were instinctive, shaped by upbringing, role models, rewards, and punishments. My understanding of right and wrong came from parents, peers, media, and societal norms, all of which carried biases and opinions. In my household, opinions about people of different faiths, sexual orientation, race, and socioeconomic statuses were voiced openly – often in a derogatory terms . These opinions, absorbed like a sponge, shaped my early worldview. When I was working in the disputed territory of Nagorny Karabagh between Armenia and Azerbaijan, some of the people I met would say that kids they went to school with, played soccer and were their friends were now their enemies. Similarly, I could image that as children we did not see difference until someone explains to you that the other person is different and that difference is what makes you better or unique than the other person. Your conscious mind is now contaminated and the seeds or difference have been sown!

As children, we trust our parents as the ultimate authority. Their beliefs become our truths. It was only later, with experience and reflection, that I began to question these inherited opinions and the systems of classification that shaped them. I started to see the world not in neat lines, but in the messy, interwoven patterns of human existence.

In today's world, the proliferation of labels and identities seems aimed at fostering inclusivity, yet often creates unexpected divisions. Some groups have sought to reclaim slurs once used to demean them, transforming these words into badges of pride. While this reclamation is empowering for many, it also adds layers of complexity to an already intricate social fabric. For those of us who grew up in a time when identities were less fragmented, the sheer multitude of labels—identities, sub-identities, and even sub-sub-identities—can feel overwhelming.

Subcultures have always existed, providing shared spaces for those with common interests or beliefs, or where a sense of safety and familiarity could flourish. But as much as these subcultures can nurture belonging, they also risk creating boundaries that divide us. Take, for example, what was once simply "gay" or "lesbian." These words described men who had romantic or sexual relationships with men, and women who preferred the company of women in the same way. The derogatory terms hurled at us in the 1970s and 1980s— words like "queer," "faggot," or "poofter"—weren't just insults; they were weapons, designed to strip away dignity and humanity.

For those of us who lived through that time, our fight for equality wasn't theoretical. It was a struggle for survival, often at the expense of family, friendships, and safety. All because of a single word—a label that set us apart. In some ways, I've wondered: if there were no labels to categorise those who love someone of the same sex, might we have found unity more easily? Without a word to isolate us, we could have simply been people, free to love who we chose.

Yet the simplicity of "gay" and "lesbian" has now evolved into an ever-expanding acronym: LGBTQIA+, with more letters and categories added seemingly every year. While this evolution reflects a broader spectrum of identities, it can feel like a step away from inclusivity and toward fragmentation. Instead of erasing the boundaries, we risk creating more. Maybe the missing acronym to make it truly inclusive is 'S' for straight!

Growing up, the word "gay" conjured images of camp, flamboyant male celebrities on television—men in women's clothing, exaggeratedly effeminate, and the source of comic relief for straight audiences. It was an image far removed from how many of us saw ourselves. To tell my parents I was gay meant confronting their perception of this stereotype, shaped by what they saw on TV. It didn't fit who I was.

I was like any other boy - playing with toy soldiers, getting into scraps, reading Marvel comics, going fishing, and camping. The only difference was my eventual preference for men, though it wasn't as simple as attraction in the usual sense. I was drawn to women's minds and ease of conversation; I had girlfriends and dealt with the jealousy of my mates. But something inexplicable led me to prefer men, though not necessarily in the physical sense. I wasn't particularly drawn to the act of sex itself, but rather to men's presence—the way they dressed, their confidence, their style. Women I liked were often strong, loved the outdoors, were equal rather than subservient and did not adhere to gender based roles as many did following tradition and stereotypes.

Looking back, I've questioned what led me down this path. Was it rooted in my early childhood? An escape from a turbulent relationship with my father? Perhaps it was the allure of older men who took me under their wing, offering attention, gifts, and a sense of belonging that I didn't find at home. As a young teenager, being whisked off to clubs and pubs in flashy cars seemed glamorous at the time, though in hindsight, it complicates the narrative of my identity.

I have had deep, non-sexual relationships with men— connections that transcended mere friendship. These bonds were marked by something profound, almost spiritual, that went beyond words. There may have been moments of unspoken tension, even mutual curiosity, but I never dared to explore them further. Putting a label on those feelings could have shifted the dynamic entirely, introducing a risk I wasn't willing to take. For me, intimacy and friendship always outweighed the physical. Celibacy, in many ways, became a natural state—especially crucial during deployments to countries where revealing your sexual preference could lead to imprisonment or worse.

When I lose a close friend or partner, it's more than losing a lover—it's losing a confidant, a companion, and the shared bond that drew us together in the first place. The sadness I carry isn't about the physical intimacy we shared; it's the loss of friendship and the memories that shaped our connection. Sex, while pleasant, has always been secondary, a fleeting aspect of something much deeper. For me, the essence of any relationship lies in the bond, the trust, and the moments that transcend the physical.

A single word can condemn or liberate. When relationships are allowed to grow unencumbered by restrictive labels or the weight of societal judgment, they can flourish in their purest form. Many potential connections, I believe, have been stifled by the imposition of a word or identity that creates separation rather than unity. How many souls have passed each other by, denied the chance to connect because of a single label that cast them apart?

Faith and religion are no less influential in defining who we are and how we perceive one another. Most of us are born into a dominant religious tradition, not by choice but by heritage or necessity. Faith often serves as a foundation, but if we strip away doctrine and the power structures built upon it, what would our natural beliefs be, formed purely through experience and introspection?

Religion, like words, can be wielded as a justification for behaviour - sometimes virtuous, but often cruel or self-serving. It can be used to elevate oneself above others or to rationalise actions that harm. I remember one of my sisters, when testifying on my father's behalf, telling the lawyer, "You can trust me; I'm a Christian." Her statement hung in the air, and I couldn't help but wonder if it carried weight with the lawyer. Did it bolster her credibility, or was it dismissed as irrelevant?

Similarly, a builder working for me, who consistently failed to meet deadlines and caused numerous issues including non-payment to sub-contractors, tried to assure me of his reliability by saying, "As a Muslim, we always pay our debts." His words reminded me of the Lannister's in *Game of Thrones*, who famously lived by a similar creed. His statement felt hollow, like a borrowed virtue, disconnected from the reality of his actions. Most of the actions I observed were un-Islamic.

At its core, religion often offers pure and noble ideals, but its interpretation frequently bends to suit those in power. Cherry-picking religious principles to fit one's lifestyle or justify decisions has become increasingly evident. While faith can inspire remarkable acts of compassion and generosity, it can just as easily be weaponised to exclude or condemn.

In the end, it is action - not labels, words, or proclamations of faith - that defines virtue. Yet even actions are not immune to the influence of words. A single term, cast in judgment or approval, can shape how those actions are perceived. Words have the power to elevate or to condemn, but it is our deeds, stripped of pretence, that truly reveal our character.

Having journeyed extensively across continents, regions, and countries - many where the separation of state and religion is non-existent or where religious influence deeply permeates state affairs, even within democratic frameworks - I find it difficult to evaluate which religious faith might be deemed the "right" one. Each faith holds the conviction that it alone is just and true, and in some places, the choice to believe otherwise is not an option.

The inner self may harbor beliefs contrary to the dominant religious norms, but for the sake of safety and social acceptance, these personal convictions often remain hidden. I cannot assert that one predominant religion in a country or region is inherently right or wrong, nor can I judge another, equally populous region with an entirely different faith. If I had never ventured beyond my hometown or country, I might have clung to the idea that our beliefs were superior.

In a light-hearted way, it's akin to the debate over who makes the best 'baklava'. Many Middle Eastern and Southern European nations fervently claim their version is the most authentic, the most exquisite. But as the old saying goes, "The proof of the pudding is in the eating." Perhaps the same could be said of faith—its truth and value are ultimately found in the lived experience, in the practice, and in the heart of the believer.

Body and Mind

The body has a remarkable way of adapting to survive. In remote environments, under stress, or amidst danger, it seems to instinctively know when to hold the line. It isn't uncommon for illnesses to remain dormant, suppressed by sheer will or necessity, until a moment of safety signals the body that it can finally let its guard down. This phenomenon has never been more apparent to me than during my years of work in conflict zones. After twelve unpredictable and some dangerous months in Afghanistan, my body and spirit were desperate for reprieve. Before heading home, I decided to embark on a two-week trek in Nepal — a place where both adventure and solace could be found.

This was my second visit to Nepal. My first trip had been a solo endeavour a few years earlier, a trek from Jomsom to Muktinath, part of the renowned Annapurna Circuit. Over the course of ten days, I covered roughly 96 kilometres, with side treks to Poon Hill and Tatopani. Travelling alone had its unique rewards: the solitude of the mountains, the rhythm of my own pace, and the unexpected camaraderie of fellow trekkers I met along the way. I spent several days trekking alongside three musicians from the Wellington Symphony Orchestra in New Zealand. We supported one another through steep passes and winding trails, sharing laughter, stories, and even bursts of song that echoed through the canyons and over the rivers of the breathtaking Himalayan landscape.

Before returning home from that first trip, I lingered in the tranquil lakeside town of Pokhara. On Christmas Day, I rented a canoe and paddled to the middle of Phewa Lake, savouring the serenity of the water and the towering mountains reflected on its surface. As dusk fell, the town's shoreline came alive with candles, lanterns, and colourful string lights in celebration of Christmas. Despite being in a predominantly Hindu nation, the festive spirit was unmistakable, and the moment was one of pure magic. The local restaurants were putting on a 'big bird' dinner and I decided to have my 'Christmas' dinner. This would one of many Christmases I would spend on my own. Everyone who attended were given a raffle ticket as they entered the establishment. After I sat down, the owner came out with a microphone and after asking one of his staff to pull a ticket from a hat, my ticket came out trumps! What did I win? Suddenly this 'big bird' roasted with its head still connected, ribbons and foil with all the trimmings was presented to me on my solo person table! I was expected to cheer and celebrate and faked a smile of gratefulness and thanks. Not sure whether it was the eyes of the 'Turkey' that was looking at me but I instantly lost my appetite. Maybe this was to be expected so that I could ask if I could share the prize with the staff (which I did) which was very much appreciated!

My second trip to Nepal was different. This time, I travelled with a colleague from the Red Cross, Martin, an agronomist from Switzerland. With his Swiss heritage, mountains and trekking were in his blood. We shared an easy friendship, forged through months of working together in Afghanistan. Martin oversaw agricultural projects, visiting Jalalabad my duty station regularly from Kabul where our work had often intersected. During a prior evacuation to Thailand following the Tomahawk cruise missile attack, we'd explored national parks together, cementing a bond built on mutual respect and shared experiences. I later visited Martin at his home in Hollihaka, Finland after marrying a Finnish nurse he met whilst on assignment in Afghanistan. I travelled with an old friend from school after we had reconnected after several years with our reunion and rendezvous being Helsinki rail station. Martin had converted an old kindergarten to a home which still had a massive wood burner that heated the whole school. Most the of the work he had completed himself. Attached to his property was a lake where we went out on his tin boat and fished for perch and pike. As is Finnish tradition, he had a sauna, a place we could chat and catch up on old times and then run along the ramp and jump into the freezing water – stark naked of course!

The trek we embarked on was longer and more arduous and diverse than my first. Martin seemed to take the hills, rocky terrain and descents with ease - fleet and sure footed across streams and climbing rocks. He always waited and encouraged me, helped with my backpack and gradually I was becoming more confident and sure footed in a similar vain. It took us through landscapes that seemed to shift with each passing day: vibrant rhododendron forests, open plains, lush vegetation, rocky plateaus, and towering peaks. Having learned from a bout of altitude sickness years earlier in Puno, Peru, we approached the climb to Annapurna Base Camp, over 4,000 meters above sea level, with caution. We ascended and descended within the same day to minimize the risk of altitude-related illness. It was a hard but wise choice, allowing us to marvel at the stunning vistas without compromising our health.

I was once told that this part of Nepal had inspired some of the landscapes and scenes in JR Tolkien's book the 'Lord of the Rings'. Having read his books as well as the Hobbit, it is easy to see why – especially the forests, rivers and snow-capped rugged mountains.

Visitors to Nepal often fall ill, usually due to foodborne issues. I had learned — sometimes the hard way - that sticking to local fare was the best strategy. A simple *dal bhat* (lentils and rice) or a steaming bowl of potato soup provided both nourishment and safety. Still, the lure of Western dishes occasionally tempted us. Trekking under the crisp Himalayan air worked up a hearty appetite, but caution was key. Some meals proved to be less than appetising; on more than one occasion, an unidentifiable object in the food — an eyelid in a pizza or rice that moved of its own accord — served as a stark reminder to trust my instincts.

When I returned to England, I began to feel unwell. I was passing blood in my stool, and it continued for days until my stool turned to just blood - sometimes in alarming amounts. Adjusting my diet to less fibrous, simple foods brought no relief. It became a social nightmare, confining me to my home and visits only to understanding friends and family. Although I underwent the usual post-deployment medical check, I was told this was likely a response to readjusting and that my body needed rest. I still felt strong and fit, going for walks and trying to stay active. Hoping for improvement, I decided to go on a retreat to relax, eat healthily, meditate, and spend time in nature. While the retreat offered sanctuary and eased the embarrassment of frequent, urgent trips to the toilet, the symptoms persisted.

I remained in contact with the medical staff affiliated with the Red Cross. Blood and other investigations failed to pinpoint the cause, though my haemoglobin levels were rapidly dropping. Despite my travel history and the well-documented health risks in the countries I'd worked in, nothing conclusive emerged until I was referred, out of desperation, to the Tropical Medicine and Infectious diseases clinic at University College Hospital in London. By then, my haemoglobin had dropped to 5.7. Remarkably, I was still active; during the retreat, I had climbed Glastonbury Tor, attributing my breathlessness to exertion rather than dangerously low oxygen-carrying red blood cells.

At the outpatient clinic, my vital signs were taken, and the doctor asked to see me after all the other patients had been attended to. His words stirred anxiety, but I complied. Once the clinic had emptied and even the staff seemed to have gone, he invited me into his consultation room. He asked if it was okay to close the blinds and if I would lie down on the examination table. Then, unexpectedly, he asked if he could pray. I agreed, feeling an unexpected sense of safety. After months of stomach cramps, bloody diarrhea, and isolation, it felt as though resolution was finally within reach.

The doctor, an Australian, reviewed my symptoms and travel history and took blood samples. He suspected a bacterial infection causing intestinal damage and was surprised that earlier tests had failed to detect anything. He made immediate arrangements for my isolation in the hospital, not because I was infectious but because the ward's other patients, many with AIDS-related illnesses, were severely immunosuppressed. Rigorous testing followed, including for HIV, Hepatitis A, B, and C, and tropical diseases. Routine in my line of work, these tests were familiar territory.

Eventually, a positive result for Campylobacter infection emerged. It was a straightforward diagnosis, yet it had been missed in an earlier stool test upon my return. Had it been identified earlier, I could have avoided eight weeks of suffering. Yet, in hindsight, I see this delay as a pivotal moment, leading to an unusual and deeply supportive experience.

The infection left a permanent mark. Delayed treatment resulted in acute colitis, now chronic but well-managed. Though occasional flare-ups occur, they are under control, thanks to effective care - again, often by Australian doctors. After a week in the hospital on intravenous antibiotics and after discharge a blood transfusion consisting of four units, I began regaining my health, strength, and the 10 kilograms I had lost.

During my stay, the admitting doctor visited me and gifted me a book, *Formed by the Desert* by Joyce Huggett. I still cherish that book today. While still recovering, I received a call from the British Red Cross's International Deployment Team. They inquired about my interest and availability for an assignment in Tajikistan. Though flattered, I was not ready for another deployment; my haemoglobin needed time to rebuild, and my colitis was being treated with prednisolone. Nevertheless, being considered for another assignment was the morale boost I needed. Conflict in the Balkans was escalating, and requests for health delegates were coming in thick and fast.

Sadly, during my hospital stay, an event unfolded that would later fracture my family in ways I could never have foreseen, the effects of which still linger today. To this day, I am unsure why my sister, with whom I had been very close, chose that vulnerable moment - when I was confined to a single room and physically weakened by illness - to say the things she did. In the privacy of my hospital room, she expressed a need for comfort and wanted to lie beside me. What she said devastated me, leaving a permanent scar. She made me promise not to tell anyone, warning that if I did, she would disown me as her brother. I felt emotionally cornered, as though my silence was being coerced.

The following day, my mentor and dear friend Jane visited me. Struggling with the weight of what had happened, I confided in her about my sister's words and the way they were shared. I told her I couldn't believe what my sister had claimed and wondered why she would say such things. Jane's response was simple but piercing: "Why wouldn't you believe her?"

Her words unsettled me, forcing me to confront the possibility of an unbearable truth. I kept silent for a number of years, but during that time, my relationship with my father began to deteriorate. Nothing explicit was said, but it felt as though he knew I knew something. The tension simmered, unspoken but palpable, and it seemed only a matter of time before it boiled over. The opportunity came when my father made a disparaging comment about my lifestyle and sexuality. His words struck a nerve, and I finally confronted him.

The confrontation backfired spectacularly. Instead of addressing the issue, I was accused of threatening my father and was asked to leave. It appeared my mother colluded with both my father and brother Mark that I had threatened him as though to protect him which to this day I cannot fathom. My brother even called me a 'terrorist' implying I was terrorising my father. My efforts to bring the matter to light were dismissed, and the family was left reeling. Like me, no one in the family could fathom the allegations being true at the time. Yet years later, the truth emerged, irreversibly shattering much of the bond we once shared as a family.

The Storm

2022 brought some of the most severe storms Victoria had experienced in decades - certainly the worst since we had bought our acreage, nestled against the Wombat State Forest, and begun our life in the quiet hamlet of Spargo Creek. We lived with the comfort of space, sky and trees, but also with the knowledge that nature here did not simply exist around you. It shaped you. It tested you. It reminded you of your place - every summer, every wind change, every lightning strike.

Bush and grass fires had long been a familiar threat. Like many who lived on the edge of the forest, we had a fire plan. We kept the area around the house clear of trees - particularly the tall, oil-rich eucalypts that could turn a spark into a firestorm. We cleaned leaves from gutters, filled the bathtub with water, kept buckets filled with water in case of power outages, wool blankets and masks close at hand. We moved vehicles away from the house and invested in diesel rather than petrol engines because of the lower combustion risk. We also engaged in the practice of planting fire resistant trees – mostly wattles and landscaping areas around the house with pebbles and stones as a protective barrier. We prepared two French steel trunks that I brought back from one of my Red Cross deployments and filled it with essentials such as some tinned food, toiletries, spade, radio, torches, spare batteries, first aid pack etc, some cotton clothing and tinned, dog crates and pet dry food. These trunks were kept close to the door so could quickly put them into the vehicles if deciding to leave.

In earlier years, homeowners relied on defence: roof sprinklers, 1,000-litre tanks fitted to utes, long hoses and diesel pumps ready to extinguish embers blown in from kilometres ahead of the fire front. The belief was simple - protect your home, stand your ground, do not let fire take what you built.

But tragedy had reshaped that belief. The new advice was uncompromising: leave early. Leave when the warnings first appear—not when the flames are already visible. Do not hesitate. Because once a fire reaches the crowns of the trees - once the oxygen is drawn from the air and the heat becomes radiant and carnivorous -there is no surviving it. There were different codes – depending on whether to watch and keep informed, act and leave or stay. The latter was when the fire was deemed so severe and potentially catastrophic that the best option was to stay, as leaving was now far too dangerous and would provide a nightmare for the rescuers and firefighters.

People had tried bunkers, wombat burrows, dams, tanks. A few survived. Many did not. In theory, you can prepare, rehearse and imagine how you will act. But when the sky turns black and the smoke thickens to something you can taste, when the roar becomes all you can hear, nothing feels rehearsed. Panic is a weather system of its own.

Dams could evaporate and water tanks become boiling cauldrons. The only structures that consistently saved lives were properly constructed bunkers with filtered air vents - but few properties had these.

Wildlife sought refuge as instinct dictated. Wombats and echidnas burrowed deep into cool soil and waited for the fire to pass overhead, though many emerged with burnt feet and faced days without food or water. Koalas were among the most vulnerable - slow, tree-bound, with nowhere to go once the flames crowned. Kangaroos too suffered, not from lack of speed, but from instinct: mobs panicked and bolted uphill, straight into the fire front. The solitary wallaby, by contrast, seemed wiser, often heading downhill to shelter where the fire burned less fiercely.

We learnt this early when a grassfire on a neighbour's property swept dangerously close to our fence line. It was my first time responding as a volunteer firefighter with the Country Fire Authority. I remember the speed more than anything—the flames jumping across patches of grass, wind and oxygen feeding the flames, the panic and freight-train movement of fire across dry ground. I remember the heat and sweat on my face through the mask, the dull thump in my chest, the racing pulse of something far older than thought. Some experiences enter the bones and never leave.

After several hot, dry summers that sharpened the fire risk, the weather broke. Rain returned - at first a relief, then a season. The paddocks became soft, then saturated. Water pooled in tyre tracks and collected in the hollows of fallen branches. The land sloped gently down to the creek behind the house, so when the dams filled, they spilled, and the water travelled in small runnels and rivulets down to the creek bed.

What had once been a quiet, two-metre-wide brook became a river. First slow and heavy, then brown and fast, then white at the mouth of rapids that had never existed before. Logs that had been still for decades lifted and turned like matchsticks. Stones rattled against each other like bones. We moved the beehives to higher ground and lifted them on bricks, hoping it would be enough to keep them safe from the rising water.

Our English Staffordshire Terriers were bold, determined, eager to join in anything we did, including swimming—but they were not built for endurance in water. Their compact, muscular bodies made buoyancy a negotiation rather than a gift. Goldie, however, believed she was unstoppable. She threw herself into the dam after Jax, our Kelpie, again and again. Jax swam with an ease that felt born, not learned. He would carry a tennis ball in his mouth, paddling calmly to the centre of the dam, while Goldie churned behind him with the determination of someone proving something to herself. More than once I waded in to pull her out when her strokes began to sink, her head dipping and lifting, eyes still fierce with the thrill of the chase. She was the smallest of our dogs, yet the bravest. Courage is not always rational.

One day, Jax and I went down to check the creek. Where I expected water, I found movement. Where I expected a stream, I found a river. It was at least ten metres wide now, and roaring. Before I could call him back, Jax stepped too close to the softening bank and slipped. The water caught him instantly.

He fought - paws slashing the surface, neck stretched toward land—but the current dragged him away.

I ran. The bank was slick and uneven, but I knew the fallen tree that formed a narrow, makeshift footbridge near the boundary fence could give me one chance to catch him before he was swept under. I reached it, grabbed a low branch for balance, leaned out over the torrent. Jax's collar flashed. I reached. For one moment - one impossible, exact second—our hands and paws and breath aligned - and I held him.

I dragged him toward me, both of us slipping, his weight sodden, the water still pulling. I hauled us back to the bank and collapsed in the mud, shaking, gasping, alive.

A second later, and I would not have reached him.

The storms of 2022 marked a turning point—not only in the land, but in my relationship with Ian. The June storm came with a violence that defied expectation. Trees that had stood for sixty or eighty years were ripped from the ground as though they had never belonged there. They fell across fences, roads, paddocks, each pointing in a different direction, as though the wind had spun a wheel and flung them indiscriminately.

We were without power for nearly a week. Clearing the fallen timber became a slow, heavy rhythm that would take almost two years.

Then November came, and another storm. Not as fierce, but the weakened trees had no strength left to resist. Branches tore loose. Fences collapsed. One of our power poles shifted and ripped its connection from the house.

We thought we had endured the worst. But storms are rarely only weather.

Jax went missing.

Dusk was closing in. The mistly rain was cold and fine. Wind threaded through the trees like something whispering. We put on coats and headlamps, grabbed hand torches and called his name into the dark. I drove slowly along the road, scanning verges, checking gate lines, knocking on neighbours' doors - houses spaced across acres. Ian searched paddocks, sheds, the sheep shelter, the far corners where dogs sometimes go when frightened.

Nothing!

Night settled fully. The house felt hollow without him.

I asked Ian again if he had checked under the deck. He said yes. He was tired. He said there was nothing more we could do and he was going to bed.

But something in me stayed awake.

It was Myshka - our cat - who found him. She darted along the deck, stopping abruptly, staring down into a narrow gap. She and Jax were bonded in a way animals understand without explanation. I called Ian back.

We called his name.

At first, all we heard were the brown tree frogs and the banjo-string call of the pobblebonk frog vibrating through the wet night air. Then - a faint, muffled cry.

I lay flat, torch angled, and saw his eyes reflect back. Jax had wedged himself deep into the narrowest space, trapped, terrified.

There was no room to pull him through. So I dug. With my hands at first, then a spade, pushing mud and stones and sticks aside until there was space enough to slide him out.

When he came free, I held him, and the relief shook through me. I cried. I hugged Ian. In that moment, Jax was all that mattered.

But the relief did not stay.

I had asked Ian, again and again, whether he had checked under the deck. Each time he had told me he had. I could not understand how he had not seen or heard him. And the fear, once it had nowhere left to go, became anger.

That night, I could not sleep beside him. I asked him to sleep in the spare room.

From that night on, more often than not, we slept separately.

The Burden of Truth

It was with great sadness that I couldn't find a way to convince my family of the truth earlier. My father exuded a kind of righteousness that rendered him nearly untouchable within the family and among his friends. Meanwhile, I was cast as the "difficult" one, perpetually at odds with him. Assumptions were made about my motivations, but the truth was far simpler—I wanted to help him confront his demons. To do that, I became his nemesis, a role I neither wanted nor took lightly.

Had I been more forceful, gone to the police sooner, perhaps the horrors inflicted upon my nieces - and previously on my older sisters - might have been addressed and prevented although risking my family loyalties. I was caught in a web of emotional blackmail. It was my sister's word against my father's, and she often backtracked on what she had confided. No matter how I approached the situation, there was no win-win outcome. For years, I suffered ostracization and the stigma of being branded the "troublemaker."

It was only when my younger sister called to tell me about an unsettling incident during a family gathering that the façade began to crack. One of my nieces, mimicking a behaviour she had experienced, revealed, in her innocent way, what our father, her grandfather, had done to her. Her mother questioned her, and in that moment, lives were irrevocably changed. My father, who had defied the odds to survive a near-death illness the previous year, would now face justice. Had he died then, his secrets would have been buried with him.

The truth emerged in pieces, but the turning point was when an older niece stepped forward, confirming her own experiences of abuse over several years -many of which occurred at Beechdale Road in Brixton, the place of my birth. Her testimony sealed my father's fate.

Writing about this period and its aftermath remains one of the hardest things for me to do. Apart from my older sister, Charlotte, and my brother, Mark, I have no contact with the rest of my family, including my mother. I remain convinced that she knew what my father was doing but chose to protect him, deflecting attention in his favour and blaming all but herself. At one time, she condemned him like the rest of the family, but she later turned, portraying herself as the victim.

In the end, I was the one who maintained a semblance of neutrality. I volunteered to take my father to court for his sentencing after the trial. Other family members, in their anger, wanted to exact their own retribution—threatening my father and attempting to take his possessions. I intervened, warning them that their actions would shift the focus away from justice and potentially land them in trouble. The irony wasn't lost on me: from being the outcast, I had somehow become the voice of reason, trusted by all parties even while living on the other side of the world.

Before sentencing, I was asked by his defence lawyer what would constitute a just punishment. I advocated for a balance - something that would provide closure to the survivors but also account for his failing health. Ultimately, the court settled on an 18-month sentence reduced from a likely 3-year sentence. Knowing this beforehand, I was tasked with preparing a bag of essentials for him - white vests, underwear, t-shirts, and toiletries. Though I knew the likely outcome, I couldn't bring myself to tell him. He was convinced he wouldn't go to jail.

Driving him to the courthouse in Canterbury was one of the hardest things I've ever done. The journey itself was fraught - a wrong turn led to a punctured tyre, and my father sat silently in the backseat, his eyes meeting mine in the rearview mirror. The look he gave me - part chastisement, part resignation - was one I'll never forget.

The family was divided, each faction seated apart in the gallery. When the respective lawyers presented the final statements and listening to what my father had done, I broke down and had to leave the gallery momentarily to compose myself. During the recess, I was asked to bring the bag to the downstairs court room where the sentencing would take place.

The sentencing was the last time I saw my father alive - frail and diminished standing behind a glass barrier – all alone. In that moment, I handed over the bag to the court officer and watched as my father, a shadow of his former self, was led away.

In December 2022, I learned of his death through a Facebook post. No one in the family had informed me, assuming I wouldn't care. They were wrong. Despite everything, I loved my father and forgave him long ago. In letters, I expressed that forgiveness. But the gatekeepers within the family - my mother, younger sister, and eldest sister - often censored or distorted our communication, further widening the chasm between us. I often reflected on how letters and messages from Prisoner of War are censored and manipulated in favour of the authorities before being sent to its receiver.

While my father fell from grace, there were moments of connection. I remember the meals he cooked when my mother was away, the 'all in one' pot (was like camping food) and the bacon and egg sandwiches he made during test cricket or Wimbledon, and the hours we spent playing tennis. He was athletic, strong-willed, and deeply flawed. I believe his recovery from near-death was no accident—it was a chance for his sins to face earthly judgment.

Even now, I grapple with the legacy of those events. But I hold to certain truths: never make assumptions, always honour your word, and strive to do your best, no matter how difficult the path.

Working in challenging and tropical environments inevitably exposes one to diseases rare or unheard of back home. Malaria, yellow fever, and Japanese encephalitis are common in endemic regions, alongside heightened risks of giardia, hepatitis, respiratory infections, foodborne illnesses, and various skin diseases. However, with rigorous pre- and post-deployment medical assessments, required vaccinations, and strict adherence to preventative measures, most health risks can be managed.

Interestingly, the most common reason for aid workers to be medically evacuated is not due to disease but to injuries - particularly those involving vehicles. Driving through hostile terrain, unfamiliar roadways, or regions still bearing the remnants of war can be perilous. I was fortunate during my assignments to avoid such incidents personally, though there were close calls. I recall escorting relief trucks through a shortcut in farmland near Gaza. Laden with supplies, one of the trucks overturned. Thankfully, no one was injured, but the situation was precarious. It was dusk, tensions between Israelis and Palestinians were heightened during the Second Intifada, and we were deep in unfamiliar territory. With assistance from local farmers using excavators and tractors, we managed to right the truck and retreat to a nearby town, where we spent the night.

During my longest assignment in Nagorno-Karabakh, the environment was less fraught with immediate danger but still shaped by the scars of war. This post-conflict setting allowed for more interaction with the local Armenian community, as hostilities with Azerbaijan were mostly contained to the border. These interactions often provided rare moments of camaraderie and levity. One evening, some colleagues, local staff, and I joined a spirited volleyball game at a nearby sports hall. Unlike the casual beach games I was used to, this was played on a polished wooden floor, and the competition was intense.

During a critical moment near the net, as I prepared to smash a floating ball, a loud snap echoed through the hall. I crumpled to the ground in excruciating pain, my vision swimming. The colour drained from my face as dizziness set in. I had ruptured my Achilles tendon.

The injury seemed dire enough to require evacuation, and I braced for the worst. However, Nagorno-Karabakh, despite its limited infrastructure, had surgeons whose expertise had been honed during the war. Their skills, coupled with rudimentary but effective medical facilities, proved sufficient. My lower leg was encased in a plaster-of-paris back slab after X-rays confirmed the diagnosis.

Though immobilised, I adapted to a mostly desk-based role for the following month, avoiding evacuation. The recovery was painstaking and required patience. It took nearly two years to regain full confidence in traversing uneven terrain, but the experience underscored the resilience one develops in the field.

The most challenging environment I faced in terms of health risks was during my time in Bangladesh, working at the Red Cross field hospital in Cox's Bazar. Nearly one million Rohingya refugees were crammed into a sprawling, overcrowded camp of just 12 square kilometres. The tropical heat, poor sanitation, and rampant diseases—such as dengue, gastroenteritis, giardia, norovirus, and other infections associated with overcrowding - meant that our staff were frequently sick. Gastro-related illnesses, particularly acute diarrhea and vomiting, were especially common, sparing no one.

As the public health delegate, much of my role focused on caring for our own team as much as the refugee population. I worked to ensure proper hygiene practices, maintain hydration among staff, establish isolation protocols, and implement infection control measures. We were fortunate to have a camp kitchen attached to our accommodation— single-bed tents - which allowed us to manage isolations effectively. Infected staff were confined to their sweltering tents during the day, with food delivered to them directly. We did our best to provide fans and other small comforts, but the conditions were harsh. Some staff, upon recovering, opted to return home before completing their assignments.

I completed two rotations as the public health delegate, somehow managing to stay relatively well although just before the end of my first rotation, my partner called me to tell me his beloved mother was near death and if I could return home. Of course without hesitation I did but I was too late to see her alive. She entered mortality whilst I was travelling home.

I was home for about 6-weeks before returning for the second rotation supporting my husband and helped him prepare the funeral and celebration of life ceremony compiling some of her favourite music with photographs of the life in a story book presentation on a screen.

This mission left me with a deep sense of accomplishment, as the preventative measures we implemented - improving water and sanitation systems, conducting early disease surveillance, and strengthening community health - genuinely saved lives, including those of newborns in the camp.

However, my turn to face evacuation came during my last deployment in 2022, when I was assigned as a regional health coordinator at the onset of the Ukraine war with Russia. Based at the regional headquarters in Budapest, Hungary, my role involved coordinating humanitarian efforts for the influx of refugees. While many border countries, including Poland, Romania, and Slovakia, bore the brunt of the exodus, Hungary's response was complicated by its government's sympathies toward Russia. Moldova, despite its small size and economic challenges, admirably supported Ukrainian refugees, punching well above its weight.

This deployment came at a time when the world was emerging from the shadow of the COVID-19 pandemic. While Australia maintained some of the most rigorous infection controls globally, Europe was beginning to relax its measures. In the cramped offices of the regional headquarters, with staff from all over the world and inconsistent adherence to infection control policies, it was only a matter of time before COVID spread. Around 50% of the staff, including me, contracted the virus.

Having avoided COVID up to that point, I was unprepared for how severely it would affect me. Alone in a small hotel room with no cooking facilities, relying on food deliveries and struggling to work remotely, I found the situation unbearable. The dizziness was so intense that I sometimes crawled to the elevator due to effects of tinnitus, fearing I might fall over the balcony or collapse. Eventually, I moved to alternative accommodation with a small kitchen and separate living space, but the symptoms persisted. It became clear that I couldn't recover without a complete break.

I returned home to Australia for medical care, supported by the Australian Red Cross, and after four weeks, I was able to get medical clearance to complete my assignment. However, my role was limited to supporting the Hungarian Red Cross from within Hungary.

This mission marked the conclusion of my international humanitarian career. By then, the psychological and physical toll of years spent in war and disaster zones had become undeniable. Symptoms of post-traumatic stress began to surface—a natural consequence of the horrors and challenges I'd faced. I had already resolved that this would be my final deployment, driven by the growing need to focus on my personal life and attempt to salvage my relationship. But deep down, I knew it was too late.

I sensed that whatever love remained from my husband had faded. When I came home to recover from the effects of COVID, my mattress stayed on the floor, the bed sheets untouched except for the damp patches where our cat's urine had seeped underneath. I was too exhausted and unwell to care, yet on some level, I knew this was a harbinger of the end. It wasn't just the physical disarray—it was the absence of care and concern that spoke volumes. Simple gestures, like coming home to a clean house or feeling someone's effort and support, mattered far more than empty words or mechanical tasks.

My husband never asked how I felt or inquired about my experiences in Ukraine. I clung to the hope that we could reconnect, that something might reignite the spark we once shared. But the reality was that our bond had eroded. We still had so much - material possessions and our beloved dogs—but those attachments weren't enough to hold us together. Without them, the cracks in our relationship became unavoidable.

I bore much of the guilt, believing my frequent deployments had driven the wedge between us. Yet those same deployments had provided the financial stability we needed at the time. It's a cruel irony that what once strengthened us ultimately contributed to our unravelling.

Now, I find myself in limbo, living alone on our hobby farm, awaiting the finalisation of our divorce and separation of assets. Only time will reveal whether this ending was part of a larger plan for the next chapter of my life. For now, I remain suspended between what was and what could be, trying to navigate the uncertain path ahead.

Of all my 23 deployments, this one left me the most disillusioned - not because of personal challenges but because of the glaring inequities it highlighted. Billions of dollars were poured into the Ukraine response, yet other crises - arguably more desperate - remained grossly underfunded. The Rohingya crisis, ongoing conflicts in Africa, and the protracted Syrian war all received far less attention and support. The disparity was stark: European countries opened their borders and provided sanctuary to Ukrainian refugees, while others from strategically and politically "less important" regions were left without refuge.

This deployment revealed how even the supposedly impartial humanitarian response was being eroded, politicised, and shaped by strategic interests rather than need. The inequities in the global humanitarian system were laid bare, and it was a sobering, if bitter, note to end my career on.

The Tank and the Dalek!

War is no joking matter but, even in the depths of despair and where life or death is at the mercy of a simple failure in communication or a misunderstanding, there are moments that seem so surreal, bizarre and at times comical. None more so when being confronted by a tank!

World War One (also known as the Great War) that left millions dead and even more injured and suffering as a result, could have been avoided through the simple act of communication. I know this sounds simplistic and maybe the war would have still happened - if not then but later. The intention was already there but all that was needed was a trigger that would act a catalyst or an 'excuse' to unleash hell.

The trigger came in the form of the assassination of Archduke Franz Ferdinand of Austria and Hungary on 28 June 1914 in Sarajevo, Bosnia. The assassin was a Bosnian Serb nationalist who was part of a group called the 'Black Hand' which sought to end the Austro-Hungarian rule in Bosnia and Herzegovina.

If you have read my earlier chapters, you will notice that these events were in the former Yugoslavia. Austria-Hungary blamed Serbia for the assassination and were given an ultimatum demanding strict compliance and measures to suppress anti-Austro-Hungarian activities. Whilst Serbia accepted most of the terms, it wasn't suffice - Austria-Hungary declared war on Serbia on 28 July 1914.

As it is now, affiliations and agreements are made between nations and, allies are formed – some for strategic reasons others due to historical and ethnic ties. Some are non-binding agreements and others are binding. Russia aligned with Serbia began to mobilise forces. Germany allied with Austria-Hungary declared war on Russian four days later on 1st August and then against Russia's ally France two day later on 3rd August.

To reach France, Germany invaded Belgium violating their neutrality. This led to Britain declaring war on Germany on 4th August 1914.

Within 37 days of the assassination of the Archduke, the Great War began that claimed an estimate between 16 to 20 million military and civilian deaths with an additional 21 million soldiers wounded and countless others left with lasting physical and psychological scars. The armistice that ended the war came four years later on the eleventh hour of the eleventh day of the eleventh month in the year 1918.

These staggering numbers highlight the devastating impact of the war on global populations. There was also the massive impact of the 'remnants and consequences' of war that some estimate to be even greater than the number killed during active combat. Diseases due to the impact of the war on public health systems, exposure to water borne diseases and diseases that manifest through poor hygiene, poor sanitation, starvation and malnutrition, mental health and living in squalor led to a surge in bacterial and viral infections – no more harmful than the influenza pandemic that coincided with soldiers returning home. The numbers are staggering that dwarf the number of military and civilian deaths.

While the assassination was the immediate trigger for World War I, it was not the sole reason – it acted a catalyst. All the ingredients were there, and it just needed to be exploited – there was already a lot of underlying tensions, unresolved deep-rooted ethnic and nationalist tensions in the Balkans. The ingredients and underlying conditions—militarism, alliances, imperialism, and nationalism—meant that Europe was already on a path toward conflict.

Preventing the assassination was theoretically possible through better planning, diplomacy, or addressing nationalist tensions. However, the broader context of political and social instability in Europe meant that even if this specific event were avoided, another flashpoint might have triggered the conflict.

Many assumed this war called the 'Great War' was *'the war that would end all wars'*. It was only called World War One when a second world war erupted with even more destructive consequences just a few decades later.

Whilst not directly the cause of World War Two, Yugoslavia's Government signed the Tripartite Pact aligning itself with the Axis powers (Germany, Italy and Japan). Many Yugoslavs were unhappy with this pact and overthrew the pro-Axis Government. This led to an invasion of Yugoslavia by Germany and Italy and their allies with the territory divided amongst Axis powers and collaborators. This invasion led to delay in Germany's planned invasion of the Soviet Union (Operation Barbarossa) by several weeks, potentially influencing the timing of the campaigns and its eventual challenges. Yugoslavia became a hotbed of resistance movements which exists today.

While Yugoslavia did not trigger World War II, its political turmoil and subsequent invasion played a significant role in the broader dynamics of the conflict. The fierce resistance and occupation there became one of the defining elements of the war in the Balkans.

I was deployed to Israel and the Palestinian Territories in 2004 – during the second Intifada. The word 'intifada' Arabic for 'uprising' was as term used by the Palestinian as an uprising against Israeli occupation in the West Bank, Gaza Strip and East Jerusalem.

The second intifada which began in September 2000 was triggered by Ariel Sharon's visit to the Temple Mount in Jerusalem – a site sacred to both Muslims and Jews. Palestinians viewed this as provocation. The second intifada lasted until 2005.

There was violence on both sides, with one side carrying out large protests, stone throwing, suicide bombings, armed attacks and the other, in response, military operations, airstrikes, curfews and the construction of the West Bank barrier. There were significant casualties and further deepening of political and social divisions between Palestinians and Israelis. During my deployment in 2004, there was widespread suffering on both sides and little resolution in sight.

Despite the uprising, Palestinians in the West Bank and Gaza were heavily dependent on Israeli-controlled services, particularly for access to certain medical treatments, employment in Israel, and essential goods. During the Intifada, this dependency created tension between the need for survival and the desire for resistance. The Israeli occupation meant that essential resources like water, electricity, and border crossings were under Israeli control

The unintended benefit although it would come at a cost, the Intifada also accelerated efforts to develop alternative Palestinian-run services, such as informal healthcare networks, underground education initiatives, and local economies less reliant on Israeli goods and services. The Palestinian Authority (PA), though limited in its capacity, attempted to fill some gaps in governance and service provision. However, its effectiveness was hampered by the conflict and internal divisions.

My role as the Health Coordinator was not confined to one side of the conflict. Many international agencies were providing support through various organisations to the Palestinian people, largely because they were perceived as the oppressed party, facing a disproportionate level of need compared to the Israelis. However, unlike the current conflict in 2024, I observed that Israel's military incursions at that time were meticulously planned to limit civilian casualties. This stood in contrast to many other contemporary conflicts, where battles were no longer fought on traditional battlefields between opposing armies but instead waged from a distance, often increasing civilian casualties.

The First Geneva Convention defines a combatant as someone enlisted in an established, governed army who wears a uniform and is distinguishable from civilians. The Israeli military fit this definition, with a well-defined chain of command and soldiers who were easily identifiable. In contrast, this distinction was not clear-cut for Palestinians. Any civilian could potentially take up arms and then revert to civilian status, blurring the lines between combatants and non-combatants.

The Israelis held a significant advantage in terms of military power, logistics, and technology, which allowed them to conduct strategic and precise armed responses, including precision strikes. During one visit to Gaza, I witnessed this firsthand. While driving through an area where the Israeli army had recently made an incursion, our Red Cross vehicle stopped at a crossroad as we saw an Israeli tank approaching. We retreated cautiously to observe from the pavement, stepping out of our vehicle to assess whether the tank would continue up the road. Almost immediately, bullets struck the pavement just in front of us - clearly a precise and deliberate warning to step back and retreat into our vehicles.

Israel's technological and military superiority enabled them to target militants with precision, even in areas where combatants, militants, and civilians shared the same space. However, when these groups overlapped, civilians, including children, were inevitably at risk. Any harm to children in these situations carried the potential for significant political fallout. Despite this, compared to other conflicts at the time, the number of civilian casualties in Israeli operations was relatively lower.

In response to Israel's incursions, curfews, restrictions on movement, and punitive measures - such as demolishing the homes of suicide bombers - Palestinians turned to guerrilla-style tactics. These involved random attacks with less sophisticated weaponry, including suicide bombings at checkpoints and attacks on civilian buses. Such attacks created widespread anxiety among Israelis, as they targeted everyday activities like commuting or shopping.

While the majority of the humanitarian sector focused on addressing the critical needs of the Palestinian population, a different type of support was required for Israelis affected by the indiscriminate and unpredictable nature of these attacks. The random targeting of civilians, combined with the use of imprecise and less advanced weaponry, exacerbated the psychological toll on the Israeli population.

A term often used in the humanitarian sector is *perfidy*. In the context of war, *perfidy* refers to deliberate acts of betrayal or deception that violate the trust or agreements between opposing parties, often to gain a tactical advantage. This is particularly relevant when deceit is employed in ways that contravene established rules of war or moral codes. For example, pretending to surrender or feigning protected status - such as displaying the emblem of the Red Cross - while intending harm constitutes perfidy. Such actions are not only deemed dishonourable but are explicitly prohibited under international humanitarian law, as they erode the principles of good faith and humanity in warfare.

Perfidy has significant consequences, particularly in relation to ambulances and checkpoints. Ambulances, like medical facilities, are traditionally trusted to be carrying individuals injured or in need of care, especially when marked with the protective emblems of the Red Cross or Red Crescent. When such symbols are misused to deceive, that trust - and the protection offered by these emblems—is profoundly undermined.

This erosion of trust has ripple effects. Increasingly, we see hospitals and medical facilities being attacked, often under the pretext that they are harbouring combatants, militants, or weapons - claims that are frequently denied. The question arises: if perfidy in these instances is not about gaining a tactical advantage, what is driving its increasing prevalence?

Finally, consider the perspective of civilians in desperate circumstances. If survival depended on disguise - perhaps using a symbol of protection - what choice would you make? In a matter of life and death, would you act differently?

Seeing a large military tank turn a street corner and head directly toward you feels like a scene straight out of a World War II film about German forces in occupied France. The streets were eerily deserted - everyone had taken cover in their homes. In the distance, it was just us, cautiously edging out from a side street at a crossroads.

This would not be my last encounter with an Israeli tank - the next one would be far more intimate.

The number of Palestinian casualties resulting from Israeli Defence Force (IDF) incursions and airstrikes was steadily rising, placing immense pressure on the Palestinian-run hospitals in Gaza. In response, we implemented a program to supply war-wounded kits, medications and provide war surgery training for hospital staff. Various organisations also contributed medical support; for instance, the Spanish Red Cross donated several ambulances to the Palestinian Red Crescent Society.

However, restricted movement exacerbated the already dire situation. Palestinians from East Jerusalem or the West Bank were barred from entering Gaza and vice versa, making it increasingly difficult for Gazans to leave the territory. Israeli civilians, due to personal safety concerns, were strictly prohibited from entering Palestinian territories. Among the few exceptions to these restrictions were non-Israelis and non-Palestinians - primarily international humanitarian workers, diplomats, and representatives from donor countries like the European Union, the USA, Canada, and Japan and international journalists.

The donation of the six ambulances would provide much needed outreach medical support that would be operated by the recognised Palestinian Red Crescent Society (PRCS), who were working towards becoming a full member of the International Red Cross and Red Crescent Movement. The equivalent, the Maged David Dom (MDA) which translates to "Red Shield of David" were also supported by the International Red Cross and were in the process of accreditation to become a full member. The full memberships were granted in 2006 after Third Additional Protocol to the Geneva Conventions in 2005, which introduced the Red Crystal as a neutral emblem. This protocol allowed MDA to operate under an internationally recognised symbol without using the Red Cross or Red Crescent, addressing long-standing emblem-related concerns and facilitating its integration into the global humanitarian network.

My intimate encounter with an Israeli tank occurred while escorting a fleet of Spanish Red Cross ambulances donated to the Palestinian Red Crescent Society (PRCS) in Gaza. Our team consisted entirely of Gazans, except for me as the sole international representative. Being a British citizen working for an impartial and neutral organisation, I could move relatively freely between Israel and the Palestinian Territories, subject to strict security measures and screening.

At the border crossing into Gaza from Israel, my Palestinian field officer, who was from East Jerusalem, was not permitted to accompany me into Gaza. Only I and my vehicle were granted access, while my field officer returned to our sub-delegation office in East Jerusalem with the accompanying vehicle. The PRCS had already secured permission for the ambulances to enter Gaza. Once through the border and customs checks, I met with my PRCS counterparts and national staff from our sub-delegation office in Gaza city. Accompanied by one of our national staff he took over the driving responsibilities whilst I exchanged seats to be in the passenger seat so I could manage the radio contact and instruct those in the vehicle behind me and maintain radio contact with our Sub-delegation in Gaza. The convoy consisted of our vehicle as lead vehicle with two PRCS Land Cruisers and six donated ambulances following.

At the time, Gaza was under curfew, and Gazans were not allowed to leave the territory. The Israeli Defence Forces (IDF) had deployed tanks and other military hardware as a mobile force to patrol the area, respond to insurgencies, and carry out retaliatory operations, such as demolishing homes of individuals connected to suicide bombings in cities like Jerusalem and Tel Aviv. The tension was palpable, and as per our procedures, we maintained regular radio contact with our radio room to update our position and status.

The roads into Gaza were challenging, marked by the passage of tanks that had churned up fields and paths alongside the road The once-paved surfaces of the road were now uneven and broken, making navigation difficult, especially for the ambulances. Soon, we encountered a dip in the road that was too severe for the ambulances to traverse safely, forcing us to halt and assess our options.

Suddenly, from a nearby field, an Israeli tank roared toward us like a charging bull elephant, its diesel engine belching smoke and dirt rising in thick clouds around its massive frame. It tore through the soft ground, following the perimeter wire fencing parallel to our convoy. With a screech of metal and grinding gears, it came to an abrupt halt at the head of the line. For a brief moment, my mind wandered to the children's story of the three billy goats trying to cross a bridge guarded by a fearsome troll. In my imagination, the tank was the troll, poised to demand in a booming voice, *"Who's that crossing my bridge?"*

The surreal thought vanished as I instinctively rolled my window halfway down, following the customary protocol for receiving instructions. The tank's turret swivelled ominously, its gun barrel sweeping across the line of vehicles. Then, over the loudspeaker, a commanding voice crackled: "Exit your vehicle."

Following the command, I stepped out of the Land Cruiser, leaving the door open behind me, and stood beside the vehicle awaiting further instructions. This was a routine I had experienced before at border checkpoints, where compliance with IDF instructions was paramount for safety. Trust, in these situations, depended on strict adherence to protocol.

The voice from the tank ordered me to step forward. I climbed onto a nearby dirt mound, standing directly in front of the tank. Only then did I see the face of its commander, partially visible below the turret and holding two flags. He began asking the standard questions: who we were, what we were doing, and why we were there. As always, our operations had been pre-approved through coordination between our office and the IDF high command, but it was a waiting game until the checks were confirmed.

As I stood face-to-face with the tank's barrel, which swung abruptly from side to side, I was struck by an odd thought - it reminded me of a Dalek from *Doctor Who*. The tank's turret resembled a Dalek's head, and the barrel mirrored its iconic eyestalk. Even its voice, disembodied and mechanical, amplified the resemblance. The absurdity of the comparison brought a brief inner smile, but outwardly, I maintained a poker face, still and expressionless.

The checks seemed to take forever, but eventually, the mood shifted. The tone of the conversation became lighter, and the tank commander even offered to assist by filling in the uneven terrain to allow us to proceed. While this seemed helpful, I quickly realised the potential implications: a headline such as "IDF Helps the Red Cross Deliver Humanitarian Aid to Gaza" would compromise our neutrality and position the IDF as a humanitarian actor, undermining the impartiality of the entire operation.

Spotting a group of labourers repairing the road ahead, I suggested we ask them to fill in the large holes instead. The tank commander approved, and I drove to the labourers, requesting their help. Armed with shovels and pickaxes, they filled the dips sufficiently for our convoy to continue.

As we prepared to leave, the tank remained stationary, its turret and its gun barrel swivelling as though watching us. At the bottom of the front of the tank there was a row of chains which looked like a beard, making the tank look even more human! Then, in a surprisingly human gesture, two small white flags waved from a window below the turret, as if bidding us farewell. We proceeded to the PRCS office in Gaza City, where the ambulances were officially handed over by our head of sub-delegation.

This encounter was just another day in the life of a Red Cross delegate—but in its own way, it was uniquely memorable, not just for the challenges but for the outcome.

A medal, the army, love and a gym

The Florence Nightingale Medal a prestigious international award which is presented to those distinguished in nursing and is named after the British nurse Florence Nightingale. The medal was established in 1912 by the International Committee of the Red Cross (ICRC), following the Eighth International Conference of the Red Cross Societies in London in 1907. It is the highest international distinction a nurse can achieve and is awarded to nurses or nursing aides for "exceptional courage and devotion to the wounded, sick, or disabled, or to civilian victims of a conflict or disaster," or for "exemplary services or a creative and pioneering spirit in the areas of public health or nursing education." In 2023, I was honoured to be awarded this medal for my services to working in war zones, disasters, public health and nurse education.

A year earlier, I received the Victorian Division of the Australian Red Cross International Award.

Both these honours came as a surprise. I was informed about the International Award directly by the Australian Red Cross. A few days later, a friend—who was herself a previous Florence Nightingale Medal recipient—sent me a message congratulating me on receiving the Florence Nightingale Medal. At first, I thought she was mistaken, as I had only been officially informed about the International Award. When I asked how she knew, she replied that it had been announced on the ICRC website. Intrigued, I searched online, and there it was - my name listed as a recipient of the Florence Nightingale Medal! Shortly afterward, the Australian Red Cross confirmed that both I and a colleague had been nominated and had received this distinguished honour.

The news filled me with immense pride. While the medal itself is a significant symbol, its deeper meaning—to be acknowledged for my work - was profoundly moving. I later learned that I was only the 62nd Australian to receive the Florence Nightingale Medal since 1920 and the first male recipient of the medal in Australia.

I was presented the medal by our Honourable Governor General David Hurley at Government House in Canberra.

Within the Red Cross and Red Crescent Movement, I had undertaken twenty-three deployments. Additionally, I worked on deployments with UNICEF, UNHCR, WHO, and Oxfam, all within a span of twenty-five years.

Receiving the Florence Nightingale Medal felt more than a personal honour; it symbolised recognition for the countless humanitarian aid workers who dedicate their time and energy to support those affected by conflict or disaster. While only a small number of us are recognised with this medal internationally each year, in truth, each award represents the collective efforts of our community.

The medal provides a powerful platform. It allows you to speak with authority about working in the humanitarian sector, to advocate on behalf of those with a lesser voice, and to offer an educated and experienced perspective in contrast to the views of armchair critics. Most importantly, it serves as a source of inspiration for the next generation of nurses and aid workers, encouraging them to step forward and make a difference.

They say that in some professions and vocations, you are married to the job. Perhaps this is true for those who dedicate their lives to a monastic or religious order, where marriage to another human is replaced by devotion to the divine. It was certainly true during my early deployments in war zones. Remaining unattached to a single person allowed me to focus fully on my work without the distraction or burden of a partner worrying about me. It gave me a sense of freedom. I know of some humanitarian workers that dedicate their whole lives to helping others and a life of service.

In many ways, it also benefited the organisation. They didn't have to navigate the aftermath of grieving relatives or loved ones if something tragic were to happen. While this was never explicitly stated, I often suspected that my situation gave them added flexibility in assigning me to tasks or roles that carried greater risks. Reflecting on some of my deployments, I realised the dangers I faced were often more significant than those encountered by many of my peers.

My height, complexion, heritage, and gender often worked to my advantage. I could "blend in" and be less visible, frequently mistaken for a local rather than an outsider. At least from an initial observation, this offered an added layer of protection and, at times, greater opportunities to navigate sensitive environments.

Many of my roles were described as 'polyvalent,' meaning I wasn't confined to a single title or function. Instead, I was expected to adapt and undertake multiple responsibilities as needed. This flexibility became a defining feature of my work, allowing me to contribute in diverse and sometimes unexpected ways.

The Path Less Taken

I have often found myself torn between the universal narrative of the "human dream" and the unique, unpredictable course my life has taken. The dream is a familiar one: finishing school, attending university, finding a job, meeting a partner, marrying, having children, building a home, and eventually enjoying a fulfilled retirement. At times, my life seemed to flirt with this ideal - moments of passion, love, and rebellion intertwined with youthful adventures in music and dance, glamorous holidays, and the thrill of living on the edge.

In my late teens and early twenties, my nights often led me to London's vibrant club scene, including *Heaven*, an iconic venue nestled under the arches of Charing Cross. It was a place alive with music, possibility, and intrigue, where special guests were invited to a private upstairs area. At the time, I was considered a "good catch" in the eyes of men, but beyond the occasional crush, this lifestyle felt like an escape—something my soul needed to experience rather than embrace. I realised that my life was being pigeonholed into a world that was not part of my dreams or my 'whole self'. The longer I stayed, the harder it became to leave. It began to define me, and while I outwardly accepted it to survive, inwardly, I longed for a way out. I saw sadness etched in so many faces, their eyes filled with longing and a fragile hope that someone - perhaps me - might be the one to change their lives.

Many of the people I met during this time, including two great loves, have since died from AIDS, a silent storm that was gradually emerging from the shadows. I vividly recall dancing alongside Freddie Mercury and Limahl, the lead singer of Kajagoogoo and the voice behind *The NeverEnding Story*. The radio host and comedian Kenny Everitt and the host of a popular chat show, Russel Harty were regular visitors as were probably many other celebrities.

There were moments when I yearned and imagined a different life - a more settled existence with a loving marriage, raising children, and giving my parents the joy of grandchildren. It was a vision of belonging, of completeness. Yet, for reasons I still cannot fully grasp, my life veered away from that path. Instead, it took me through experiences I never imagined or wanted, but which were essential in shaping the person I was to become.

My reality diverged sharply from my childhood dreams. My life became a tapestry of experiences that would never have unfolded had I followed the traditional path I had imagined. I often ponder whether this divergence was part of a divine plan or the will of my own soul seeking its unique journey.

Life could have been simpler, perhaps, but I wonder - would it have been unbearably dull? There were times when I longed for that simplicity, particularly when I mourned the absence of fatherhood. The chance to raise children, to experience the joy and challenges my own parents faced, remains a poignant longing.

When I look at my sister Charlotte, I marvel at her resilience. Despite a turbulent childhood, broken marriages, and the trials of being a single mother, she raised four children and now cherishes her role as a grandmother with her soul mate. Her journey was far harder than mine, yet she found beauty and meaning in her struggles.

In contrast, my path was driven by a sense of purpose - one I believe was chosen by my soul. My life, shaped by experiences both planned and unexpected, sought meaning beyond convention. My desire to be married did occur but not in the way I envisioned when I was young. It could also have been an arranged marriage, one borne out of convenience or circumstance, or a union marked by poverty or displacement. The expression *be careful what you wish for* resonates deeply - our desires, when fulfilled, rarely appear as we imagine.

Moments of loss and grief have brought clarity and spiritual awakening. Routine and complacency can strip away one's spiritual essence, binding us too tightly to our human roles. It is often through life-altering events that we reconnect with our deeper selves.

I have loved deeply, though sparingly. My first love was in my late teens, my second in my early twenties - a love I then believed to be my greatest - and my third nearly two decades later that I took for granted would be until 'death do we part'. Between these were fleeting attractions and brief romances, none of which compared to true love. Yet, I discovered that love need not be physical or romantic. My greatest, enduring love has been one with a friend in which we had a deep spiritual connection. A friend I seldom saw after our lives were separated when he married. We shared a lot and our connection was not physical or intimate but it was one of caring and understanding. Whilst we seldom see or hear from each other, he is seldom away from my thoughts and was probably the greatest influence in making Australia my home. When we do catch up, it is like time has stood still and memories of our experiences together, are etched into our souls. Other loves may take the form in another human, an animal such as a pet or unseen but omnipresent - an unspoken connection beyond the bounds of intimacy.

A turning point in my relationship with my family and particularly my mother came when I confronted my father, leading to distancing from my family to protect my own health and mental wellbeing. This unjust blame and ostracism, painful as it was, became a gateway to freedom. It allowed me to break away from unhealthy dynamics and take responsibility for my own life. Sometimes, the greatest act of love is letting go.

In my search for solace and understanding, I experienced a spiritual awakening. A deep yearning drew me closer to God, culminating in an unexpected calling. I found myself undergoing an assessment for the Church Missionary Society (CMS) in an abbey near Birmingham. The process involved prayer, meditation, and reflection under the watchful eyes of a bishop, a monk, a nun and a layperson. At its conclusion, I was told I had a calling. The laypersons words stayed with me: "You are very special." The monk suggested that I would suit the monastic life.

A Japanese female friend once told me, "When you have two or more paths in front of you, take the hardest one." Another friend countered, "Whatever path you choose is the right one - there is no wrong path, even if it leads to grief." I decided not to pursue the path to missionary work - which I think in hindsight was the easier path. I took the path that was the right path.

My life has been far from the "perfect dream." It has been messy, unpredictable, and often challenging. Yet it has been deeply fulfilling, guided by something greater than my own understanding. In the end, I have come to see that the life I lived - full of twists, heartbreaks, and spiritual revelations - was the life I was meant to live.

Personal Sacrifice and Four Words That Changed Everything

My last traditional relationship spanned seventeen years. When it ended, the devastation was profound. All the dreams I had nurtured - of a secure future, fulfilling travel, and a comfortable retirement - were shattered by four simple words: *"I want a divorce."*

There was no discussion, no shared reflection - just a unilateral decision delivered like a bombshell, dismantling the life we had built together. In that moment, the path I thought I was on vanished, leaving me to navigate uncharted terrain. While those words set the wheels of change in motion, it was up to me to take action, to bring meaning and resolution to what was otherwise just an abrupt declaration.

The timing of the statement could not have been worse. I had already decided to retire, bringing my international career to an end. I had invested all my savings into a fitness business - a venture we both shared but one I was deeply committed to, supporting it financially during my deployments and even through the challenges of the COVID-19 pandemic, which had crippled countless small businesses, especially in the fitness industry.

Yet, in hindsight, I recognise that the seeds of our relationship's undoing were sown long before those words were spoken. My international work—particularly deployments to conflict zones - had taken a toll, not just on me but on us. Symptoms of post-traumatic stress were already manifesting, adding an invisible weight to our lives.

Seemingly ordinary events would trigger exaggerated reactions. Once, a fleeting play of light during the night and sound convinced me there were gunmen in our garden. The crack of a branch and the flash of a torch scanning for foxes became, in my mind, bandits in the shadows. I was living in the country where night patrols and gunshots were common. I acted out how I would working in a conflict zone. I woke my partner, told him not to put on the lights, keep low and not to make a sound whilst I crawled to the door and then the window to peak through the blinds. I was frantically calling '000'. He followed my instructions without questioning and made no mention of this when we awoke the next day and continued our usual routine.

Nightmares were a constant, often mixing the past with the present in disturbing ways. Particularly upsetting were dreams involving my four-legged family -abduction, fire, and harrowing escapes from intruders or encroaching infernos rolling from the forest toward the house. I felt safe knowing my partner was next to me but somehow, I wasn't sure if he would jump into burning house to save me as I would do without hesitation to save him. I know my mother would put herself at risk to save others but wasn't sure I could trust the same of my father unless out of vanity or chivalry.

One recurring dream that continues to haunt me over decades: knowing there were bodies hidden in a cellar or attic, their remains long decomposed and undetectable. In these dreams, I was the killer. I would stand beside those inspecting the supposed scenes of death - family members, strangers considering the property -knowing they would find nothing. My heart would race as they searched, and then I'd wake, overwhelmed by a sense of relief as the parallel world faded into nothingness.

These vivid and often terrifying dreams weren't just a private burden; they crept into my waking life, affecting my behaviour and, inevitably, our relationship. It was part of why I made the decision to leave my international career. I had hoped to focus on our business and build the future we had once envisioned together. But by the time I made that decision, it was too late. The damage - seen and unseen - had already taken its toll.

Still, amidst these struggles, there were moments of unexpected beauty, even in dreams. Occasionally, I would find myself flying - soaring effortlessly over rooftops and treetops, fully in control of when I ascended and descended.

I marvelled at the intricacies of the world from a vertical perspective, one impossible to grasp from the ground. It fascinated me to see the world as a bird might, with breathtaking clarity and detail.

In those fleeting moments of flight, I felt a freedom that eluded me in my waking life, a reminder that even amidst chaos and loss, the mind could conjure a vision of transcendence.

The unilateral decision to divorce felt profoundly unjust, considering the sacrifices I believed I had made - and was still making - to transform what had become an unhealthy dynamic back into the relationship we once cherished. I was working to rebuild what we had, only to find myself facing an irreversible decision made without my input.

People often assume or ask whether I was, or had ever been, in the military. This assumption likely stems from the structured nature of the nursing profession and my international work, my interest in both World Wars, the Hellenic wars and the military in general – especially Naval ships. Both professions often operate within hierarchical systems and sometimes overlap with military environments. My overseas roles frequently required engagement with armed forces and understanding the 'military mind' proved to be a distinct advantage. It allowed me to anticipate behaviours, navigate the chain of command, and approach challenges strategically by presenting problems that required solutions rather than dictating how things should be done. I learned that asking for help or presenting a challenge was often met with enthusiasm and resourcefulness. Conversely, telling someone 'how to do their job' was almost always the wrong approach.

In truth, the answer to whether I was in the military is both "yes" and "no." Yes, in that I accepted an offer to become an officer in the Royal Australian Army, and no, because I ultimately chose my partner and our life together over a career as a reservist. At the time, I was poised for a role that would have quickly elevated me to the rank of captain, with a long-term goal of becoming a Major. I had successfully passed the rigorous entry requirements, including fitness and psychiatric testing, been issued my rank insignia, army personnel number, uniform, and title as Lieutenant Nicholas Prince, and was set to begin officer training at the Royal Military College, Duntroon. Before then, in the UK and visit to the RAF recruitment and information office at the Ministry of Defence in Whitehall, London, they were keen due to my experience in the Middle East to consider applying for a Nursing Officer role in the RAF.

My partner, stating he was a pacifist did not agree that I would be carrying arms. I explained that whilst my role would not be infantry it was standard practice for all military personnel to carry and know how to use weapons – especially in self-defence. Even nurses, chaplains and others away from the front line come under attack and there may be a last resort decision to defend your colleagues or yourself. Being defenceless and without a weapon didn't lessen your chance of being wounded or killed. A gun was a deterrent. A question that is common during recruitment is whether when faced by a child soldier carrying a weapon would you shoot the child? I know that I gave the right answer (or at least the answer they were wanting to hear). After I made the difficult decision to resign and the reasons why, I was kept on 'stand-by' for five years in case I decided to return or be summoned to active service if we went to war. Ironically the same person who presented me the Florence Nightingale Medal in his role as Governor General was previously an army general. We talked about this and the shared space between the military and humanitarian organisations during my private audience with him.

Given that the Australian Army had not yet established a dedicated Civil-Military Cooperation (CIMIC) corps, my nursing profession allowed them to accept me as a Nursing Officer. However, in practice, my role would have been more aligned with Signals. I had a natural affinity with army personnel and, compared to most of my peers, a much higher level of field experience working in conflict zones. My knowledge would have been invaluable in the theatre of war.

However, there was a stark contrast between the roles I had fulfilled as an aid worker and the duties of an officer in the armed forces. As a humanitarian, my protection came from the emblem I wore, enabling me to interact with all sides of a conflict. In the military, there would be no such neutrality; I would belong to one side alone. The army carried the advantage of protective equipment and defensive mechanisms, while as a humanitarian, my tools were dialogue, neutrality, impartiality, and independence - principles reinforced through education about the Red Cross, international humanitarian law, and the Geneva Conventions, to which states were signatories.

Prior to this, I had already represented the International Red Cross at military-led training and educational seminars alongside officers from the Australian Defence Force, regional militaries, and the United Nations. While Australia did not, at that time, have a dedicated CIMIC corps, most European armed forces, UN peacekeepers and NATO did. These units were invaluable in disaster relief and combat settings where militaries and humanitarian organisations often shared the same operational space. Such collaboration was essential to saving lives, even if the principles and values guiding each group remained vastly different. Later, I was invited to the Army Staff Training College in Canberra as a subject matter expert to assist military personnel undertaking a disaster-relief subject as part of the officer master's program. Many participants were from international, regional, or allied forces, and the exchange of knowledge proved invaluable.

The logistical power of an army can bring critical relief in the aftermath of warfare or natural disasters, making coordinated efforts indispensable. Armies are generally familiar with their respective Red Cross or Red Crescent National Societies and even more so with the International Committee of the Red Cross (ICRC), which holds a unique mandate to assist in armed conflict zones. As the custodian of the Geneva Conventions and international humanitarian law, the ICRC bridges divides to deliver aid where it is needed most.

Beyond my career aspirations, other sacrifices were made in the name of the relationship I had chosen to prioritise. I suspended my doctorate studies in Public Health, believing the added workload was creating unnecessary strain on my partner. It reduced the time I could contribute to domestic responsibilities, and I wanted to ease that burden. Whenever my partner needed me, I was there, willingly setting aside opportunities that I thought paled in comparison to the greater one: sharing a life with someone I loved.

I know understand better how women particular forsake their own careers and independence to support their partner, give birth and raise children. Whilst this is becoming increasing a shared responsibility, it was less common in previous generations. My sacrifices, whilst significant for me were choices that women rarely had.

When I look back on that relationship, I realise how much it was shaped by the need to fill a void. After years of being single and periods of celibacy, I sought emotional and intimate connection. Yet, for me, physical intimacy has never been paramount - it has always been the spiritual connection that truly matters. Reflecting on those seventeen years, I see now that the relationship lacked the depth of spiritual intimacy I craved. Instead, it was rooted in traditional structures: the assigned roles, the pursuit of financial security, and the comfort of a predictable, ordered existence.

Life became a cycle of routines - 9am to 5pm work routine, shared meals, TV shows, and weekend errands, gardening, walking and playing with the dogs and an occasional visit to a market, see a film at the local cinema and go for a meal or a drink at the pub. While there's nothing inherently wrong with this rhythm, my work in war and disaster zones, where camaraderie and purpose thrived amidst chaos, made the mundanity of routine feel stifling. Living between these two parallel worlds - one marked by raw human struggle and the other by safety and order created an internal conflict that I struggled to reconcile.

At times, this conflict erupted in anger or frustration. I found myself wrestling with how much we, in our insulated lives, take for granted. The complaints I heard about petty inconveniences grated against the stark realities of displacement and survival I had witnessed. While I could often mask my frustration, the occasional ignorant comment would spark a sharp response. It was as though my experiences had made it impossible to see the world through the singular lens most people rely on—a lens shaped by the media and devoid of the complexities I had encountered firsthand.

Perhaps life would have been simpler without the weight of those opposing worlds without the constant push and pull between them. Yet, as challenging as it has been, this duality has shaped me. It has forced me to question, to reflect, and to grow in ways I never would have in a life untouched by such extremes.

When I committed myself to another person, my commitment reading was taken from a chapter in Khalil Gibran's book 'The Prophet'

In *The Prophet*, Khalil Gibran offers a poetic and profound meditation on the nature of love, painting it as a force both exquisite and tumultuous. Love, he writes, crowns you with joy but also crucifies you with pain. It is not merely a gentle embrace but a tempest that shakes the very foundations of your being. Through this duality, love compels you to confront your vulnerabilities and ultimately transforms you, shaping you into your truest self. It is through love's trials that we are refined, much like wheat is threshed and sifted before it becomes flour.

Gibran reminds us that love demands selflessness and surrender. It is not about possession or control, but about giving yourself fully, without expectation of return. Love does not bind; it liberates. To truly love is to set another free, to allow them to flourish as an individual while still remaining connected. Yet, this freedom does not diminish the depth of love; rather, it strengthens it, for love thrives in openness and sincerity, unclouded by fear or domination.

Love, he suggests, is not a sanctuary from hardship but a crucible in which we are tested and purified. It requires courage to endure its trials, for love will often break you open, revealing parts of yourself you did not know existed. This breaking is not an act of destruction but one of creation, as love compels you to grow in ways you could not have anticipated.

Despite its transformative power, love does not ask you to lose yourself. Gibran beautifully describes the balance of unity and individuality within love, likening lovers to the pillars of a temple. They stand together, supporting the same structure, yet remain distinct, each holding their unique space. Love unites without erasing, connecting two souls while honouring their separate identities.

Perhaps most striking is Gibran's vision of love as eternal and unwavering, transcending the transient nature of human emotions. Love, he asserts, is not confined by time or circumstance but seeks a deeper spiritual purpose. It calls for devotion, not as an obligation but as an expression of the soul's yearning to connect with something greater than itself.

Ultimately, Gibran's vision of love is one of profound freedom and commitment. It is not the fleeting romance of possession or desire but a spiritual journey that invites us to embrace both the ecstasy and the trials it brings. Love, in its purest form, is both a challenge and a gift - a force that unites us with others while helping us discover who we truly are.

My long career working in the theatre of war and disasters shaped my identity in ways that often overshadowed my personal self, especially among friends and colleagues. It was rarely my humanity that intrigued them, but rather the practical markers of societal worth: *"What's your job?"* or *"Do you own a house?"* These questions seemed to dominate potential suitors' conversations, with the inevitable *"What do you do?"* proving particularly fraught for me. It was an impossible question to answer succinctly and, if I did, it often sent people running.

At times, I leaned into this professional identity, especially when it served a purpose delivering lectures, fundraising, attending ceremonies, or earning a degree of standing and respect. Yet, once the uniform was shed and I resumed my civilian guise, I often found myself struggling to fit into certain societal groups. Small talk and trivial conversations felt alien, even hollow, leaving me searching for something more meaningful.

I found solace in deepening my connection with nature and the sanctuary of our hobby farm. My partner and I left the bustle of the city behind, settling on an acreage in regional Victoria. Over time, we transformed this space into a nature's paradise. We planted native trees, shrubs, and flowering bushes, creating a vibrant microclimate that has drawn a dazzling array of native birds and animals. At times, the property bustled with life - sheep, lambs, chickens, six dogs (excluding the occasional puppies), a cat, reptiles, goats, and even alpacas. This haven more than compensated for the high-stakes work I was doing overseas.

It was a life I could have truly embraced, one that nourished my spirit. Yet, the toll of working in war zones and the lingering impact of post-traumatic stress posed challenges that could not be ignored. This place was my refuge, a testament to resilience and renewal, even as I navigated the shadows cast by the work that had shaped me.

As the dream of a hobby farm and self-sufficiency fades after my divorce, new dawns emerge. Since 2018, I have owned a fitness club - a concept that had simmered on the backburner for years before becoming a reality. This opportunity arose after I returned from an assignment in South Sudan, where I was deployed with the World Health Organisation. At the time, South Sudan was embroiled in a civil conflict, creating ideal conditions for a cholera outbreak alongside famine-induced warfare.

Upon returning home, I needed to rebuild my strength and fitness. Regular exercise, especially between assignments, had always prepared me for the physical and mental demands of working in highly stressful and unpredictable environments. I joined a newly opened gym nearby that offered everything I needed, including long hours and seven-day-a-week access. With a straightforward membership process, a fortnightly payment plan, and an access fob allowing entry anytime, it was an ideal fit.

Over time, I got to know the owner, who was seeking personal trainers. As a qualified personal trainer, I discussed the opportunity and was invited to join the team. The gym was part of a franchise, and through my involvement, I met the company founder – a top Australian triple jumper and former Commonwealth Games competitor. The franchise was expanding, and I expressed interest in becoming a franchise owner. This aligned with my need for a succession plan, as I knew my humanitarian work would eventually conclude, and reintegrating into the nursing and health sectors could be challenging, given the vastly different demands and the reverse culture shock.

Working in humanitarian settings, where health services were often limited, had shaped my perspective. In Australia, we enjoy abundant healthcare resources, both public and private, with many services free or subsidised. However, this abundance can be a double-edged sword, fostering dependency and a lack of accountability. The healthcare system often becomes a conveyor belt for 'repeat offenders'—individuals who use services to address preventable conditions caused by lifestyle choices, only to return to the same behaviours. This cycle places a strain on healthcare resources, diverting funds from critical areas such as research and more complex medical cases.

In contrast, in the developing countries I worked in, illness or injury could have dire consequences, including loss of income, livelihood, or social standing. A trip to a health clinic or hospital could require a day's journey and be financially costly. With these challenges, people generally prioritised their health to avoid getting sick. Preventive measures were not just a choice but a necessity.

Preventive health has always been a passion of mine. During my time working in clinical settings, including emergency rooms and surgical wards, I witnessed the consequences of diseases and injuries stemming from poor behaviours or lack of safety measures such as not wearing car seat belts or wearing motorbike helmets that are standard practice today. Alcohol, drugs, gambling and fast food are now some of the biggest causes of lifestyle related diseases and injuries filling up the emergency rooms and hospital beds. Many diseases and injuries could have been prevented or delayed through health promotion and preventive care. Opening a gym allowed me to adopt a different approach - creating a community where members invested in their health through regular exercise, strength-building, and improved nutrition. This contributed to reducing the burden on the healthcare system, enhancing quality of life, and improving mental health and mood - benefits often overlooked by society and government.

Unfortunately, the contribution of well-run gyms to population health is often underestimated by health departments and local, state, and federal governments. There remains a heavy focus on treatment models, which are financially advantageous for governments and industries such as pharmaceuticals. In many ways, sickness is treated as an economic asset, much like wars are sometimes perpetuated to sustain arms and construction industries.

Preventive health, unless linked to a business income opportunity and substantial profit margins such as vaccination, rarely receives the funding it deserves. While immunisation is the second-largest contributor to saving lives after access to clean water, it also generates substantial profits for vaccine manufacturers. In contrast, behaviour change - such as adopting healthier lifestyles to reduce reliance on medication - poses a threat to profits and government revenue. Only when the cost of treatment outweighs the revenue generated by taxes on harmful products like tobacco do governments act decisively, as seen with smoking bans and restrictions.

After five years, when the term of my franchise agreement ended, I successfully negotiated to become independent.

Thanks to a good-faith approach and mutual loyalty to the brand, the transition from the franchise model to independence was smooth and amicable. My gym is now called *Savuti Health and Fitness*—a fitting name! Its logo is a lion! Interestingly, my hobby farm, which I shared with my partner, was called *Savuti Gardening and Hobby Farm.*

With succession plans now in place and the gym operating independently, I've adapted the business to better meet community needs and promote the growing awareness of the importance of exercise - not just for longevity but for enhancing the quality of life. I feel I've adjusted well to this local contribution. As part of this new chapter, I plan to downsize to a more manageable home. This change will enable me to focus on supporting my staff and building a strong foundation in the fitness industry.

By reducing the energy and time required to maintain private land, I can now dedicate more of my efforts to exploring the vast landscapes around me, confident that I've left my little piece of land ready for its next custodian to cherish and nurture further.

I take comfort, however, in recognising that personal challenges are shaped by the expectations of our community and our own perspective, which is itself moulded by experience. Ultimately, I have choices - choices that so many in this world are not afforded. Countless individuals are born into lives of poverty, pain, or disability, their view confined to the immediate reality around them. Yet, while I observe their struggles through the lens of my own expectations - expectations rooted in the benchmarks of health and opportunity in my own country - they often find joy even in the darkest of moments.

It's like standing outside a zoo, watching animals in cages, compared to being in Africa, confined to a vehicle that resembles a cage, where the roles are reversed - I am the one being observed. Are we truly the witnesses, or are we the ones being watched? Those we perceive as needing assistance may, in fact, be quietly assessing how we act toward humanity and those in need. I often make comment about our treatment towards refugees as one day the roles maybe reversed.

Many of you may recall, as children, being told that gifts from Father Christmas or the tooth fairy depended on your behaviour - that all your actions were being watched. Parents often invoked a figure, whether rooted in faith or folklore, to reinforce the idea of reward and punishment through an unseen third party. How many times were you warned that if you didn't behave, Father Christmas wouldn't bring you any presents, or at least not the ones you wanted? This carrot-and-stick approach subtly suppresses our natural human instinct to love freely and unconditionally.

As newborns, we instinctively love our carers, the people who nurture us, and the person who carries us through conception to birth. Yet this innate capacity for love becomes disabled by doctrine, the concept of sin, and the insidious imposition of 'difference' by society. Before these constructs take hold, we are all the same souls born into different circumstances, each embarking on a journey of experience, growth, and eventual enlightenment.

The soul, I believe, chooses its next journey before birth - a path designed for learning and understanding. Perhaps your soul has chosen to experience grief and loss, to endure poverty, to live under dictatorship, to be a criminal, face imprisonment, or even stand before a firing squad. Perhaps it has chosen to experience disability, to be a minority, to lose a child, or to live a life of wealth and privilege.

Can you change this path or make adjustments? I believe you can—if you can find a way to connect with your soul and understand its purpose. By listening to your inner voice and recognising the lessons your soul seeks to learn, you may influence the direction of your journey and move closer to peace and enlightenment.

Whatever happens in this life, is meant to happen, the people you meet – even if fleetingly as they may be a messenger or angel that may influence your decision, keep you safe or bring you closer to your soul mate. A perceived enemy may in fact be your friend! Your journey in this life was planned and agreed before you were born. Your physical body is just vessel for what your soul wishes to experience! The challenges we face are ones we set ourselves to grow and to know what it is like to be human. Whilst we often consider humans to be superior race, its action towards fellow humans is primitive compared to many other species that show only love and forgiveness for your failures. Consider your pet dog that will never judge and loves you unconditionally and becomes your life companion but cruelly taken away from you due to its short lifespan. I believe the soul can decide what form it wishes to take and not necessarily a human form.

Whatever grief, misfortune, or injustice I feel pales in comparison when I witness the suffering of others. Yet, even suffering itself is shaped by perspective, by a doctrine that dictates 'right and wrong' as if we lack the capacity to discern this for ourselves. Suffering is suffering, regardless of its form or circumstance. A child lost to famine in Central Africa evokes the same primal grief as a child lost to a technological failure in the West. The reactions and coping mechanisms may differ, shaped by cultural and environmental factors, but the pain is universal. And yet, the world so often judges suffering according to perceived priorities.

I have seen the brightest smiles and profound happiness in what I would have considered places of squalor - places far below the standards deemed essential for health, development, and prosperity. At the same time, I have seen the saddest eyes and deepest unhappiness in those surrounded by material wealth and privilege. This stark contrast reveals that joy and despair do not hinge on circumstances alone but on something far more profound, something rooted in the soul's ability to find meaning beyond the tangible.

As this final chapter of my life concludes, I look ahead with a sense of purpose and contentment. The experiences I've gathered, the connections I've built, and the contributions I've made reflect a life shaped by challenges, growth, and a commitment to leaving things better than I found them. This is not an end, but a continuation—a steady rhythm that carries forward into whatever comes next.

Authors Note:

My mother, Evelyn Dolly Somai (nee Prince) born 30 June 1933 passed away on 30 September 2025, at the age of ninety-two, after spending a week in hospital. I was told of her passing two days later. Though I learned she had asked about me before she died and often told others she loved me, I did not know of it until I spoke with my sister and her daughter. I was therefore denied the opportunity to journey to England to see her one last time.

Within days of her passing, I began to write new chapters — *'Fractures', 'The Fragile Thread' and 'Divided Bloodlines'* each partly reimagined from earlier chapters, *Body and Mind* and *The Burden of Truth*. These chapters have become essential to this memoir, shaping its emotional centre and giving voice to my own sense of dislocation and longing.

It is a quiet irony that so much of my professional life has been devoted to those who are displaced — by war, disaster, or circumstance — people who have crossed borders seeking refuge, belonging, or the fragile hope of a new beginning. In writing these chapters, I realised that displacement is not always physical. Sometimes it lives within us, an echo of loss carried across generations.

I have decided to keep these chapters for a second book

I was born on the 4th August the same day and month as the day Britain declared war on Germany in World War 1 leading Australia's entry into the war. My Grandfather Charles Henry Prince, interned by the Germans in St Denis, Paris was born on the 11th day of the 11th Month the same day and month as the Armistice that brought The Great War to a halt!